Simon Kordonsky

SOCIO-ECONOMIC FOUNDATIONS OF THE RUSSIAN POST-SOVIET REGIME

The Resource-Based Economy and Estate-Based Social Structure of Contemporary Russia

With a foreword by Svetlana Barsukova

ibidem-Verlag
Stuttgart

Bibliografische Information der Deutschen Nationalbibliothek
Die Deutsche Nationalbibliothek verzeichnet diese Publikation in der Deutschen Nationalbibliografie; detaillierte bibliografische Daten sind im Internet über http://dnb.d-nb.de abrufbar.

Bibliographic information published by the Deutsche Nationalbibliothek
Die Deutsche Nationalbibliothek lists this publication in the Deutsche Nationalbibliografie; detailed bibliographic data are available in the Internet at http://dnb.d-nb.de.

Cover picture: The panorama of Soligalich town, Kostroma region. © copyright 2016 by Juri Plusnin.

∞

Gedruckt auf alterungsbeständigem, säurefreien Papier
Printed on acid-free paper

ISSN: 1614-3515

ISBN-13: 978-3-8382-0775-9

© *ibidem*-Verlag
Stuttgart 2016

Alle Rechte vorbehalten

Das Werk einschließlich aller seiner Teile ist urheberrechtlich geschützt. Jede Verwertung außerhalb der engen Grenzen des Urheberrechtsgesetzes ist ohne Zustimmung des Verlages unzulässig und strafbar. Dies gilt insbesondere für Vervielfältigungen, Übersetzungen, Mikroverfilmungen und elektronische Speicherformen sowie die Einspeicherung und Verarbeitung in elektronischen Systemen.

All rights reserved. No part of this publication may be reproduced, stored in or introduced into a retrieval system, or transmitted, in any form, or by any means (electronic, mechanical, photocopying, recording or otherwise) without the prior written permission of the publisher. Any person who does any unauthorized act in relation to this publication may be liable to criminal prosecution and civil claims for damages.

Printed in the EU

Soviet and Post-Soviet Politics and Society (SPPS)   Vol. 152
ISSN 1614-3515

General Editor: Andreas Umland,
Institute for Euro-Atlantic Cooperation, Kyiv, umland@stanfordalumni.org

Commissioning Editor: Max Jakob Horstmann,
London, mjh@ibidem.eu

EDITORIAL COMMITTEE*

DOMESTIC & COMPARATIVE POLITICS
Prof. **Ellen Bos**, *Andrássy University of Budapest*
Dr. **Ingmar Bredies**, *FH Bund, Brühl*
Dr. **Andrey Kazantsev**, *MGIMO (U) MID RF, Moscow*
Prof. **Heiko Pleines**, *University of Bremen*
Prof. **Richard Sakwa**, *University of Kent at Canterbury*
Dr. **Sarah Whitmore**, *Oxford Brookes University*
Dr. **Harald Wydra**, *University of Cambridge*

SOCIETY, CLASS & ETHNICITY
Col. **David Glantz**, *"Journal of Slavic Military Studies"*
Dr. **Marlène Laruelle**, *George Washington University*
Dr. **Stephen Shulman**, *Southern Illinois University*
Prof. **Stefan Troebst**, *University of Leipzig*

POLITICAL ECONOMY & PUBLIC POLICY
Prof. em. **Marshall Goldman**, *Wellesley College, Mass.*
Dr. **Andreas Goldthau**, *Central European University*
Dr. **Robert Kravchuk**, *University of North Carolina*
Dr. **David Lane**, *University of Cambridge*
Dr. **Carol Leonard**, *Higher School of Economics, Moscow*
Dr. **Maria Popova**, *McGill University, Montreal*

FOREIGN POLICY & INTERNATIONAL AFFAIRS
Dr. **Peter Duncan**, *University College London*
Prof. **Andreas Heinemann-Grüder**, *University of Bonn*
Dr. **Taras Kuzio**, *Johns Hopkins University*
Prof. **Gerhard Mangott**, *University of Innsbruck*
Dr. **Diana Schmidt-Pfister**, *University of Konstanz*
Dr. **Lisbeth Tarlow**, *Harvard University, Cambridge*
Dr. **Christian Wipperfürth**, *N-Ost Network, Berlin*
Dr. **William Zimmerman**, *University of Michigan*

HISTORY, CULTURE & THOUGHT
Dr. **Catherine Andreyev**, *University of Oxford*
Prof. **Mark Bassin**, *Södertörn University*
Prof. **Karsten Brüggemann**, *Tallinn University*
Dr. **Alexander Etkind**, *University of Cambridge*
Dr. **Gasan Gusejnov**, *Moscow State University*
Prof. em. **Walter Laqueur**, *Georgetown University*
Prof. **Leonid Luks**, *Catholic University of Eichstaett*
Dr. **Olga Malinova**, *Russian Academy of Sciences*
Prof. **Andrei Rogatchevski**, *University of Tromsø*
Dr. **Mark Tauger**, *West Virginia University*

ADVISORY BOARD*

Prof. **Dominique Arel**, *University of Ottawa*
Prof. **Jörg Baberowski**, *Humboldt University of Berlin*
Prof. **Margarita Balmaceda**, *Seton Hall University*
Dr. **John Barber**, *University of Cambridge*
Prof. **Timm Beichelt**, *European University Viadrina*
Dr. **Katrin Boeckh**, *University of Munich*
Prof. em. **Archie Brown**, *University of Oxford*
Dr. **Vyacheslav Bryukhovetsky**, *Kyiv-Mohyla Academy*
Prof. **Timothy Colton**, *Harvard University, Cambridge*
Prof. **Paul D'Anieri**, *University of Florida*
Dr. **Heike Dörrenbächer**, *Friedrich Naumann Foundation*
Dr. **John Dunlop**, *Hoover Institution, Stanford, California*
Dr. **Sabine Fischer**, *SWP, Berlin*
Dr. **Geir Flikke**, *NUPI, Oslo*
Prof. **David Galbreath**, *University of Aberdeen*
Prof. **Alexander Galkin**, *Russian Academy of Sciences*
Prof. **Frank Golczewski**, *University of Hamburg*
Dr. **Nikolas Gvosdev**, *Naval War College, Newport, RI*
Prof. **Mark von Hagen**, *Arizona State University*
Dr. **Guido Hausmann**, *University of Munich*
Prof. **Dale Herspring**, *Kansas State University*
Dr. **Stefani Hoffman**, *Hebrew University of Jerusalem*
Prof. **Mikhail Ilyin**, *MGIMO (U) MID RF, Moscow*
Prof. **Vladimir Kantor**, *Higher School of Economics*
Dr. **Ivan Katchanovski**, *University of Ottawa*
Prof. em. **Andrzej Korboński**, *University of California*
Dr. **Iris Kempe**, *"Caucasus Analytical Digest"*
Prof. **Herbert Küpper**, *Institut für Ostrecht Regensburg*
Dr. **Rainer Lindner**, *CEEER, Berlin*
Dr. **Vladimir Malakhov**, *Russian Academy of Sciences*

Dr. **Luke March**, *University of Edinburgh*
Prof. **Michael McFaul**, *Stanford University, Palo Alto*
Prof. **Birgit Menzel**, *University of Mainz-Germersheim*
Prof. **Valery Mikhailenko**, *The Urals State University*
Prof. **Emil Pain**, *Higher School of Economics, Moscow*
Dr. **Oleg Podvintsev**, *Russian Academy of Sciences*
Prof. **Olga Popova**, *St. Petersburg State University*
Dr. **Alex Pravda**, *University of Oxford*
Dr. **Erik van Ree**, *University of Amsterdam*
Dr. **Joachim Rogall**, *Robert Bosch Foundation Stuttgart*
Prof. **Peter Rutland**, *Wesleyan University, Middletown*
Prof. **Marat Salikov**, *The Urals State Law Academy*
Dr. **Gwendolyn Sasse**, *University of Oxford*
Prof. **Jutta Scherrer**, *EHESS, Paris*
Prof. **Robert Service**, *University of Oxford*
Mr. **James Sherr**, *RIIA Chatham House London*
Dr. **Oxana Shevel**, *Tufts University, Medford*
Prof. **Eberhard Schneider**, *University of Siegen*
Prof. **Olexander Shnyrkov**, *Shevchenko University, Kyiv*
Prof. **Hans-Henning Schröder**, *SWP, Berlin*
Prof. **Yuri Shapoval**, *Ukrainian Academy of Sciences*
Prof. **Viktor Shnirelman**, *Russian Academy of Sciences*
Dr. **Lisa Sundstrom**, *University of British Columbia*
Dr. **Philip Walters**, *"Religion, State and Society", Oxford*
Prof. **Zenon Wasyliw**, *Ithaca College, New York State*
Dr. **Lucan Way**, *University of Toronto*
Dr. **Markus Wehner**, *"Frankfurter Allgemeine Zeitung"*
Dr. **Andrew Wilson**, *University College London*
Prof. **Jan Zielonka**, *University of Oxford*
Prof. **Andrei Zorin**, *University of Oxford*

* While the Editorial Committee and Advisory Board support the General Editor in the choice and improvement of manuscripts for publication, responsibility for remaining errors and misinterpretations in the series' volumes lies with the books' authors.

Soviet and Post-Soviet Politics and Society (SPPS)
ISSN 1614-3515

Founded in 2004 and refereed since 2007, SPPS makes available affordable English-, German-, and Russian-language studies on the history of the countries of the former Soviet bloc from the late Tsarist period to today. It publishes between 5 and 20 volumes per year and focuses on issues in transitions to and from democracy such as economic crisis, identity formation, civil society development, and constitutional reform in CEE and the NIS. SPPS also aims to highlight so far understudied themes in East European studies such as right-wing radicalism, religious life, higher education, or human rights protection. The authors and titles of all previously published volumes are listed at the end of this book. For a full description of the series and reviews of its books, see
www.ibidem-verlag.de/red/spps.

Editorial correspondence & manuscripts should be sent to: Dr. Andreas Umland, c/o DAAD, German Embassy, vul. Bohdana Khmelnitskoho 25, UA-01901 Kyiv, Ukraine.
e-mail: umland@stanfordalumni.org

Business correspondence & review copy requests should be sent to: *ibidem* Press, Leuschnerstr. 40, 30457 Hannover, Germany; tel.: +49 511 2622200; fax: +49 511 2622201; spps@ibidem.eu.

Authors, reviewers, referees, and editors for (as well as all other persons sympathetic to) SPPS are invited to join its networks at www.facebook.com/group.php?gid=52638198614
www.linkedin.com/groups?about=&gid=103012
www.xing.com/net/spps-ibidem-verlag/

Recent Volumes

143 Инна Чувычкина (ред.)
Экспортные нефте- и газопроводы на постсоветском пространстве
Анализ трубопроводной политики в свете теории международных отношений
ISBN 978-3-8382-0822-0

144 Johann Zajaczkowski
Russland – eine pragmatische Großmacht?
Eine rollentheoretische Untersuchung russischer Außenpolitik am Beispiel der Zusammenarbeit mit den USA nach 9/11 und des Georgienkrieges von 2008
Mit einem Vorwort von Siegfried Schieder
ISBN 978-3-8382-0837-4

145 Boris Popivanov
Changing Images of the Left in Bulgaria
The Challenge of Post-Communism in the Early 21st Century
ISBN 978-3-8382-0667-7

146 Lenka Krátká
A History of the Czechoslovak Ocean Shipping Company 1948-1989
How a Small, Landlocked Country Ran Maritime Business During the Cold War
ISBN 978-3-8382-0666-0

147 Alexander Sergunin
Explaining Russian Foreign Policy Behavior
Theory and Practice
ISBN 978-3-8382-0752-0

148 Darya Malyutina
Migrant Friendships in a Super-Diverse City
Russian-Speakers and their Social Relationships in London in the 21st Century
With a foreword by Claire Dwyer
ISBN 978-3-8382-0652-3

149 Alexander Sergunin, Valery Konyshev
Russia in the Arctic
Hard or Soft Power?
ISBN 978-3-8382-0753-7

150 John J. Maresca
Helsinki Revisited
A Key U.S. Negotiator's Memoirs on the Development of the CSCE into the OSCE
With a foreword by Hafiz Pashayev
ISBN 978-3-8382-0852-7

151 Jardar Østbø
The New Third Rome
Readings of a Russian Nationalist Myth
With a foreword by Pål Kolstø
ISBN 978-3-8382-0870-1

Contents

Foreword 9

    The shadow economy of the USSR 13
    Contemporary Russia: re-emergence of the estate system 20

The cyclical nature of Russian history 27

    The political economy of socialism and its legacy 31

The resource-based state 35

    Resources and threats; the specific Russian nature 37
    The ontological status of threats,
    their identification and ranking 39
    The threat framework mirrored in the state structure 41
    The institutional structure for neutralizing threats in Russia 43
    Corporations for utilizing the resources
    allocated to neutralize threats 49
    The population, threats and markets 52
    Goods and money in a resource-based state 55
    Types of resources in the contemporary resource-based state ... 59
    Resource self-management: redistribution and plundering 61
    The social stability mythologem as a
    form of legitimizing resource plundering 67
    The world economy and the resource-based state organization .. 69

**Social justice and the social structure
of a resource-based state** 71

    Social stratification as a specific task
    of the theory of classification 82
    Estates and classes: concept operationality 85

Russian classes and Russian estates 97

    The estate system in Imperial Russia 102
    Soviet estates 105
    Earned and unearned income, administrative trade,
    and shadow economy 117

Repression as a form of regulating
inter-estate relations in the USSR 124
The collapse of Soviet inter-estate relations 127
Contemporary service (titular) estates and state service 132
Relations between titular estates 139
The hierarchy of titular estates and corporate relations 144
The service of titular estates 149
Non-titular estates 152
Relations between titular and non-titular estates 163
Estate stratification with regard
to service, facilitation, and support 169
Administrative bargaining as a way of social life 171

Political groups as integrated estates: government, the people, active population, and the marginalized population 177

Model of the estate component
of Russia's social structure: reference conditions 194
The hypothesis underlying our calculations 195
Formalized model of the social structure 197
Discussion of the presented model 203
Limitations of the presented model 207

Some aspects of how the contemporary estate-based structure functions: Search for a national idea, repression and depressions 211

The national idea as justification
for the need to mobilize resources 213
Resource depressions and repression
as a way of "restoring order" in the use of resources 215
Stagnation and depression as phases of public life 220
Relations of the estate-based order with the external world:
"forming the resource base", importing and adopting 225
Importing worldviews and knowledge of the society—
the art of imitation 230
Socialization and its institutions in an estate-based society 243
Democracy and estate stratification 246
Daydreaming. Instead of a conclusion 252

Appendix 1. Classification of threats 257

    Ranking threats and evaluating
    the relative amount of resources for their neutralization 261

**Appendix 2. Order of the Administrative Directorate
of the President of the Russian Federation 265**

Literature 281

Foreword

Do not delude yourself. Our market and the classes it generates languish in the shadow of a resource-based economy socially organized as a system of estates. In an extremely concise and simple way, Simon Kordonsky's views can be reduced to the above assertion. I suspect it is "simple" for me, because I have read his book **Socio-Economic Foundations of the Russian Post-Soviet Regime**. For the readers, I would like to highlight the key aspects of the work. However, trying to convey Kordonsky's idea, I am constantly tempted to present my own views on the subject. Retelling any good book is a challenge, since it trains the mind rather than the memory.

The author distinguishes two analytical models—the market and resource-based economy. Classes form the social foundation of the market, whereas the social structure of the resource-based economy is reduced to a hierarchy of social estates. The competitive creativity of the market—economists call it competition—generates new products (resources). The successful get richer, the losers get poorer. This determines the division of people into classes distinguishable obviously by their consumer behavior.[1] The people themselves clearly and uniquely identify themselves in this space, since such classes are levels of a consumer hierarchy.

---

[1] Here we should mention that the concept of "class" has a long and complicated intellectual history. At times, when it found its way from scientific treatises into the consciousness of the masses, this history was even bloody. It is sufficient to recall the different meaning attributed to this term by Karl Marx and Max Weber. Simon Kordonsky, however, is an author without reverence. When he believes something is "off the point", do not expect an honorable place in the footnotes. He takes the concept of class from the works of American functionalists (1930s) without lengthy explanations about other usages of the word. Readers spoiled by education are at times challenged. They are haunted by Karl Marx's politicized and revolutionized classes derived from the ownership of the means of production, as well as classes supplemented by parties and statuses in Max Weber's three-component model. For Kordonsky, however, what people themselves perceive as social demarcation is far more relevant than what is written in books. And the people, watching and comparing consumer models, quite distinctly divide the world into the rich, the poor and those in the middle. Noting this, American sociologists applied the already occupied term "classes" to such groups.

However, there is another algorithm—to concentrate resources in a single center and distribute them to those who by deed or word have proved their usefulness to society, or in other words, to the state, which are fundamentally inseparable in this scenario. O. Bessonova calls such an economy distributive, since relations of "give-receive" rule the day rather than the simplified market motto of "buy-sell".[2] S. Kirdina paints a similar picture. She distinguishes two types of "institutional matrices" with characteristic economic, political, and ideological components.[3] Kordonsky defines such an economy as resource-based, emphasizing the fundamental importance of dividing resources among the estates as the core process of social life.

The market economy is balanced through the pricing mechanism. The resource-based economy has other signal channels forcing the center to adjust the "distribution" mechanism. When in the process of distribution somebody's interests are ignored or somebody appropriates what he is not entitled to, complaints flow to the center, and the mechanism is adjusted using techniques specific for the period—from cutting heads to criticizing at communist party meetings. When the tide of complaints ebbs, the "distributive" mechanism is considered to be "socially fair", which means that the majority of people agree that different activities receive resources commensurate with their contribution to the common cause of serving the state.

Service, not labor is compensated in an estate society. The difference is fundamental. One can work a lot or not much, but one can serve only well or poorly. Ultimately, market behavior targets new consumption peaks, thus implying quantitative measures of labor and

---

[2] When in the midst of radical "market construction", in the 1990s, O. Bessonova wrote about the imminent reinstatement of the "distributive economy", she was reproached for not seeing revolutionary changes of the reality because of the commitment to her idea. Now there is little doubt that the idea was worth it. And the reality lived up to the idea; it was just a question of waiting some 15–20 years; see: Bessonova O.E. 2006. *The Russian distributive economy. Evolution through transformation.* M.: ROSSPEN.

[3] According to S. Kirdina, the institutional matrix of the "Western" type is characterized by a domination of private property, democracy, and supremacy of "I" over "we", whereas the triad of public property, authoritarianism, and the unconditional subordination of "I" to the will of "we" constitute the institutional base of the "Eastern" matrix; see: Kirdina S.G. 2000. *Institutional matrices and the development of Russia.* M.: Teis

performance. Estate service transforms the notion of labor into performance of duties imposed by the society. Therefore, the nature rather than the measure of labor is important, because the nature of service holds a code to the individual's social status, rights, duties, privileges, moral norms, and relations with law. Poor service is fraught with downgrading. This is likely to cause a decline in income—not because there is less work in a lower position, but because the service is less responsible. Labor is paid, and service is rewarded. The rewarded are people who serve. They are divided into *estates*—groups that have different responsibilities to the center (sovereign) with a respective differentiation in rewards and rights. Some serve the state "directly" (at present, these include prosecutors, judges, police officers, the military, state civil servants, etc.) and are referred to as *titular estates* with numerous internal rankings. They have visual insignia (uniform), formal evidence of belonging to the services (official IDs), legislatively stipulated privileges (e.g., deputy immunity from prosecution), and informal regulators of estate behavior. Some serve "indirectly", providing conditions for the activity of the service estates (doctors, teachers, scientists, lawyers, the clergy, prostitutes, and others)—these are the so-called *non-titular estates*, the second echelon of serving people with an appropriate prestige and pay. A class hierarchy relates to the world of consumption, whereas an estate hierarchy—to the space of rights and privileges.

Various activities, such as collecting and inventorying resources, ensuring their integrity, jailing or frightening those who attempt their unauthorized "carve-up", protecting from the enemy, and others, determine the diversity of the estates' functional designation. However, this visible distinction in the types of activity conceals a single driving force of every service—to demonstrate exceptional usefulness for the general cause, irreplaceability, and, with luck, the ability to replace others, which eventually determines the amount of resources allocated to an estate. Please note: not in proportion to the work, but according to the significance of the service. The activity of the estates is not focused on creating resources (what determines market activity). Instead, it is focused on redistributing ("carving up", as the author of the book calls this process) the available resources and expanding the space of rights and privileges stipulated by law or tradition.

In the modern world, neither the market, nor the resource-based economy exist in pure form. They *coexist*. For several centuries, we have been looking up to countries with a sustainable balance between the market and "distribution", where market activities dominate. The estates remain, but belonging to them is more a question of prestige than income level. Due to the domination of market principles, classes triumph over estates. In particular, wealth is no longer linked to the estate status. An aristocrat may be poor. In an estate-based society, however, the hierarchy of estates influences the income of their members. A high-ranking official cannot be poorer than members of lower-ranking estates. At least, that is what he believes. Similarly, a police officer is certain that enforcing law and order is more important than engaging in "buying-and-selling". Simply, he establishes this law and order for the benefit of private clients rather than as a public benefit. However, since no one formally recognizes the triumph of service hierarchy as the core principle of social organization, servicemen are forced to "restore social justice" by all means, even risking to be prosecuted for various "abuses".

In Russia, the resource-based economy dominates, giving up its positions only when the existing resource distribution patterns collapse or the resources run out. However, as soon as market initiative starts bearing fruit in the form of an expanding resource base, the service estates reinstate their positions. Principles of the market and resource-based economy coexist in diachrony, i.e., the periodic brief triumph of the market gives way to long-term concentrated "carve-up" of resources behind the facade of zealous service. "...This produces the phenomenon of cyclicity in Russian history—a certain 'groundhog century'".

The social map of present-day Russia is extremely mixed: relict estates of bygone ages loudly claiming what they believe "they are entitled to"; newly established estates mobilized to fight the "threats of the XXI century", real or imaginary; and classes desperately trying to break free from the web of estate exactions.[4] The latter find themselves in a difficult position—from every podium they hear assurances that "we are building the market", but actual experience and calculations indicate some other reality. Governed by the simple principle to call a spade a spade, Kordonsky provides a name for this reality. Estates engaged in "carving up" resources—that is the essence of our social life. What we call politics out of habit, is the process of finding a compromise to align the interests of classes with the resource appetites of the estates through mechanisms of political and economic lobbying.

"I believe that Russia is a country where the estate world order based on inequality of citizens before the law and different rights and obligations to the state dominates in times of stability, when there are no revolutions or reforms. It was and still is a resource-based state where the resources are not increased but distributed—shared between the estates. Resource growth is achieved by an 'expansion of the resource base' rather than through production of goods and turnover of capital".

The shadow economy of the USSR

The general theory provides a rather interesting explanation of the phenomenon, which the official lexicon refers to as the shadow economy of the USSR. Centralized planning implied complete triumph of the resource-based economy—the people were supposed to live within the space of benefits to which they were "entitled". Besides pay, they were entitled to lots of other benefits determined by their estate status—health resorts, departmental pioneer camps, and others. The revolutionary slogan "Land to the peasants, factories to the workers" was replaced by stipulated rights to a legitimate part of the estate rent—rations for the military; "feeders" for scientists; Black Sea resorts for those engaged in the defense industry, subsidized utility tariffs for

---

4   Research performed by O.I. Shakaratan and colleagues confirms that social stratification of contemporary Russia is a web of estate-based hierarchy and elements of the class structure; see: Shkaratan O.I., Yastrebov G.A. *The social and occupational structure of Russia's population.* Mir Rossii. 2007. No. 3, pp. 3–49.

police officers, etc. Apart from centralized channels, scarce benefits were also allocated through trade unions, which in fact acted as consolidators of the estate system.

Recollections of my life in Novosibirsk Akademgorodok (Academic Town) abound in such details. Candidates and doctors of science bought food in various closed distribution outlets and had only a vague idea about the food basket of their colleagues with a different estate status. By the way, students with young children got the same shopping opportunities as candidates of science. In terms of demographic policy, this measure was much more effective than the current maternity capital. "Non-core" servicemen (doctors, teachers, and drivers) purchased in ordinary shops, this being a much clearer manifestation of their "backstage" position than the difference in salaries. Housing conditions also differed formally. Defending a Ph.D. thesis gave nonresident scientists a high chance to move from the dormitory to a tiny apartment (Khrushchyovka); a doctoral thesis meant keys to a spacious apartment; and the title of academician transferred its holder to the only street in town built up with villas. This differentiation was absolutely legitimate, since the so-called *earned income* consisted of salaries in conjunction with legitimate estate privileges.

However, unfortunately for the architects of this coherent tower of estate differentiation, the people did not want to limit themselves to earned income. They wanted to storm consumer heights, to consume in excess of what they were "entitled to". The Moral Code of the Builder of Communism and repressive legislation forced people to conceal such aspirations, but did not block them. In a market economy, competition in consumption implies competition in labor efforts with free access to a variety of resources. In a resource-based economy, the only way to exceed the limits of consumption determined by estate affiliation was to divert the resources allocated by the center—in other words, to apply a creative approach to the formally designated methods of their circulation. Diversion of resources, including their theft, constituted "Soviet-style business", or, more conventionally, the shadow economy of the USSR. In other words, estate logic governed access to resources, but Soviet people used these resources like ordinary representatives of a class society, i.e., according to their own socio-economic interests.

Only repression could curb such aspirations. Cruel and widespread repression, when fear paralyzes. Because the desire to live is stronger than the desire to live well. Shadow economy as a widespread phenomenon with an extensive involvement of the popular masses did not exist under Stalin. The ideological component, enhanced by the talent of creative intellectuals of that period, also played its role. The "law of three spikelets"—that was the nickname people gave to the decrees of 1932 and 1947, which allowed the authorities to punish anyone who encroached on the property of enterprises or harvest from collective farm fields, regardless of the age and hunger of the pilferer. How should they have been afraid to joke like that! By the way, at that time Sergey Prokofiev was composing the music to the *Three Oranges* ballet. Genuine equality—some get "three oranges", the others—"three spikelets".

After Stalin's death, the machine broke down. Everyone tried to benefit from the resources available to them. Do not think that we are talking only about directors of food stores. Everyone had at least a resource of working time paid for by the state. Since the people served or supported service rather than worked (that was the main reason for regular failure to implement economic self-sufficiency and various forms of self-financing), their earnings depended more on the place of work than on the measure of labor. An adjuster of equipment at a defense enterprise received substantially more than his counterpart at a garment factory did—not because sewing equipment was less complicated, but just because defense was more important for socialist construction. A good position meant no need to sweat. If the position was not especially good, any extra efforts on the job were even more stupid. People received their legitimate part of the estate rent not for the quality of their labor, but for the fact of belonging to a social group. Therefore, they tried to reduce the measure of labor as much as possible. "Top performers" were an exception. They demonstrated the real possibilities of the resource base available to everyone, and for that reason were disliked (to put it mildly) by their colleagues. In fact, the top performers were no different from the other workers—they all tried to make use of the marginal utility of the resources allocated from above. Only the ones surrendered the results of their creative efforts to the state, whereas the others kept them to themselves. That was the only difference. For example, you can plow an additional kolkhoz field in excess of the norm, or you can plow your own or your neighbor's land plot. Please note: using the allocated equipment, fuel and lubricants. The state will express its gratitude in the form of a bonus or commendation, whereas the neighbor will share his future crop or pay in booze on the spot. The implementation of this multi-factor model gravitated toward the shadow economy.

"Using working time for personal purposes" was the most common Soviet-style pilferage, because working time was the only resource, which the state provided to everyone. The other resources were differentiated by estates, thus also differentiating the amounts and algorithms for converting them into so-called *unearned incomes*. The potential for such conversion was no less important for evaluating a job than the associated earned income. The famous alienation from labor, which Karl Marx attributed to capitalism, was overcome under socialism in a peculiar manner: people experienced an "alienated" indifference to the process and results of labor, but treated the resources allocated for these purposes, as their own.

I cannot refrain from memories. In the 1980s, for the purpose of labor education, high school students spent one day per week at industrial training facilities, where they were supposed to acquire occupational skills. Once there, the coaches briefly instructed them and sent out to work, thus filling the gaps in the personnel policy. The humor of the authorities consisted in the fact that, for example, training for the occupation of a "chemical engineer" actually meant standing at the conveyor of a chemical-pharmaceutical plant in the role of a bandage packer. The pay for all types of work was purely symbolic. So, the schoolchildren "chose an occupation" based on the opportunity to appropriate something at the workplace. For the first time in my life, I was demotivated in my studies—as top of the class, I was sent to master the occupation of a "chemical engineer", whereas the underachievers became sales personnel in food stores. Justice, nevertheless, prevailed—they have eaten their stolen cream a long time ago, whereas my bandages will last for ages. Senior comrades showed sophisticated ways of "shoplifting" through the checkpoint. That was the essence of Soviet-style introduction to labor.

It is indicative that the legislative amendments that accompanied Khrushchev's "thaw" were by no means liberal. The authorities had to take tougher measures, because as repressions slackened, the shadow economy broke out. The people, however, chose to live under the motto "You can't catch us all" and enhanced the skills of living in two parallel economic worlds—the official and shadow economies. Actually, these worlds were not parallel, since they intersected. The main intersection was the common resource base, access to which was determined by the estate status. The weakening ideological component of the regime also played a role in the growth of the shadow economy. Because of the intelligentsia's key intellectual project—de-Stalinization (esthetically as talented as the former praising of Stalin's victories),—the ordinary people were disillusioned with the idea as such, which gave them reason to morally justify economic sabotage against the state.

Here it turned out that the estates differ not only by the amount of pay and benefits, which constitute their legitimate estate rent. The main and decisive factor of their stratification is the ability to distribute resources. Distribution of resources is the essence of power in an estate society. Kordonsky introduces the notion of *administrative currency* as a measured right (legitimate or illegitimate, legal or illegal) to influence the alienation and distribution of resources, which gives its holder access to a variety of benefits. Administrative currency was a side effect of the estate order. Real power was measured not by the list of official functions, but by the capacity to influence the trajectory of resource flows. Thus, a letter on a Communist Party letterhead carried more weight than that on a letterhead of the Soviet authorities. This indicated the actual rather than the declared hierarchy of the party and the Soviets. The key informal rule of the resource-based economy reads as follows, "Do not have a hundred rubles, but have the right to allocate them". Since everything was being allocated—specialists, tractors, holiday vouchers, medical drugs,—the field of administrative bargaining buzzed like a beehive.

We should not think that self-interest was the only driving force. Quite often, administrative bargaining was the only way to fulfill a plan imposed from above. Similarly, it was often the only way to raise resources for a particular region, because the construction of a new facility in the area served to develop the transport and social infrastructure, create jobs, and, consequently, enhance the positions of the regional leaders in their negotiations with the center. Therefore, the reasons to participate in administrative bargaining could vary, reaching far beyond simple enrichment through theft of allocated resources.

Two segments were clearly distinguishable in the shadow economy of the Soviet period: spontaneous shadow activities of particular individuals (pilferers, speculators, black marketeers, etc.) and large-scale activities organized by tsekhoviki (illegal entrepreneurs who set up production of scarce goods). The former were distanced from the authorities in the sense that the authorities were not "in on the act"; they did not purposefully allocate resources for shadow utilization. Therefore, pilferers and speculators were caught, denounced, expelled, criticized, that is, condemned in a variety of ways.

Tsekhoviki, on the other hand, were the blast furnace for smelting the "administrative currency" into the consumption level of the power elite. Therefore, they were caught only under campaigns aimed at removing a stratum of the governing nomenklatura to clear the space for new contenders. Sometimes, however, the proceedings revealed details not anticipated by the initial scenario, when traces led to offices that were not supposed to be disturbed. Closed court hearings served as insurance against such unexpected revelations, which gave Themis the chance not to punish beyond the allowed level. Setbacks occurred only shortly before the collapse of socialism, when unruly journalists, commissioned by intra-party factions, made public some top-level cases.

The case of the "knitwear manufacturers" at the time of the Krushchev "thaw" illustrates the close links that tsekhoviki had with the authorities.[5] That was a high-profile case both by the severity of the sentence, and the scandalous nature of the revelations. The beginning

---

5 See: Evelson E. 1986. *Court cases on economic crimes in the USSR (the nineteen sixties)*. London: Overseas Publications Interchange Ltd.

was quite innocent. Believing in the ennobling force of labor, psycho-neurological clinics introduced occupational therapy for patients in the format of "medical-labor departments". Thus, they were allowed to produce knitwear, which was extremely scarce at the time. For this purpose, they were allocated raw materials and equipment. The doctors, however, had neither wish nor skills to engage in knitwear manufacturing; the machine tools slowly corroded, and moths fed on the wool. The situation changed dramatically with the appearance of a certain Roife—resourceful native of Bessarabia. He undertook to arrange the process, thus earning the gratitude of the doctors, patients, and superior organizations. Soon it became clear that a smart approach could turn this activity into a real bonanza. A creative use of raw materials and equipment generated unaccounted output. This was achieved by using smaller clothing patterns, adding synthetic yarn, adjusting the machines to produce looser jersey fabric and so on. The enterprising manager arranged deliveries of functioning machines under the guise of decommissioned ones and high-class raw materials—under the guise of cheap ones; he replaced the patients with free laborers whose employment records were filed with some personnel department. Production grew and soon expanded beyond the hospital walls. Please note: no one stole the machines and raw materials from state warehouses in the dark of night. They were obtained quite legally. And the knitwear was sold not on the black market, but through state-owned stores with the traders getting their share of the pie. Arranged police escorts served to avoid undesirable inspections on the road. The investigation revealed that representatives of different agencies, including rather high-ranking officials, were involved in the "knitwear manufacturers" case. These included deputy ministers, senior functionaries of the State Planning Committee, store administrators, and law enforcement officers. Capital punishment was a reaction to the scale of the business, but also served the purpose of burying the witnesses of the system's total corruption. That was a high-profile case, but it was not unique. A similar pattern existed in Georgia in the 1960s. It involved producing fashionable clothing from capron fabric.

Only naive romantics could regard the tsekhoviki as market petrels, as economic rebels fighting the system. In fact, they were associated with the system by the resource-based principles, not to mention the fact that shortage of goods generated by centralized planning guaranteed high demand for their products.

Although generated by the Soviet order, the tsekhoviki, nevertheless, accelerated its end. Using the "administrative currency" of government patrons to build their businesses, shadow entrepreneurs destroyed the foundation of the society—the estate system, because they promoted the emergence of classes, which differed in the space of consumer hierarchy regardless of the estate status. "The class structure is like cancer for the estate organization of a society-state". A military officer was now worse off than a "huckster" was because shadow processes adjusted the initial distribution of resources between them (earned income, including the legitimate part of the estate rent). This destroyed the people's confidence in social justice, which an estate-based society understands as distribution of benefits according to the significance of state service.

Perestroika set in—a time when a new estate topography started emerging. This always happened at times of unrest and revolutions.

Contemporary Russia:
re-emergence of the estate system

The reforms of the 1990s, quite reasonably referred to as market reforms, changed the Soviet estate order irreversibly, because service in the USSR consisted in building socialism—communism. This affected both titular and non-titular estates. Numerous communist party functionaries, teachers of scientific atheism, State Planning Committee employees, and other direct servitors of the discarded idea had to seek a new place under the social sun. Activities neutral to the communist idea also lost their former status. The abundance of goods "downgraded" commercial workers and trade unionists; the military lost their aura of saviors of the Motherland (which since the days of Lenin had been in constant danger) and dragged down the social ladder workers of the defense enterprises. New laws and broken traditions changed the existing estate order, thus depriving people of social guidelines.

In such circumstances, the logic of the market economy starts dominating. The population is rapidly differentiated by income, and entrepreneurs appear on the scene. The wealth of others is the only thing people now hate more than their own poverty. Business income, even legal under the laws of that time, seems completely illegitimate to the population that observes the developments through the prism of their estate philosophy. In terms of estate values, the market is a priori "unfair" because market resources do not land in the treasury, whereas the procedure of splitting up this treasury among the estates determines the conventional, albeit conflict-prone way of life. Numerous appeals to "restore order in the country" actually mean appeals to restore the clear and usual rules and procedures, preferably without communist trinkets. Nostalgia blocked out negative manifestations of the estate order leaving warm memories of a difficult, but socially just life.

Three processes converged in space and time: a mass of people in search of new service opportunities, whose previous experience consisted in utilizing resources allocated from above; a social mandate for a "firm hand" capable of outlining new services; and, finally, developing entrepreneurship, which generated new resources. Quickly enough, by the early 2000s, these processes resulted in the re-emergence of the estate system—the army of servicemen ready for the "carve-up" received political support and new resource opportunities created by business. The resources and the banners under which they could be "carved up" were in place.

With two reservations. First, market processes bore fruit, and a complete return to unconditional estate-ness was no longer possible; the social structure was a mix of estate and class positions, and the estates themselves were now different. Second, the new estates were too young and, more importantly, bashfully pushed behind the decorations of market-building, to develop their estate identity and become the basis of social self-identification for their representatives. "People refer to themselves and members of their own estate in estate terms and to members of other estates—in class terms". Kordonsky defines the situation, which emerged, as "underdeveloped classes and half-baked estates".

Entrepreneurs underwent metamorphoses, which are very indicative. Presumably, they are not servicemen, since they operate in a market rather than a resource logic, which means that they actually create resources, rather than collect, guard, and distribute them. Finally, they work for their own benefit rather than for "the good of the country". In other words, an entrepreneurial estate is like a round square. However, the market bravado of independent entrepreneurs diminished with the reestablishment of the estate order. It was becoming increasingly difficult to do business without close links with representatives of the state in their inconceivable variety. Firefighters, sanitary and tax inspectors, customs officers, prosecutors, various controllers, and other guardians of public interests advanced in a united front. Fighting was senseless because of the opponent's superior forces, and being friends meant recognizing the servicemen's right to *estate rent* or their own duty to pay *estate tax* (not to be confused with tax as an instrument of fiscal policy). The estate that in its capacity of public resource manager limited business opportunities collected estate tax into its corporate cashbox instead of the state budget. The right to coercion was a special resource, which the state nearly lost to racket in the early 1990s. Victory over the alternative coercion agent dramatically raised the rate of estate tax charged by law enforcement bodies.

Gifts, bribes or "kickbacks" offered by entrepreneurs either individually in payment of estate tax or impersonally in the form of the business's "social responsibility" served in recognition of the estate rules of the game. Social responsibility meant that business contributed to the budgets of various authorities and participated in consolidating funds for purposes that the authorities deemed relevant for a specific region. This could include "sponsoring" a police station, participating in the construction of sports facilities, restoring churches, transferring works of art to museums, planting flowers in front of the city hall, and other financial investment in cooperation with the authorities. In response, the police provided "protection" ("krysha"), prosecutors removed competitors, and the mayor's office helped secure government contracts. Justifying such pay-offs by lack of alternative, many entrepreneurs relaxed and started enjoying the situation, because they realized that cooperation with the authorities was a specific business. Instead of competing for consumers in the market for goods and services, they began competing for the right to be included in the resource "carve-up"' network controlled by the authorities.

Within a legislatively uniform group of entrepreneurs, a column of business people stood out, who were actively engaged in supporting the budgets of titular estates (i.e., using their "protection") and in response receiving the right to "carve up" budget resources. Entrepreneurs generated by the market mutated into merchants crushed by the estate system. "In contrast to entrepreneurs, who are orthogonal to the estate structure, merchants are engaged in a specific administrative business with its bribes, "kickbacks" and "carve-ups" of budgetary resources allocated for facilitating services". If entrepreneurs personify the market, merchants supporting the activities of titular estates become characters of the estate hierarchy themselves. In other words, they become a post-Soviet non-titular estate.

However, the servicemen also experienced a curious mutation. They suddenly revealed entrepreneurial aspirations and talents of an owner creatively seeking ways to enrichment. However, exclusively with regard to budgetary resources allocated from above. As for resources held by other services or, sadder still, by entrepreneurs, they demonstrated plain concern of state-minded officials preoccupied with finding the best ways of managing such assets. Obviously, the best way is to take such resources under their custody. An owner with regard to public property and an active raider with regard to the property of others—this is the portrait of our contemporary serviceman.

Taking a business away from an entrepreneur is no longer a problem. The algorithms are all in place. Monopolistic managers of state coercion, the so-called "siloviki" (force structures), were especially successful. Growing separatism, drug abuse, terrorism, pedophilia, banditry, hacking, and poaching make their service to the state extremely significant, thus legitimizing their rising estate rank. Consequently, they are "entitled" to a lot. But they are no penny-pinchers to suck from the budget—the budget is for pensioners and large families. Like real men, they will settle their problems themselves. They will find where to take what they are "entitled to"—not by law, but according to justice. In an estate-based society, justice is always above the law.

When a public servant takes away someone's business, this means that the class structure is collapsing under the onslaught of the estate order.

Taking away resources from another department is more challenging. And here, oddly enough, word games, which have seized the country, come to the rescue. Importing analytical constructs from other socio-political realities, everyone began talking about abuse of power, corruption, violation of the equality before the law principle, and about other things devoid of meaning in an estate society, the essence of which consists in differentiating the rights of estates, including the right to collect estate rent and not abide by the law.[6]

The market for "status" license plate numbers, various identity cards, and departmental permits fixed directly to the windshield exists because the traffic policeman differentiates the applicability of traffic rules to car owners with different estate status. A bribe as a type of estate rent is levied only on those whose status is lower. For this reason, resourceful people try to mimic high-ranking estates and buy fake IDs, which are regularly confiscated during raids. One former State Duma deputy told me he had lost a fortune in fines once he became an "ordinary citizen"—he had completely forgotten the traffic rules during the years of serving as deputy.

We must take word games seriously. They shape practice. The current administrative competition for resources is taking place under the banners of fighting corruption and abuse of power. Journalists keep reporting about rogue cops and other rogues. Exposing a corrupt agency or its representative (which also undermines the position of the agency) means killing two birds with one stone. First, it demonstrates commitment to the new values dominant in politics and rhetoric. Second, a request is thus placed to redistribute public resources, this being the essence of social life in an estate-based society. The more resources, the more informal rights an estate receives, including the right to collect estate rent. Therefore, the game is worth it. And so the country is busy following news about who committed what crime.

---

6   Kordonsky is quite skeptical about intellectual adoptions in social sciences. He dedicates a special chapter to this topic, *Importing worldviews and knowledge of the society - the art of imitation*.

Using the case of the "Three Whales" [furniture smuggling], customs pushed prosecution down the estate ladder. Chekists removed from the "feeder" police officers who covered gambling. Discussions about the need to fight corruption in higher education resulted in the introduction of the unified state exam, thus entitling schoolteachers and their administrative supervisors to estate rent. The struggle, the essence of which is redistribution of resources among the estates and intra-estate groups, is framed in "Newspeak" and righteous indignation. Someone actually believes this. The best of us, of course. The others work with it.

Inventing "new threats" and requesting the state to allocate resources to combat them is another approach to redistribution. It is like in a pioneer camp: whoever tells the most horrific tale is the leader. In fact, we are talking about blackmail—if you do not allocate the resources, you will suffocate from smog, fall into an abyss, perish from viruses, drown in ice-holes, and poison yourself eating American chicken. And journalists present these resource claims in the form of spectacular stories.

Tightening resource constraints are the reason for increased competition for resources, which manifests itself in scandalous public revelations. Almost all gas is exported not even reaching the villages near Moscow; most entrepreneurs have been turned into merchants and forced to seek various "protection"; the militia has been renamed to police creating a pretext to reduce the number of servicemen in the course of performance assessment. In the meantime, the resource base for "carving up" becomes increasingly conflict-prone, and the budget as a resource bank is alarming. Business—the only actor creating resources—is slipping into the shadow economy, withdrawing capital from Russia, selling itself to foreign investors, merging with multinational corporations, i.e., resisting seizure of assets, thus demonstrating complete "social irresponsibility". Increased allegations of corruption and abuse indicate a growing shortage of resources and a crisis of the estate order, which usually refrains from using such weapons from fear of "war of all against all".

Simon Kordonsky's book gives little hope that the slogans flooding Russia will be realized. Political rhetoric and actual public administration are pulling Russia in different directions. There is no doubt as to who will have the upper hand. That is no reason, however, to read only other books and walk about smiling happily like a blindfolded person.

Prof. Dr. Svetlana Barsukova
Department of Sociology
National Research University Higher School of Economics
Moscow, Russia

" ... Yet what is truly "historical" in Russia today? With the exception of the Church and the system of communal land tenure among the peasants, which will be discussed separately, absolutely nothing, apart from the absolute power of the Tsar, a relic from the time of the Tartars which hangs in mid-air in quite unhistorical "freedom", now that all those "organic" institutions have crumbled away which gave Russia its characteristic stamp in the seventeenth and eighteenth centuries. A country which, in its most "national" institutions, strongly resembled the monarchy of Diocletian until barely a century ago is indeed incapable of undertaking "reforms" which are both viable and at the same time historically oriented."

Max Weber. 1906

The cyclical nature of Russian history

Russian history never manages to become proper history. It has been politically relevant for many years. Indeed, despite the fact that times of change are yet again replaced by stagnation, and the state alternately disintegrates and then further re-integrates, Saltykov-Shchedrin remains a contemporary writer, the travel notes of Marquis de Custine resemble reports, and Chaadaev's letters are still politically relevant. The texts of some contemporary columnists could well belong to ardent revolutionaries of the 1920s or the reactionaries of the reign of Emperor Nicholas I.[7]

---

[7] In times of stagnation people live by memories – sometimes their own, but more often of others – of "real" life: restless youth and great achievements; valor at the battlefront and feats at the grand construction sites of socialism; struggle for freedom and against anti-national regimes, as well as other crap. In times of depression, rather than living their own lives, they try to assume the roles of well-known characters from the ever-relevant history - imperial aristocrats or politicians; De-

Generations pass, and in every one of them the senile sense of the "tread of history" exists alongside the infantile urge to build yet another "bright future". The next period of "consolidation of the statehood" gives rise to the desire for change, which, in turn, gives way to the yearning for stability (including, protection from thieves, bandits and the despotism of petty bosses) typical of the times of depression—political thaws, reforms, revolutions. Various fundamental studies describe the cycles of our history; however, they do not clarify these phenomena and provide no explanation why the histories of other states lack such pronounced cyclicity.[8]

External observers interpret Russian phenomena with a certain stretch of imagination. In our everyday life, they discern various features like national character archetypes, signs of anarchy and democracy, totalitarianism and autocracy, developed economy and subsistence farming,[9] and construct theories that no one but they can understand. The observers are confident that they know how it "actually" was and is. Only everyone has his or her own "actuality".

These same observers, especially those subject to self-reflection, usually present Russian history as a linear sequence of events—from the Time of Troubles to autocracy; from autocracy to the revolutions; from the revolutions to stagnation; from stagnation to perestroika, and

---

cembrists or Narodniks [Populists]; landowners or clergy; Cheka or White Guard officers; noblemen, Bolsheviks, Mensheviks, Constitutional Democrats, or dissidents; war, revolution and counter-revolution heroes; farmers and peasants. They play the old roles as outlined by learned social scientists and dream of going back to the past, which sometimes becomes the present, not least due to their efforts.

8   Rozov N.S. *The cyclicity of Russian history as an ailment: Is recovery possible?* http://www.nsu.ru/filf/rozov/publ/cycles1.htm; Pantin V.I., Lapkin V.V. *The philosophy of historical forecasting: Historical rhythms and global development prospects in the first half of the twenty-first century.* Dubna, 2006; Ilyin V.V., Panarin A.S., and Akhiezer A.S. *Theoretical political science: Reforms and counter-reforms in Russia. Modernization cycles.* M., 1996.

9   Indeed, Russian phenomena somewhat resemble book prototypes; however, they are not identical with them due to their "specific Russian nature". The observers identify what they expect to see, but their actual discoveries turn out to be far from canonical, thus upsetting their expectations. The disappointment is sometimes so great, that even quite balanced people behave inadequately, believing, perhaps, that Russia is to blame for not conforming to their perceptions. A columnist, well known at the time of perestroika, exclaimed in reaction to LDPR's [Liberal Democratic Party of Russia headed by Vladimir Zhirinovsky] success at parliamentary elections, "Russia, you have gone crazy!"

so on.[10] The periodic transition from prospering dictatorships to reforms-crises remains at the margins of their attention, and they tend to treat the reproduction of the past in the present as incidental. The observers focus on the bright future; therefore, they perceive a repetition of the past as God's punishment and the consequence of power falling yet again into the hands of self-interested politicians.

Such future-focused people believe that contemporary Russia is an ordinary country, which at a certain stage built socialism, but is currently undergoing modernization and starting to resemble other countries. According to them, Russia is already a market economy, where government intervention is still substantial. Deregulation of the economy will make Russia similar to other countries. They attribute deviations from the standard picture to the fact that the top leadership lacks economic expertise and resorts to Soviet methods of governance. With proper guidance, everything will be more than normal, and economic growth rates (the principal indicator for apologists of modernization) will be the same as in contemporary China. As a result, Russia will even more resemble the United States.[11]

Reformist speculation is an essential component of "prosperity—depression" cycles. The Russian perception of the environment is not self-sufficient; for centuries it was based largely on cross-country comparisons. Different versions of the slogan "catch up and overtake" used to and still determine the actions of the authorities and the thinking of the elite. In different historical periods, reformers wanted Russia to resemble Holland, Germany, Sweden, France, Portugal, Argentina, Poland, Chile, and other countries. Such attempts always ended in catastrophic failures. As a result, disaster survival remains the everyday existence of the population.[12]

---

10 Gaidar Y.T. *Long time. Russia in the world: Essays of economic history.* M., 2005.
11 Andrei Illarionov. *Dangerous turn. The State is a loser in business* // Rossiyskaya Gazeta. 23 September 2005.
12 Reforms of Peter the Great, emancipation of the peasants, collectivization, industrialization, privatization, nationalization, and the monetization of social benefits. The loser complex haunts observers obsessed with progress. They yearn for the best and purest: a strong and respected state, true democracy, a civil society, and market economy. However, their recommendations implemented by the authorities generally result in global mistrust accompanied by the not unfounded

Russia is unique, just like any other country. I believe its uniqueness consists in the phenomenon that practically everything its citizens undertake governed by good intentions backfires. The people who are used to this say that everything is accomplished through the ass. Quoting a famous executive manager, politician, and diplomat, "We tried our best, you know the rest".

Why does this happen? I tried to answer this question indirectly by assuming that exaggerated administrative and market-based mechanisms were a specific Russian feature.[13] However, the synchronic administrative market theory cannot explain why the authorities' titanic efforts to consolidate the state eventually lead to some form of totalitarianism, and equally tremendous democratization efforts weaken the state and sometimes result in its dissolution. Olga Bessonova attempted to provide an explanation based on ethnic determinants of the socio-economic structure of Russia and its history.[14] There are other ways and attempts at explanations, but they mostly represent versions of the "conspiracy theory", which are not interesting.

The gap between the observed and its interpretation is astounding. The phenomena of our life have little in common with expectations

---

fear of the "Russian bear", a helpless autocracy, Soviet power and civil war, the fight against terrorism and sovereign democracy, a ridiculous political system, enemies of the people and harmful nongovernmental organizations, widespread theft and corruption. The observers always pin responsibility for this on the authorities who failed to implement their brilliant projects and concepts properly.

13 Kordonsky S. *Markets for power. Administrative markets of the USSR and Russia.* M., 2006. I am of the opinion that such phenomena are marketed in Russia, which are not considered goods in other countries; which are either not exchanged for money at all or exchanged on a much smaller scale - power, for example. Administrative-market approaches describe the state apparatus and are not intended to explain why a vast country requires such cumbersome and inefficient power structures and why the government should manage the enormous material and human flows, while other countries - economically successful and politically stable - have nothing of the sort.

14 Bessonova O.E., *The theory of distributive economy - a new approach to Russia's economic development* // Obshchestvo i ekonomika. 1998. No. 8–9, pp. 241-255. This concept integrating the experience of socio-economic field research with the author's interpretation of the specific historical process in Russia substantiates the existence of realities that escape the attention of researchers who rely on representations and interpretations traditional for economics. My approaches to depicting Russian reality are largely similar to those proposed by Olga Bessonova; however, I do not see the need for such a profound reduction to the ethnic origin of our problems. (http://ieie.nsc.ru/~rokos/nesch/RAZEC.html)

based on generally accepted theoretical patterns.[15] However, even the simplest descriptions of domestic realities, which are not accentuated ideologically or politically, are still rare. Moreover, substantive knowledge about what is happening in the country causes reactions such as "this cannot be, because this should not be" and "there is no need to know it, because it will disappear in the course of reforms". Instead of conducting research, people thoughtlessly replicate imported theories, assuming in strict accordance with progressist stereotypes that Russia is similar to those countries where the techniques have been developed.

However, when presenting the results of their research, apologists of imported theories (if they are honest) have to admit that the subject phenomenon is completely different from what they a priori imagined or simply does not exist.[16] An independent researcher conducting an empirical study of the country first determines that standard concepts and methodologies cannot be applied to describe the observed.[17]

The political economy of socialism and its legacy

I am of the opinion that Russia never had an economy as defined in standard textbooks. What external observers believe to be economy is most likely just a resource-based arrangement of public life.[18] As far

---

15   Therefore, largely due to this, an ordinary intellectualistic discourse is built on the contrast between what "is" (awesome, wrong) and what "should be" according to the theory professed by the debater.
16   This was the case with the search for Russia's middle class. See: Tarusin M. *The middle class and stratification of the Russian society. Lecture of 27 January 2005* // Public lectures Polit.ru: http://www.polit.ru/lectures/2005/02/02/mid.html
17   Nefedova T., Pallot J. *Unknown agriculture. Why one needs a cow.* M., 2006.
18   I did not find an adequate definition for such a system in economic literature; therefore, I use the term "resources" and "resource-based state" without reference. The absence of definitions is all the more interesting at least because the term "resources" inevitably emerges in everyday relations and professional discussions whenever "Russia's destiny" is touched upon. There is a completely unintelligible from my point of view approach of identifying Russian socialism with the "Asiatic mode of production", where the issue of resources is somehow addressed. See, e.g., Zakharov A.V., *"Real socialism" and the "Asiatic mode of production"* // Obshchestvennye nauki i sovremennost'. 1993. No. 3, pp. 164–172.
Yury Yaremenko felt the resource-based nature of socialism very well: "In describing these processes, I feel some dissatisfaction with the lack of adequate description language. Basically, we are not talking about economic phenomena -

as I know, the theories professed by progressive economists do not analyze such a phenomenon. Respectively, the conceptual framework of these theories is hardly applicable to depict the resource flows orchestrated by the state. Goods in Russia are not exactly goods, money is not exactly money, production is not exactly production, and even consumption only appears to resemble the classical consumption outlined in standard economic textbooks.

V. Ilyin defines the distinction between resources and capital as follows: "The categories of resources and capital are related but they are not identical. A resource is an opportunity, which will not necessarily become a reality. Any capital is a resource, but not every specific resource becomes capital. Capital is a market resource realized in the process of adding value. Therefore, the holders of the same material resources may be differently related to capital, and, consequently, occupy a different place in the class structure. Money under the mattress is treasure; money circulating in the market and bringing profit is capital. Such transformation of a resource into capital is possible only in the context of a market society. In the absence of a market, no increase in the market value of resources is possible."

In Russia, an attempt was made to build a social system without capital, based only on resources. In a sense, the attempt succeeded. Therefore, by default, the social structure is still depicted in terms of classes as related to the means of production rather than classes based on consumption—higher, middle, and lower,—as is traditional for contemporary foreign science.

---

they should be rather comprehended in terms of sociology. The secondary nature of our economy in relation to the reproduction and expansion of the administrative and social structures that I mentioned is a problem that yet no one has properly understood and appreciated because we are used to live in the speculative world of economic determinism. We find it difficult to realize that rather than resembling Europe or America, our society was more like ancient Egypt, where the construction of the pyramids was the consolidating element of the entire Egyptian civilization. Similarly, our economy in its development had no intrinsic sense. It was simply an environment for the reproduction and expansion of administrative structures" (Yaremenko Yu. Economic conversations. Dialogues with S. Belanovsky, M., 1999). However, Russian economists failed to develop the ideas of Yury Yaremenko. They were carried away by translations of the "classics of world economic thought" and by attempts to squeeze our realities into a conceptual framework, established God knows when and by whom.

From my point of view, the resource-based state system escaping the attention of classical science is specified in classical works devoted to building socialism in the USSR. In a sense, the ideal constructions designed by the political economy of socialism have become reality in the course of the past century. They are so familiar that it is an ungrateful and substantially non-trivial task to recognize the socialist stigmata in our current, ostensibly capitalist, life. Fundamentally new phenomena emerged in the process of building socialism, such as classes of workers, peasants, and employees, branches of the national economy, and the administrative and territorial division of the country. They are objectified categories of the political economy of socialism and can be understood only within its conceptual framework. However, from the point of view of classical science, our objective realities are complete nonsense that should not and cannot exist.

Soviet socialism was a holistic resource management system, rational, coherent, and integrated into government. Contrary to the opinion of most domestic ideologists, politicians, and economists, socialism is not dead. Moreover, cleared from Soviet rhetoric, it is re-emerging as largely anti-Soviet socialism. Many current ideological discussions are based on the conflict between the supporters of different forms of its ideological reincarnation (from internationalists-statists and orthodox socialists to national socialists). Even those politicians who are considered liberal, seek acceptable forms for implementing essentially socialist ideas, such as the need for industrial policy, planning, fair distribution, and price control. This socialism has little in common with the traditional European one, as it relies on a resource-based (or distributive, according to Olga Bessonova) state system, rather than capitalist production, consumption, distribution, and exchange. **In such a system, everything distributed by the state becomes a resource.**

The situation is more complex when it comes to economic science and social practice based on it. The political economy of socialism is far beyond the scope of economics taught in universities and business schools, therefore "real economists" currently perceive its concepts as a certain curiosity. In turn, Russian entrepreneurs consider odd the economic science taught in such universities and business schools, since this knowledge is completely out of touch with their actual practice.[19]

The principal idea of Soviet socialism, partially inherited by the Russian one, is that the economy and the social organization of the state must be merged into a single mechanism for equitable distribution of resources. Production should be a component of social life, and social life should be organized as state-of-the-art production.[20] The syncretic system must ensure a crisis-free seamless and sustainable development of the society based on rational concentration and distribution of resources owned by the state of the whole people.

Life in Russia demonstrates that the system based on categories of the political economy of socialism did not disappear with the collapse of the USSR. Therefore, the works of the founders of the political economy of socialism—Lenin, Stalin, Bukharin, Sokolnikov, and Strumilin,—as well as of such practitioners of socialist construction as Stalin's People's Commissars Voznesensky, Zverev, and Lyubimov, remain an adequate depiction of our reality, adjusted naturally for time, style, and lack of ideology.

---

19 Foreign languages and mathematics are the core subjects in such educational institutions. Special courses generally include recitals of translated books and articles that have no referents in our life. The impression is that students are trained for work abroad.

20 In Lenin's days, life was modeled in line with technologies of the second industrial revolution. Currently, information technologies are on the agenda, and their proponents strive to record, assess and control all resource flows. It is well known that the recent attempt to apply these technologies to control alcohol business flows resulted in the first shortage crisis in contemporary history. However, a start has been made.

The resource-based state

The Russian state pursues (and used to pursue) the goal of mobilizing and managing resources that are not goods and the value of which cannot be expressed in monetary terms. Resource wealth is measured in kind, by "iron and steel per capita". In the socialist ideal, resource mobilization means that the state completely controls all material and human flows. Our state has emerged as a tool for managing resource flows that it itself had generated. It creates conditions for a seamless movement of resources and first removes all hindrances, i.e., internal and external enemies.

Russian-style resources are rather treasures, which are either concealed or pointlessly wasted by nature or people, whereas they should be mobilized and used to achieve the great goal. The administrative-territorial, sectoral and social organization of our country is a derivative from the exploration, production, accumulation, distribution, and utilization of resources. In this system, social ties are flows of resources between elements of the state structure. The population is a resource for the construction of the Soviet, or currently Russian, socialism. Education is a resource[21], the health of the population is a resource, and land is a resource. In this framework, labor is also a resource rather than goods. The term "labor resources", invented by political economists of socialism, precisely reflects the place and role of the population in producing and processing other resources, and hence in the social system. Like Midas, the state turns everything that it needs at a specific time into resources.[22]

---

21 Hence, for example, talk about the "drain of intellectual capital".
22 The territory, minerals, flora and fauna, and finally the people are no more than resources. Instead of developing the economy as a system for producing wealth, the socialist state accumulates and manages resources. The purpose of this activity, like in a popular Brezhnev-era joke, is to overtake global leaders, who, according to official propaganda, are standing on the edge of an abyss. Resources have intrinsic value, and their possession is everything. Those who have more resources are socially significant; if you do not have access to resources, you are nobody. Production is the development of resources, and social life is their accumulation. Politics is a struggle for resources, including such resources as territory, geopolitical position, outer pace, and ocean depths. Economy is replaced by re-

The resource-based state system is fractal, i.e., it reproduces its principal features at every structural level. Every fragment of the state system, including people, is a resource for another fragment. The state "charges" each fragment with the task of becoming a resource, i.e., serving the purpose of achieving the great national goal, which is specified down to an individual.[23]

Utilization is a form of using resources. An enterprise, industry or region must utilize the allocated resources. The result consists in meeting certain regulatory requirements or manufacturing a product.

No goods emerge from such utilization. The mere fact of spending or consuming the resources evidences their use. The used resources are written off, and they cease to exist as an accounting unit.

Warehousing is a form of storing resources. Any person who has lived under socialism knows that store is no sore; therefore, the amount of resources accumulated by the state and its population is immense. However, it is impossible to assess this wealth in terms of goods and money due to the very nature of the state.[24] There can be no question of using economic tools for assessing performance in a resource-based state. Value and cost-effectiveness are meaningless, since the paradigm of the political economy of socialism does not envisage them. Any mention of these indicators is a symptom of the

---

    source management, the effectiveness of which is measured by the progress on the way to achieving the great goal.

23   The great national goal is decomposed into a set of separate goals for each fragment of the state structure (administrative-territorial units, branches of the national economy, and the statistical social groups of workers, peasants, and employees) built as parts of the machine steadily advancing towards the established target. Five-year plans for the social and economic development of the USSR approved at congresses of the CPSU Central Committee were broken down into annual, quarterly, and monthly plans for every fragment of the state structure—from republics to village councils, and from branches of the national economy to work teams. Government planning authorities allocated resources to implement these plans. Physically, material resources were provided by public supply agencies, and labor resources - by the State Committee for Labor and the NKVD-Ministry of the Interior.

24   A simple example illustrates the amount of accumulated wealth: plundering of metals stockpiled by the USSR and their export from Russia have secured over the past 15 years a comfortable life for various experienced managers from a dozen states. According to expert estimates, salt, matches, soap, preserves, and sugar stashed away by the population at the time of the latest shortage of goods (1970s–1980s) were used up only by the mid 1990s.

erosion of the great idea and the beginning of the transition from the latest stability to the yet another depression.

The management procedure combining various by-laws, regulations, and instructions governing resource accumulation, storage, utilization, and write-off determines the use of resources. Any violation of such instructions, standards, and regulations constitutes a crime against the management procedure.

Resources and threats; the specific Russian nature

It appears that the economy of the USSR was totally resource-based and oriented at neutralizing various threats related to existing and potential resource shortages. The outstanding technological development of the USSR was the result of such a policy because the state mobilized all the resources and planned their allocation to neutralize the threats associated with lagging behind the "main adversary", primarily in the military field. Contemporary Russia largely succeeded the USSR; therefore, it can be classified as a resource-based state, where economic development is secondary to activities aimed at identifying, structuring, and neutralizing those factors that threaten state integrity and social stability. Investment in neutralizing such threats accounts for a significant part of the Russian economy. Economic development performs a service function in relation to neutralizing threats.

Appropriate resources are needed to neutralize the threats. The Russian state withdraws such resources from the market and distributes them among its structural elements (regions, ministries, municipalities, public and private corporations) according to the accepted and agreed upon perceptions of the scope and relevance of the threats. Thus, the resources that can be made available to the structural elements of the state depend, largely, on the threats that a particular structural element can actualize and present to the state. Thus, if confirmed by respective agencies, information on a threatening epidemiological situation, will result in resources being allocated to the Office of the Chief Sanitary Inspector (Federal Service for Protecting Consumer Rights and Public Health—Rospotrebnadzor), the Ministry of Health, the Ministry of Internal Affairs, the Ministry for Emergency

Situations, regional authorities, and other structures charged with fighting epidemics. Government-authorized information about the threat of unemployment will lead to an additional flow of resources to the Ministry of Labor and Social Development, which will distribute them to those regions where the number of registered unemployed is relatively higher than in the other regions.

Every structural element of the state is interested in increasing the flow of allocated resources and therefore seeks to formalize and institutionalize the threats that exist or may arise if this particular element does not receive the requested resources in the required amount. Driven by this logic, all structural elements of the state have to generate information (intended for resource managers) on the threats, the reliability of which is quite different. As a result, the highest levels of government are flooded with information that various external and internal agents are threatening people, organizations, regions, the political system, etc., and that additional resources are needed to neutralize their activity.

In such circumstances, inventing new different-level threats—from the federal to the local (municipal) one—becomes a method of obtaining additional resources from the state. The myth about the "Orange Revolution" threat is an example of a rather successful invention. Classifying this threat as a relevant one resulted in the establishment of new structural units (such as the "E" Directorate within the Ministry of Internal Affairs) and the emergence of various "patriotic" youth organizations. The state allocated resources to those who combat this threat. The latter have formed themselves into a sort of corporation that seeks continued public funding for its activities and therefore uses any pretext to actualize the "Orange Revolution" myth.

Since the state has no independent (from its structural elements) algorithm for classifying, assessing, and ranking threats, it reacts to new threats by withdrawing more and more resources from the market (thus limiting the opportunities for increasing capitalization) and allocating them to those structural elements, which according to the officials and politicians are designed to neutralize the most dangerous threats. The downside of such activities are shrinking markets. Economic and political agents refocus from risk-based market operations to utilization of resources allocated by the state for neutralization of threats, some of which are apparently unsubstantiated.

It is common for domestic social practice that the state withdraws resources from the market and uses them to maintain its integrity, enhance security and social stability, which the politicians and officials claim to be threatened. However, there is no explicit definition of "threat", and the system of threats is depicted only in the political *National Security strategy of the Russian Federation until 2020*.[25] Individual threats are described in such documents as the *Information Security Doctrine of the Russian Federation*,[26] *Food Security Doctrine of the Russian Federation*,[27] *National Strategy for Economic Security of the Russian Federation*,[28] and the like.[29] There is a system of state apparatus units, various ministries and agencies, designed to neutralize specific threats.

The ontological status of threats, their identification and ranking

The ontological status of threats is not defined. It is generally considered that they arise (or exist) outside of any social, political, informational or other contexts. However, something becomes a threat only if it has "threatening consequences". Thus, tsunami and fires become threats due to their consequences—if they threaten the economy, politics, and could result in loss of life. Such phenomena occurring outside the inhabited world serve to satisfy the curiosity of ordinary people or the professional interest of specialists, but they pose no threat.

In turn, threatening consequences do not exist by themselves; they are relevant only for the parties concerned. Consequences must

---

25 https://docs.google.com/viewer?url=http%3A%2F%2Fstra.teg.ru%2Flibrary%2Fstrategy%2F4%2F0%2FNB.docx
26 http://www.scrf.gov.ru/documents/5.html
27 http://www.kremlin.ru/news/6752
28 http://www.scrf.gov.ru/documents/23.html
29 http://www.scrf.gov.ru/searchhl?url=documents/sections/3/&mime=text/html&charset=utf-8&hldoclist=http%3A//www.scrf.gov.ru%3A17000/%3Ftext%3D%25D0%25B4%25D0%25BE%25D0%25BA%25D1%2582%25D1%2580%25D0%25B8%25D0%25BD%25D1%258B

be differentiated not only by type, but also by specific social groups, local communities, for the entire state or its individual institutions.

This means that it is necessary to identify the threats, i.e., detect and name them. The identification process includes determining the range of threats, their likelihood, localization, potential damage, and social and other consequences.

Following identification, the threats have to be classified. The theory of management distinguishes between natural and anthropogenic threats, which, in turn, include political, economic, technological and other threats. Generally, such classifications are more illustrative than substantive. The wording of the national security concepts, where the empirical listing of threats performs purely political functions, is such an example[30]. It is evident that there are no generally accepted theoretically substantiated methods for classifying and ranking threats.[31]

After completing classification, it is necessary to rank the threats, i.e., determine which threats are more significant, and which are less so.

Following classification and ranking, the threats have to be neutralized through mobilizing the respective resources and utilizing them in such a way as to mitigate the consequences of the threats. A historical framework of government organizations responsible for neutralizing threats serves this purpose. Its components result from the practical classification of threats. These organizations consolidate, distrib-

---

30 Analytical report of the Institute of Sociology of the Russian Academy of Sciences, *The national security of Russia as assessed by experts* http://www.gosbook.ru/node/47171;
http://www.armscontrol.ru/start/rus/docs/snconold.htm; *National security doctrines and concepts of the USA, France, and Japan* http://www.budgetrf.ru/Publications/Magazines/VestnikSF/2000/vestniksf117-05/vestniksf117-05030.htm#HL_12;
Xiong Guangkai. *Comprehensive concept of the national security of China*, http://www.globalaffairs.ru/number/n_13205, *The national security strategy of the United States of America*, https://docs.google.com/viewer?url=http%3A%2F%2Fmerln.ndu.edu%2Fwhitepapers%2FUSNSS-Russian.pdf,
A Strong Britain in an Age of Uncertainty: The National Security Strategy http://www.direct.gov.uk/prod_consum_dg/groups/dg_digitalassets/@dg/@en/documents/digitalasset/dg_191639.pdf?CID=PDF&PLA=furl&CRE=nationalsecuritystrategy

31 This in itself is quite a serious threat, as it eventually leads to a dispersal of resources allocated by the state to neutralize threats and confuses politicians, entrepreneurs, and the population.

ute, and utilize the resources required to neutralize the threats. The higher the rank of a threat, the more dangerous it is, which means that the state must allocate a greater part of the limited resources to an organization for its neutralization. The greater the amount of resources used when neutralizing a threat, the higher is the status of the organization in the state hierarchy.

The threat framework mirrored in the state structure

The very structure of the state can be considered as an objectivation of certain practical perceptions of the threats, as an institutionalization of their applied classification. The state structure responds to different threats by establishing respective institutions. Thus, the existence of natural hazards is countered by ministries and agencies responsible for neutralizing their consequences, whereas military threats are addressed by structures within the military establishment. A resource-based state can be represented as a set of agencies created to neutralize threats, and the amount of resources utilized by these agencies—as a result of the official ranking of these threats: the more dangerous the threat, the greater amount of resources must be allocated to the respective agency.

State structures are formed historically, and quite often they reflect practical threat classifications, which are no longer relevant. That is why the state's reaction to current threats is not always adequate. Moreover, agencies once established with the purpose of neutralizing certain types of threats, are able to react to new threats only in the way they reacted to the former old ones.

Preserving the established framework of agencies and other structural units designed to neutralize threats is equivalent to the state legitimizing the invariance of the sources of threats, with all the ensuing political and economic consequences. This means that the existing management structure designed to neutralize the threats is by nature extremely conservative.

Under such management arrangements, rapid response to new "inter-agency" (not envisaged by the existing institutional structure) threats is achieved by establishing emergency bodies—

headquarters,—which include by virtue of office heads of the relevant agencies, and by holding various meetings attended by the officials responsible for neutralizing the threats. The work of the headquarters and the meetings serve to coordinate the activities of various services for neutralizing "inter-agency" threats.

The resources for such activities are provided from different funds managed by the officers in charge of the headquarters: ministers, governors or other officials.

Besides official documents, such as various security concepts and reports of the agencies responsible for neutralizing threats, information about the threats, their emergence and relevance is currently available in the information space, in the Internet, where scientists, journalists, experts, officials, and ordinary citizens express their more or less substantiated opinions about the most urgent threats. The spectrum of these opinions is extensive and ranges from predictions of global nuclear war and meteor attack to possible pandemics, hunger, water shortages and the collapse of Western civilization under the influence of the "Islamic factor".

It is extremely difficult to extract reliable information about the existence and relevance of threats from this information noise. Moreover, the agencies responsible for neutralizing threats use accentuated selections from such information to support additional resource requirements.

The resource-based nature of the state and the established institutional mechanism for generating and neutralizing threats is self-sustaining and self-perpetuating. For governmental and public organizations, political parties and associations, regional and municipal authorities, inventing threats and demonstrating them has become a major tool for extracting resources from the budget. Informal corporations emerging in the administrative market for the purpose of utilizing budgetary resources allocated to neutralize threats, are essentially closed for description and study precisely because of their informality.

The institutional structure for neutralizing threats in Russia

The need to neutralize all kinds of threats is an essential part of Russian public administration. Besides ministries designed to neutralize natural and anthropogenic threats (Ministry for Emergency Situations), foreign threats (Ministry of Foreign Affairs), military threats (Ministry of Defense), threats to social stability (Ministry of Internal Affairs), threats of law violations (Ministry of Justice), the administrative structure of the state includes special institutions called federal services. The federal government has thirty-five federal services with different subordination, ultimately responsible for neutralizing specific threats.

Of the above services ten are subordinated to the president, ten—to the Cabinet of Ministers (the prime minister), and fifteen are departmental (ministerial) services.

Thus, by its very structure the state classifies threats at least into four categories: threats to the existence of the state (neutralized by ministries subordinated to the president—Ministries of Defense, Foreign Affairs, Internal Affairs, Justice, Emergency Situations); threats to the governance procedure (neutralized by services subordinated to the president); threats to the functioning of the state (neutralized by services subordinated to the prime minister); and threats to the functioning of sectors of the economy (neutralized by services subordinated to ministries).

All ministries and federal services have territorial, regional, inter-regional, municipal, district, and inter-district branches, which represent them in the administrative-territorial hierarchy and which are responsible for neutralizing threats within their departmental and territorial jurisdiction. Every service has its own budget, which is used by its subordinate structures that are eventually localized in the municipalities.

The activities of the services aimed at neutralizing threats can be regarded as managing flows of budgetary resources distributed to their own personnel and to other groups of the population. It is natural to assume that both the personnel of the services and the other beneficiaries are interested in increasing the flow of resources distributed to them.

As the amount of resources allocated to the ministries and services depends on the severity and magnitude of the threats, the services are interested in both expanding the range of threats within their competence and in exaggerating their scale and danger. On the other hand, the groups for whose protection the resources are allocated, are also interested in increasing their amount and, therefore, in exaggerating the threats.

The classification of threats is inherent in the framework of government bodies and their ranking is manifested in the amount of resources allocated to the service or department for the purpose of neutralizing threats: the more significant the threat, the more resources are allocated to neutralize it and the more people are involved in the relevant services and supporting entities.

Table 1   Empirical classification of threats and agencies responsible for neutralizing them

Ministries subordinated to the president that neutralize threats to the existence of the state	Federal services subordinated either directly to the president or to the ministries subordinated to the president that neutralize threats to the governance procedure	Federal services subordinated to the prime minister that neutralize threats to the functioning of the state	Federal services subordinated to ministries that neutralize threats to the functioning of sectors of the economy
Ministry of Internal Affairs Neutralizing threats to internal stability		**Federal Anti-Monopoly Service** Neutralizing threats to market monopolization	**Federal Service for Labor and Employment** Ministry of Labor Neutralizing threats of unemployment, etc.
Ministry of Civil Defense, Emergencies and Disaster Relief of the Russian Federation Neutralizing natural and anthropogenic threats, ensuring mobilization readiness		**Federal Customs Service** Neutralizing threats to the customs border	**Federal Service for Intellectual Property** Ministry of Economic Development Neutralizing threats of breaching laws on intellectual property
Ministry of Foreign Affairs of the Russian Federation Neutralizing threats related to international relations		**Federal Tariff Service** Neutralizing threats related to tariff regulation	**Federal Accreditation Service** Ministry of Economic Development Neutralizing threats related to infringement of rights to different activities

Ministry of Defense of the Russian Federation Neutralizing military threats	**Federal Service for Military and Technical Cooperation** Subordinated to the Ministry of Defense Neutralizing threats related to violations in military-technical cooperation	**Federal Financial Markets Service** Neutralizing threats of financial market disruptions	**Federal Registration Service** Ministry of Economic Development Nneutralizing threats related to breaching the state registration of title to land
	Federal Service for Technical and Export Control Subordinated to the Ministry of Defense Neutralizing threats related to non-compliance with standards for military and dual-use goods and services		
Ministry of Justice of the Russian Federation Neutralizing threats of non-compliance with laws	**Federal Penitentiary Service** Subordinated to the Ministry of Justice Neutralizing threats related to the behavior of convicts and criminals	**Federal Service for Alcohol Market Regulation** Neutralizing threats related to uncontrolled turnover of alcohol and alcoholic products	**Federal Tax Service** Ministry of Finance Neutralizing threats related to tax and duty payments
	Federal Bailiff Service Subordinated to the Ministry of Justice Neutralizing threats of non-compliance with court decisions		
	State Courier Service of the Russian Federation (federal service) Neutralizing threats of potential leakage of classified information when delivered by ordinary means of communication	**Federal Service for Environmental, Technological, and Nuclear Supervision** Neutralizing threats related to the technical state of engineering and environmental systems	**Federal Service for Fiscal and Budgetary Supervision** Ministry of Finance Neutralizing threats related to diversion of public funds

Foreign Intelligence Service Neutralizing threats related to the geopolitical activity of other states	**Federal Migration Service** Neutralizing threats of uncontrolled migration	**Federal Treasury (federal service)** Ministry of Finance Neutralizing threats related to the turnover of budgetary financial resources
Federal Security Service Neutralizing threats related to terrorism and intelligence activities of other states	**Federal Service for Protecting Consumer Rights and Public Health** Neutralizing threats to public health and consumption	**Federal Service for Supervision of Transport** Ministry of Transport Neutralizing threats related to transportation
Federal Drug Control Service	**Federal Service for Defense Contracts**	**Federal Service for Veterinary and Phytosanitary Supervision** Ministry of Agriculture Neutralizing threats related to epizootics and phytopathology
Federal Guard Service Neutralizing threats to senior government officials	**Federal State Statistics Service** Neutralizing threats related to registering social, demographic, and economic indicators	**Federal Service for Supervision of Communications, Information Technology and Mass Media** Ministry of Communications Neutralizing threats related to disruptions in communications, information technology, and the information space
Federal Financial Monitoring Service Neutralizing threats related to the cross-border turnover of financial resources		**Federal Service for Supervision of Natural Resources** Ministry of Natural Resources Neutralizing threats of violations in the use of natural resources

		Federal Service for Hydrometeorology and Environmental Monitoring Ministry of Natural Resources Neutralizing threats related to the uncertainty in climatic conditions	
		Federal Service for Supervision in Education and Science Ministry of Education Neutralizing threats of infringing rights to education	
		Federal Service for Supervision of Healthcare Ministry of Health Neutralizing threats of infringing rights to medical care	
	Federal services subordinated to the president within ministries subordinated to the president. Federal services subordinated directly to the president; their functions	Federal services subordinated to the prime minister (government); their functions	Federal services subordinated to ministries; their functions
Ministries subordinated to the president that are responsible for neutralizing threats; their functions			

However, such a classification of threats objectified in the very state structure represented by government agencies is hardly efficient when the consequences of the threats are outside the competence of particular services or their totality.

For example, the 2010 wildfires were a special case, where the competences of different government organizations responsible for neutralizing the threat of fires overlapped. As mentioned above, the threats are important not by themselves but by their consequences. In turn, these consequences can become independent threats, where other services not directly related to neutralizing fires will be functionally responsible for their neutralization. This was the case with the above-mentioned wildfires—their sources were located in areas controlled by the forest department and were outside the competence of the Ministry for Emergency Situations. Consequently, the institutional structure for neutralizing threats in Russia is based on a historical and political classification, which is largely attributive. It requires at least an analysis of its mechanism and operating procedure, if not substantial streamlining.

It is practically impossible to perform an economic (i.e., resource-based) analysis of the institutional structure for neutralizing threats at the federal level, as the relevant items of the federal and regional budgets are classified, and the inter-budgetary relations regulating the provision of resources to respective government agencies are not transparent.

Corporations for utilizing the resources allocated to neutralize threats

Specialized federal services and ministries are not the only entities engaged in neutralizing threats. Such activity is immanent in all structural elements of the state. They would hardly receive sufficient resources for their routine operations without demonstrating the threats that could result from a shortage of allocated resources.

Thus, because of the resource-based life arrangement, educational, healthcare, and social security institutions have to accentuate the threats (growing sickness rate and unemployment, declining rate of literacy, etc.) and demonstrate to the resource allocators that they need additional resource flows to avoid various problems that could eventually result in higher social tension or a breach of social justice.

Practically any municipal budget starts with a preamble accentuating such threats as bad roads, dilapidated housing, damaged municipal and residential infrastructure, growing numbers of patients and people on welfare. The very structure of such a budget reflects the range of threats that municipal officials and deputies use in their attempts to increase the flow of resource (in the form of grants and subventions) receivable by the municipality from regional and federal allocators.

Besides moving up the hierarchy of public administration, this flow of practically unverified information about the existing and potential threats spills out into the information space, the mass media and social networks. As a result, they are overflowing with information about the problems of individuals, municipal and natural disasters, the plight of municipalities, regions, culture, healthcare, education, social security, the military establishment and the ability of the state to withstand external and internal aggression.

Field research shows that virtually all interviews with officials and ordinary people start with complaints that everything is bad and that the resources allocated by the authorities are not sufficient to address the basic problems of local life. This general poormouthing attitude is reflected in the media, which draw a catastrophic picture of the situation in the country. The domestic media and social networks act as a certain resonator tuned to amplify and generalize information about threats. "Facts" created jointly by disgruntled citizens and the journalists, should they emerge at the right time in the right place, accumulate unverifiable interpretations and transform into something that can be dangerous for everyone, i.e. they become an obvious (the TV broadcasts this) threat, and the state has to intervene in order to neutralize it. Media content can be regarded as a flow of complaints addressed to the state against itself and indignation as to the state's reaction to these complaints.

Based on this "frightening" information generated to obtain additional resources, the municipal authorities jointly with officials of the federal services represented in the municipality, lobby an increase of resources allocated to the municipalities by the federal and regional budgets. They can motivate their requests either by growing unemployment in the municipality or the deplorable state of the utilities infrastructure, which requires immediate investment in order to prevent municipal disasters or other calamities. Hence, formulating threats is an element of resource flow management.

When the interests of public services designed to protect from threats coincide with those of the groups to whom resources are allocated to neutralize the threats, informal corporations emerge whose goal is to obtain public resources allocated to neutralize threats. Precisely such corporations are agents in the administrative market for apportioning resources intended for the neutralization of threats.

Such corporations emerge subject to certain conditions. In particular, the state should institutionalize the threat, recognize it, and allocate resources from the budget or from other sources to neutralize it. Next, it is necessary to designate a core agency that will be responsible for neutralizing the threat and determine the criteria for localizing the impact of the threat: area, social group or element of the administrative-territorial division.

When these conditions are met, a threat-neutralizing corporation generally emerges, which as a matter of course includes the municipal residents or members of the social group with whom the respective public agency and its associated organizations are working on neutralizing the imminent threat. Since the total amount of resources in the budget is limited, various corporations compete for their share of the resources. The competition is not a market one. It is administrative competition, where one of the elements is creating competing threat images in the information space—images with more vivid properties in the form of consequences for the whole state, its certain areas or social groups.

One can say that striving to increase the flow of resources allocated to neutralize threats, the residents of the municipalities and the municipal and regional authorities establish specific informal corporations competing in the administrative market with other similar corporations for a share of the federal or regional budgets.

Generally, the municipal budget already provides for the resources that the municipality expects to receive for the purpose of neutralizing threats. Therefore, an analysis of the budget structure shows what threats are relevant for the municipality, and the relative amount of resources allocated for their neutralization gives an idea about their significance. Theoretically, the more important the threat, the more resources are allocated to neutralize it.

In the process of utilizing public resources allocated for neutralizing threats, corporations using the respective budgets expand by including groups of the population that are final recipients of the above resources. Thus, actualizing the threat of unemployment is important not only for officials of the Labor Ministry but also for the recipients of unemployment benefits, who are generally included in different survival schemes, have hidden sources of income, and are unemployed only in the sense of being registered with public employment services.

It is very likely that similar corporations interested in stirring up threats to maintain or increase the existing resource flows emerge not only in the municipalities, but also in all other elements of the state structure. The corporate structures created for neutralizing threats have no interest in any research as to the logic of their functioning. Moreover, they tend to withhold any information about their activities, since public disclosure may reveal that certain threats, along with the respective corporations established to utilize the resources for their neutralization, are no more than a pure bluff.

The population, threats and markets

Russia is specific by its disproportionately large public sector, which operates primarily in a threat-neutralizing mode. In other words, neutralizing threats is the operating mechanism of the authorities. Outside Russia, administrative markets are localized, and threat-neutralizing activity focuses primarily on state and military security. Instead of an administrative market for neutralizing threats, a normal market exists, where the population's individual and group fears are converted into business and corporate incomes.

Market agents influence demand by convincing people that they will be in danger of premature old age, sickness, loss of social status, or social exclusion if they fail to consume the agents' goods and services, such as antioxidants, antidepressants or fitness centers. End consumers pay for their fears themselves. The main thing is to generate and maintain these fears, which is achieved by inventing threats and exaggerating their significance.

Due to the resource-based nature of the Russian state, market agents cannot operate here as they do in other countries. They interact, in one way or another with the public services, which are designed to neutralize the threats, and influence the introduction of new types of threats (through the World Health Organization, for example), assessment of their danger, and, consequently, the amount and selection of public resources necessary for their neutralization. In so doing, they force the state to procure from them precisely those goods and services that such agents produce. This means that in order to introduce new "effective" drugs against ageing or cellulitis into the product range consumed by Russian people, these drugs have to be approved by Rospotrebnadzor and the Ministry of Health.

After the state approves such innovations, administrative public procurement markets for these wonder drugs emerge, on the one hand, and demand for them is engineered through mass media, social networks, and healthcare providers, on the other hand.

However, such strategies do not always succeed in Russia. Thus, for example, *Tamiflu,* a panacea from flu recommended by the World Health Organization, lost the administrative competition to the domestic panacea drug *Arbidol,* the miraculous properties of which were advertised by the Ministry of Health with the political support of the federal authorities. However, the strategy of generating fear of various exotic forms of flu among the Russian population bore fruit and secured a substantial growth in the sales of both Tamiflu (retail sales) and Arbidol (retail sales and public procurement).

People with their fears that natural, technical, and social agents are threatening their life, health, social status, etc. are of special interest to the researcher. Outside the sphere of his technical expertise, any specialist (either in a certain field or in management) becomes a layperson, who uses his professional knowledge to explain phenomena beyond his competence, i.e. he reduces reality to a professionally understandable level. Thus, a politician sees everywhere political intrigues, whereas an economist tends to explain everything in terms of goods, money, and markets. Such educated people are particularly susceptible to intelligently constructed threats affecting areas of their professional interest that seem understandable.

From the conventional point of view, natural threats are manifold. They include natural disasters and various apocalypses like "the end of the world". For example, the multistage commercial operation "end of the world in December 2012", which targeted primarily the general public, lasted three years and was quite successful. This period witnessed an emergence of various specialized markets, namely, commercial artworks (movies, books); long-life goods and life support tools and devices (should the world actually end); construction of underground shelters and hide-outs.

However, people are primarily afraid of death, old age, and sickness. Global informal corporations with the participation of public healthcare institutions, including Russian ones, emerged driven by the people's desire to live longer, cure illnesses or be always healthy. Industries specializing in curing old age and non-existent sicknesses, offering "anti-age" cosmetics, leisure, fitness, dietary supplements and vitamins are organized very cleverly: from mass media and social networks circulating information on possible ways of neutralizing threats of old age and sickness to public figures—media and pop "stars", doctors, healers, and medicine men, who for substantial remuneration impose on their audience and patients certain behavior and nutrition styles, various sports, "oriental practices", and raw food diets.

The public is also afraid of "man-made threats", which include anthropogenic climate changes, depletion of flora and fauna species and "extinction of rare species" due to technical activities, genetic engineering, etc. Global fundamentalist corporations, such as Greenpeace, World Wildlife Fund, and the Kyoto Agreements that benefit from public concerns about the threats formulated and institutionalized by these corporations replicate all these threats.

Besides nature and technology, people and their relationships can also pose threats, such as foreign policy and military threats; threats related to political activity; threats due to operating errors; threats emanating from alien social groups; threats of abnormal behavior; resource-based, ideological, and information threats. Each type of threat, if the state accentuates it and allocates budget resources for its neutralization, can result and results in the emergence of global and informal corporations vitally interested in at least maintaining, better still increasing, the flow of resources. For this purpose, members of such corporations must exaggerate the threats or invent them.

Goods and money in a resource-based state

In order to concentrate resources, distribute them and control their use, it is necessary to define fragments of the state structure, localize them, and describe their mission in terms of achieving the great goal and realizing the national idea. Defining an object in terms of the socialist world order means specifying its boundaries. Where belonging to a fragment was uncertain, the authorities took measures to establish a definite identity.[32]

In general, the relations between distinguished fragments of the socialist universe were planned as inter-fragment resource flows; in practice, they took the form of socialist exchange relationships. Specifically socialist, since socialist money and goods are virtual; they are no more than a method of registering resources crossing the boundaries between different fragments of the state.[33] The socialist boundary is an infinitely thin line with resources on both sides of it. Such resources are considered goods and money only at the moment when

---

[32] For example, when at the beginning of the 1980s, Soviet sociologist A. Alekseev quit his main job for the sake of a participant observation as worker at a plant, sanctions were imposed against him, since one person could not simultaneously have the status of worker and researcher. See: Alekseev A.N. *Dramatic sociology and sociological self-reflection.* In two volumes. SPb., 2003.

[33] The idea of completely abolishing money was very relevant in the first years of Soviet rule. Different ways of replacing money, including by energy and physiological labor measurement units, were widely discussed. See: Brutskus B.D. *The socialist economy. Theoretical reflections on the Russian experience.* http://www.finbook.biz/description.html?prm=118.

they are exactly on the line. Commodity-money measurement of resources under socialism arises only at the moment of crossing the boundary. According to the political economy of socialism, fully developed socialism will have no more boundaries; therefore, there will be no more need to measure resources on an exchange basis.

The resource-based state resembles a honeycomb: many separate cells with resources flowing across their boundaries. The cells are nested in each other, with the state being the largest cell. The boundaries between the cells are needed to register and control the resource flows. In order to arrange fair distribution, the population, industries, and regions must be divided into cellular groups according to their importance for the achievement of the great goal. This division creates the boundaries between the fragments. In order to cross these boundaries, it is necessary to transform the resources virtually into commodities and money.

The establishment of boundaries violates social justice and introduces inequality between the delimited fragments of the state structure. The ideological task of the state in general (as opposed to the state apparatus) is to eliminate all boundaries, establish socialist equality of everything and everybody, and ensure social justice. The task of the state apparatus is to maintain boundaries, since they allow registering, controlling and managing resource flows, and pave the way for administrative bargaining when it comes to their distribution and redistribution. In fact, this inconsistency between the purpose and the means for achieving it, between the state ideology and the government machine was the principal contradiction under Soviet socialism.[34]

The socialist state statistics and accounting agencies monitored every fact of transforming resources into commodities and money, and back. The sum of such transactions constituted the commodity and

---

34 Bargaining in the administrative market (redistribution of resources) is intended to restore social justice, infringed by boundaries between the cells of the resource-based state, and determine the ratios for transforming resources into goods and money, and back again. An array of mark up and mark down factors, as well as various offsets served this peurpose.

financial balance of the state. In Soviet times, this balance was more or less maintained and adjusted on a routine basis.[35]

However, resources are always scarce. This is their nature. Builders of socialism engaged primarily in getting hold of resources, since what circulated in the distribution system could hardly be called goods. Rather, it was a commodity shortage. Resources were procured "by pulling strings", often not due to necessity, but just for the sake of demonstrating one's administrative-market status, the capacity to "procure".[36] Secured resources had to be utilized. Utilizing resources was no less important than procuring them, since unused resources jeopardized the chances to secure them in the next activity cycle.

These invariant ratios between standard (planned) resource requirements and the methods for meeting them emerged around every social statistical unit: sectors of the economy and individual enterprises, regions of all levels—from the village council to a republic within the USSR. Planning as such created scarcity. Re-distribution of resources emerged as an institution for balancing regional and sectoral shortages. The socialist system functioned in a way to make everyone equally poor and disadvantaged.[37]

---

35   Following is an example of a situation where an individual socialist working person served as the smallest unit of measure when drafting the balances. A wage rate scale fixed the wages of workers, peasants and employees. These wages were adjusted by various factors. Total payments under every wage rate category in a specific cell—region were planned in advance and had to match (taking into account the deposits in the savings bank) the available resources, i.e., the goods that people could buy in stores and in the kolkhoz markets. In the event that the amount of money paid out exceeded the value of available goods, the difference was covered by vodka put on sale around payday. Such alcohol-based regulation reached up to 30% in the total turnover of money. When vodka (and tobacco) became scarce, the USSR collapsed.

36   The distribution of "printed matter" vividly illustrates the status symbol of distribution; collecting a library of scarce volumes was a matter of honor for every successful working person under socialism. The administrative market for re-distributing books that emerged around wholesale and retail bookstore directors was no less significant than the one around meat shops and kolkhoz markets.

37   Generally, administrative bargaining focused on agreeing upon the rates applicable to a specific resource when it crossed a specific boundary. For a producer, applying a higher rate for milk fat when delivering milk to Gossnab (State Procurement Committee) structures (i.e., when crossing the boundary between the resource producer and the state) meant receiving for the same resource additional tonnes of butter in funds. Since types of resources were numerous, and

At times when distribution dominated completely (wartime deliveries to fragments of the state), internal boundaries were abolished and socialist goods and money disappeared. Only resources remained, which were distributed under funds or ration cards. A universal shortage of resources was specific for such times. During depressions—reforms and liberalizations—boundaries between fragments of the socialist world order expanded and formed a socialist quasi-market environment. Shortages retreated, and periods of abundance set in. Thus, in the 1990s, fragments of the state ceased to be targets of planning, distribution, and control. Local socialist laws of commodity and money circulation that used to function only when crossing boundaries, became general rules for dealing with resources. Resources hovered at the boundaries, turned into commodities and money, and remained in that status without transforming back into resources. Thus, in the course of a few years, a substantial part of the USSR resources turned into commodities, and money circulation developed.

In the 1990s, there was an illusion that by a stroke of the pen of the official who canceled funding and price control, the resource-based state turned into a normal market (capitalist) one. However, this is no more than an illusion caused by the fact that boundaries between fragments of the resource-based state materialized and became so broad that they triggered the uncontrollable growth of socialist parasites, whom the "foremen" of perestroika and other progressive economists took for supporters of capitalism.

As a result of "liberal economic reforms", resource recipients, particularly basic institutions of the state, such as the armed forces, law enforcement bodies, education, healthcare, regions, and social groups of public sector workers found themselves simultaneously excluded from the deficient market and the distribution of resources. They were forced to re-distribute the resources stocked earlier and then to plunder them. In the 1990s, this became the main occupation of the military and defense industries personnel, police officers, teachers, doctors, and others employed in the public sector. Leasing premises pro-

---

rates even more so, administrative bargaining was universal. Life was in full swing.

vided by the state, deriving personal profit from production equipment, speculating on status capacities, directly selling public resources were widespread activities vital for the survival of the resource-based state cells. The boundaries between the latter became transparent for goods and money, but impenetrable for resources. As a result, national defense, public health and education became areas of concern, to put it mildly, since all the resources available to the respective fragments were traded for goods and money in order to survive.

By the end of the century, probably only patriotic emigrants—romantic builders of capitalism in Russia—retained hopes that the invisible hand of the almighty market would resolve all problems. To address current matters, it was necessary to restore resource flows to the fragments of the state structure. Therefore, the invisible hand of the resource-based state started "putting things right" by restoring the resource mobilization and allocation system.

Types of resources in the contemporary resource-based state

Restoring order started in 1995–1997 by establishing the financial system as a resource-based one. Due to the efforts of the "young reformers", money became the principal resource of the post-perestroika state. The state now accumulates money, plans its distribution, funds allocation, and controls its supply as tightly as strategic resources under Soviet power. It allocates rubles to publicly funded entities irrevocably like a resource rather than real capitalist money. The entities must use the allocated money. Unused money is an evidence of the poor work of the resource recipient. Administrative trade in the process of distributing monetary resources among different-level budgets, ministries and agencies is now quite legitimate when drafting and approving budgets by representative bodies.

Rubles become real money only when "crossing boundaries", primarily after being converted into "conventional currency units". The value of the "wooden" ruble depends on numerous internal boundaries established by the state and the corporations; therefore, it is impractical to invest rubles without converting them into "conventional currency units". In our country, doing business largely means converting financial resources received from various budgets into "conventional currency units" and investing them into anything (even a football club) abroad.

Another resource is natural raw materials, especially energy commodities. The substance of privatization was a change in the status of oil, gas, timber, fish, and metals—they were transferred from public ownership under the jurisdiction of corporations and individuals. Loans-for-shares auctions legalized such plundering of raw materials, which provided resources for the "new Russians". The reverse process of converting the previously plundered assets into public resources constitutes the substance of the present stage of development of our state. State-controlled corporations gradually concentrate resource management. The policies of these actors of new socialist processes are no longer driven by the interests of mythical businesses, but by the interests of state representatives—corporate board members and directors.

Unlike the early 1990s, the circulation of resources is subject to various state (tariffs, duties, and regional and sectoral boundaries) and corporate (internal prices and other instruments) regulations. At the same time, no attempts of direct public distribution of energy resources or "essential foodstuffs" have yet been successful. This is natural. The system has a long way to go to reach the Soviet prototype, although in general, socialist life is getting back on track, and the state regularly pays out pensions and wages in the public sector.

There is a significant difference between the present resource-based arrangement of the state and the Soviet one—the power status has become a convertible resource. The distribution of statuses in the state structure (as opposed to the USSR, where the political establishment (nomenklatura) and the talent pool represented an intricate but efficient system) is perhaps the most profitable resource-based business. Other resources, including money, have little meaning without a respective status. Civil service positions, as well as positions in the regional and local authorities, political parties and organizations, and representative bodies are the most cost-effective investment of resources accumulated in the course of plundering-privatization and, therefore, subject to "political risks".

The number of rich people in government bodies, as well as the number of people that have become rich thanks to the power status demonstrates the awareness of the active part of the population that wealth not supported by status is as virtual as rubles. It is the public status, the position, that provides access to other resources, i.e., to participation in public life.

Resource management is the principal, politically most acceptable and promising form of arranging social life in post-Soviet Russia. It is based on the new post-socialist resources: money, raw materials, and power status.[38] Their function in our social system is such, because the resource-based organization of the state is still in place. It is imitating a market, but the market forms are too narrow for it.

Resource self-management: redistribution and plundering

In periods other than total mobilization, the USSR government machinery did not function fully in line with the expectations of its ideologists. Primarily, because as soon as repressions abate, fragments of the resource-based state start formulating their own goals, which are aligned with the national ones only partly. These goals consist in managing any available resources.

Thus, the regions aimed for a higher status in the administrative-territorial system, which meant getting access to the same amount of resources as the more significant regions. The industries strove to increase their share in resources allocated by the State Planning Committee (Gosplan). The officials sought to expand their administra-

---

38 The trend is developing to assign the status of resources to an increasing number of goods. The fragments of the post-socialist world order are covertly competing to establish their own resource base. Even grain, meat and local industry products are becoming resources. Transporting them beyond the boundaries of certain regions is already strictly regulated. Lines are being drawn between different fragments of the state, and this demarcation serves the cause of building socialism. The state gradually introduces boundaries, thus narrowing the area where goods and money can freely circulate. The recent reinstatement of border zones and a ban for senior officials to have dual citizenship are an illustration thereof.

tive resource. Ordinary citizens tended to increase current consumption and/or stockpiled products (at least, salt, sugar, soap, matches, and canned food) preparing for the next emergency situation individual for each generation—from famine and war to prison and poverty.

Eventually, redistribution turns planning, funding, and control over resource allocation into mere formalities that nevertheless provide officials with funds for inappropriate (not as originally planned) use. At certain stages in the existence of a resource-based state, diversion of resources becomes the principal objective of its public servants. Importantly, the government machine that must ensure the most effective allocation of resources in terms of achieving the great goal, serves as the vehicle for their redistribution.[39]

The administrative market is primarily a vehicle for diverting resources. The state does not establish such relationships between the statuses; they emerge spontaneously when the structural elements of the state interact for the purpose of re-allocating resources. As such, resource reallocation is a trade between officials with political and administrative resources, who match them in the process of carving up everything possible.

At times of stability, the administrative market is very rigid. The administrative currency is unified, and administrative trade is limited by predefined conditions, i.e., by guidelines on organizing resource flows. The results of carving up resources are generally proportional to the administrative weight, i.e., the position of the negotiating parties in the system of administrative-market statuses—government ones in times of stability and power ones during depressions-reforms. The one with a higher political and administrative resource receives proportionately more other resources, including material ones. In the course of trade, the officials' administrative weight changes, the administrative resource is accumulated/spent, and the administrative-market status of the administrative market agent grows/falls.

---

[39] It is necessary to distinguish between diversion of resources and plundering. Diversion means changing the direction of resource flows within the hierarchy of public purposes, whereas plundering means using the resources for purposes not mandated by the state.

The desire to increase the administrative resource and preserve or enhance administrative-market status is the basic instinct of administrative market agents. The status determines the amount of resources that its holder can re-distribute, including resources for personal consumption, for example, direct (not by means of money) access to consumer goods and services, such as foodstuffs, publicly-funded vacation homes for private use, and high-quality healthcare.[40]

At times of depression, the supreme coordinating authorities deteriorate, since nationwide goals lose their mobilizing and sacrifice-justifying force. Like in the 1990s, decision-making on re-allocation of resources shifts down to the lowest levels of coordination, sometimes taking the form of gangster negotiations ("tyorki") and rendezvous ("strelki"), where all the concerned gangs formulate their objectives quite "concretely", and physical force is what secures mobilization and re-allocation of resources.

One can say that the administrative market is a form of organizing the interior space of a resource-based state. Outside such states, the administrative market exists only in the areas where the state accumulates and distributes resources with off-market objectives. As soon as off-market allocation of resources appears, the administrative market emerges as a vehicle for their re-allocation.

***

---

40 In Soviet times, the military and representatives of various industries (the defense "nine", "consumer goods" producers, and agrarians) engaged in administrative bargaining for economic development priorities, i.e., for their industry's share in the total amount of distributed resources. The weight of the industry and the administrative weight of its leaders was determined by the amount of consumed resources - the higher the consumption, the greater was the industry's significance for the economy of the resource-based state. Even the correlation between the great goal and ways of achieving it (distribution of resources among industries and territories) was a matter of bargaining. The importance of different sectors of the economy for the construction of socialism varied: at times, the state channeled resources mainly to the defense sector, sometimes - to agriculture, and less frequently - to science and technology. Within an industry, directorates, industrial complexes, and individual enterprises bargained among themselves. The relations between enterprises under one ministry also represented a kind of administrative bargaining. Similar bargaining for the share of resources received from centralized sources or placed under public control took place among republics, regions and territories, cities and districts.

In principle, socialist resources can be converted into goods and money very easily: by plundering-stealing, stockpiling above standard levels for further exchange or sale, alienating by force, or by mugging. In terms of political economy, resource plundering is an illegitimate way of re-distributing resources for personal or group consumption.[41]

In times of stability, when the state is thriving, the plunderers are latent, pervasive, but scattered. Nevertheless, the state fights them. During Soviet socialism, the number of people repressed for economic crimes was significantly higher than that of political prisoners.[42]

As soon as the consolidating idea loses its mobilizing effect, plunderers start their own life that has nothing to do with the great goal. At times of profound depressions, such as the 1920s and the 1990s, resource plundering is widespread and legalized.

Plunderers differ by the way they alienate resources from the state. Some are thieves, who are widespread among those employed in sectors of the economy. Some are bandits, who specialize in mugging; they mostly originate from power structures. Some are appanage princes, who specialize in appropriating nominally public resources by pocketing them or concealing from the state.[43]

---

41 The socialist state began its history by including endemic Russian theft and banditry in the building of communism. The likes of [Bolsheviks] Kamo, Kotovsky, and Golikov implemented the ideology of expropriating property and transforming it into state resources. Most members of our socialist society share a philosophy of seizing assets from the state and other citizens and turning them into their own resources. The methods by which the oligarchs built their oligarchies are fundamentally the same as those used by the Bolsheviks to establish the USSR.

42 According to V.N. Zemskov, as at 1951, GULAG camps "housed" 579,918 political prisoners and 2,528,146 prisoners convicted for general crimes, most of them for economic ones: http://www.pereplet.ru/history/Author/Russ/Z/Zemskov/Articles/ZEMSKOV.HTM

43 The terms "appanage prince-landowner", "thief", and "bandit" have no evaluative meaning. These definitions are no more than a statement that people with a respective mindset and ways of action are the main actors in our Russian drama at times of depression. Russian theft is not about pickpocketing in a tram. It is primarily a way of thinking and a perception of the world, and only then a practice. Resources must be pilfered - from the state or in its favor. Everything that can be stolen should be stolen, and it does not really matter whether the loot can be sold. The appetite with which plunderers are now grabbing resources that they evidently cannot use demonstrates that such activity is not directly related to economy and politics. It is a theft instinct that surfaces in actors of the theft-based administrative market at times of depression. The bandits' functions are not about mugging passers-by. First, it is a way of thinking in terms of social justice based

When the state prospers, plunderers are hidden in the social nucleus, disguised in the state.[44]

---

on a rigid social stratification into suckers and stand up guys, the proletarians and the bourgeoisie, whatever they were called at different times. Only then is it an issue of using force to redistribute assets in favor of the "stand up guys", the proletarians and those socially close to them. Moreover, redistribute in a way as to meet the specific concepts of social justice. By their psychology, the present law enforcers are not much different from the revolutionary sailors, who robbed the assets of well-to-do citizens of the Russian Empire. Appanage principalities demonstrate their mafia nature not by the law of "omerta", but by setting "locals" against the "aliens" who are rejected. Appanage princes live from resources available in the areas they control. They try to keep control over these resources and to increase them by overstating standard requirements, juggling tariffs and ratios for converting resources into goods and money, arranging "shady" resource flows, etc. Resources can include any products manufactured by the enterprises of any industry in the area. Although appearing to be criminal, such relations are legal. No laws are violated. Rather, it is a question of locally managing resources, which the state had not included or had excluded from its management procedure.

44   In times of stability, when the state provides its citizens with a ration, to which they are entitled according to criteria of social justice, and humiliating rituals replace politics, basic "criminal" relations manifest themselves first of all in culture. Historically, three cultures exist in Russia: those of appanage princes, merchant thieves, and aristocratic bandits. Peter the Great called all merchants thieves. Merchant thieves belong to different categories-guilds. There are local thieves, and there are federal thieves. Thieves are sociable people; they pay taxes and bribes. Taxes for them are a form of kickback, and the state budget - a form of common cash pool. They also invest in themselves - they enhance their environment by erecting neat and ornate buildings, seeking to keep the streets clean, and providing decent drinking establishments. Their parties are boisterous; they drink with taste and feast in style. Their song culture includes chanson and patriotic bard lyrics. Historically, authoritative thieves settled in Moscow—Russia's thief capital.

Another culture is the bandit, mugging, aristocratic one. Bandits are as stratified as the thieves are. The lower strata live off protection racket and "carve up" municipal budgets. The higher strata get kickbacks from the federal and regional budgets, and for "protecting the state and its interests". Unlike the thieves, the bandits are concerned about the fate and fortune of the country, its greatness, culture, and military supremacy. They pay no taxes and have no common cash pool. For them, the public budget is first of all a pocket providing funds for the prosperity of the country and their organized gangs. As for leisure, they have a taste for high art, opera and ballet; they like ballerinas, subtle chanteuses, and "freaky" singers. Their favorite places are the Mariinsky Theater and the Hermitage. Bandit lyrics are represented by [rock groups] DDT and Leningrad. Bandits drink moderately; they have nothing against cocaine and are tolerant to innovations in this field.

St. Petersburg with its ornate barracks - monuments of imperial architecture and communicating courtyards between straight avenues and streets is the bandit capital. St. Petersburg is the ideal place for all types of highway robbery: from mugging people in the street to large-scale projects, such as reforms of Peter the

However, when the state weakens, previously adequate functionaries start stealing, selling their loot, and mugging, as if they had been preparing for this their whole life. Because according to definition, they can perform no other function than concentrate and distribute resources. The groups in whole and their members individually seize any opportunity to pilfer state resources—aimlessly and devoid of any ideology—and accumulate their own. Alienating resources from the state becomes an end in itself for them.

Generally, the resource plunderers are interconnected. At times when the state prospers, vertical inter-level relations arise normally only between different categories of "expert" plunderers. For example, regional thieves were connected with "lower" level district appanage princes, and were protected from "above" by republican and federal law enforcers.

The Communist Party of the Soviet Union was particular about preventing the emergence of any inter-level associations consisting entirely of thieves, law-enforcing bandits or, heaven forbid, of appanage princes—Party and Soviet bosses. The experience of the Belavezha Accords demonstrated what danger the latter pose. Many Soviet political processes were based on proven episodes of the existence of such inter-level associations. Times of instability facilitate ties between the same categories of plunderers on different levels,

---

Great, the Great October Socialist Revolution, and the voucher privatization. Revolutions targeting redistribution of resources are conceived and launched in St. Petersburg, where mugging techniques are in the blood of its inhabitants. Then comes the turn of Moscow, where theft techniques are refined.

Unlike the thief and bandit subcultures, appanage principalities have received extensive coverage. For example, by [Russian writer] Saltykov-Shchedrin, as well as the major crime investigators of the USSR Office of the Prosecutor General - on the example of the Uzbek, Dnepropetrovsk and many other criminal cases. Their specific features are banya [Russian sauna] as an institution, vodka as the main beverage, and conversations of the "do you respect me?" type as a form of communication. The subcultures of appanage principalities are unique as an aggregate of consumer institutions. Every appanage prince has his special attractions: banya, fishing, hunting, and a special brand of vodka. Besides, by all available means he "procures" "overseas" food and goods, which are placed on the table (in the broad sense) before high-status guests. The combination of local and imported constitutes the uniqueness of each appanage principality. A special environment uniting local cultural workers, artists, scientists, and scholars forms around the appanage prince. Resource plunderers turn to this environment at times when they need to substantiate their plundering ideologically.

which results in the emergence of "criminal groups". Inter-level associations consisting entirely of appanage princes, thieves, or bandits have significant competitive advantages when "carving up" resources. "Organized crime" means alliances between different-level plunderers of public resources.

In times of depression, resource plunderers who used to know their place and stole according to rank, start converting resources into commodities and money on a large scale. Regional leaders and the regional elite (appanage princes) pocket resources, industry managers "rat" or "badger", depending on the situation. The law enforcers first "play the hog" (like a "dog in the manger"), and then turn to ordinary mugging, as according to them, a thief deserves to be robbed. As a result, crime grows, since the new resource managers are much tougher than the state in persecuting those who violate the procedure of using the resources.

The social stability mythologem as a form of legitimizing resource plundering

Plunderers become protagonists in times of depression pilfering public resources and stashing them privately or corporately. They establish resource-based states in miniature—oligarchies, which are miniature socialist states with vertical and horizontal power structures, resource flows, and their own plunderers: corporate thieves, bandits, and appanage princes.[45]

However, there is an irreconcilable conflict between resource management forms and the emerging practice of nationalizing the use of resources. Those, who have financial resources, power, and raw materials at their disposal realize that any further concentration of

---

45 Oligarchies emerge along sectoral and regional lines, inheriting the Soviet resource flow management structure. Oil and gas, metals, and chemical oligarchies on a federal scale are well known. Since governors are no longer elected but actually appointed, the constituent entities of the Russian Federation are gradually turning into regional oligarchies. Such territorial-sectoral oligarchies as the Krasnoyarsk Territory, Tver Region, and Chukotka are in a sense unique. However, oligarchies are much more widespread: practically every administrative district and every town have their own oligarchs who control the distribution of resources.

resources by the state will inevitably result in socialist regulation, purges, and repressions for them. Primarily, because their wealth is based on stolen public resources. The eternal debate within the elite of our society focuses on the issue of how to stay rich without losing one's freedom. The rich try be all means to convert part of their wealth into power statuses in the hope that belonging to the new nomenklatura or membership in yet another "party of power" will protect them from inevitable repressions. However, experience shows that it is quite difficult to transform stolen resources into property and capital.

Investment in land and real estate domestically no longer guarantees the security of resources pilfered from the state and provides no opportunity to convert them into real capital. The active part of the population has realized that any private disposal of resources is illusive in our state. By all available means, people transfer the assets accumulated at the time of privatization abroad. Rumor has it that there is no single entrepreneur with a capital exceeding 10 million "conventional currency units" who has not obtained foreign citizenship or property abroad. Socialist entrepreneurs are constantly engaged in exporting resources converted into goods and money from villages to the cities, from cities to the capitals, and from the capitals abroad. The agents of these processes believe that by relocating the appropriated resources they reduce the risk of the state re-mobilizing them.

Not only the rich and powerful are alarmed. Resources stolen from the state in the past 15 years have turned into assets of tens of millions of people, who have no intention of giving them back. Any attempt to "restore order" in this niche will cause inevitable resistance. Many people have something to lose. "Kulak [prosperous peasant] uprisings" of the early 1920s demonstrate what happens in such cases.

The authorities strive to ensure continuity in the use of resources. Due to lack of continuity, those involved "in the process" are exposed to well-known risks, including loss of wealth and status. The authorities aim to maintain "social stability", i.e., to secure and legalize the financial resources, raw materials, and affiliation with the power group for "credible" public servants. The "dacha [summer cottage] amnesty" and adoption of the inheritance law canceling inheritance tax are only some steps in this direction.

Perhaps, the time is near when the state will allow the owners to keep everything acquired in whatever way, but from then on will ensure fair distribution of resources, i.e., as it deems expedient. However, this requires an ideological framework that would enable socially close people to legalize their right to dispose of the appropriated resources, and at the same time introduce the basis for mobilizing the resources currently in the possession of socially distant persons. This task is indeed difficult to accomplish.

The world economy and the resource-based state organization

During the depression marked by the collapse of the USSR, a specific reality, mediating the relations between the resource-based organization of the state inherited from the USSR and the global economy, formed in Russia. Many external features allow outside observers to consider Russia a market economy. This opinion reflects the reality—up to the point of specific investment activities, when the investors face resource-based management stereotypes, the administrative market, and the surviving distribution mechanisms of social justice.

Theoretically, one can compare streamlining the use of resources in post-Soviet states with economic recovery in a conventional economy. The similarity allows reform-minded observers to describe the Russian reality in terms of economic growth rates, GDP, and other economic indicators. However, the similarity goes no further. The current recovery of the national economy is unlikely to have complete matches in conventional economies. The resource-based system of public life is growing mainly because the state has started concentrating resources and planning their distribution—the mythical market economy has nothing to do with it.[46] It is no coincidence that foreign

---

46   See, e.g., Rykov A.I., The situation in industry and measures for its recovery (http://www.magister.msk.ru/library/politica/rykov/rykoa012.htm);
Voznesensky. N.A., The defense economy of the USSR during the Great Patriotic War (http://militera.lib.ru/h/voznesensky_n/14.html).

investment in Russia is now taking forms similar to those of the late 1920s—import of manufacturing facilities, technology, and ideas on setting up production. At that time, the USSR was experiencing growth after a major depression of the resource-based state system, which, in particular, resulted in the collapse of the Russian Empire. Russia is currently experiencing similar growth. It is well known what followed "economic growth" in the USSR at the end of the 1920s—the 1930s with their collectivization, industrialization, and repressions. Strictly speaking, Russian capitalism exists only in that cell of the resource-based state, where the "conventional currency unit" and the ruble are converted without restrictions. This cell is still large, albeit shrinking, causing the concern of progressive economists.[47]

Corporate management systems increasingly resemble public organizations. Ostensibly capitalist, businesses self-organize more like socialist enterprises than traditional business units. The domestic "capitalists" themselves have turned into resource users trusted by the state and into "heads of directorates" of the re-emerging branches of the Russian national economy. Those who fail in trust have to pay dearly. Government raiding has become the principal tool for revising the results of privatization. It is largely similar to selective repressions.

Russia is reinstating the resource-based state system—contrary to prevailing opinion about the development of the market economy and domestic business practice, which is unable to accept the fact that "the space is shrinking". Business does not want to believe the obvious. Despite the evident risks, business does not intend to give up the 80% p.a. margin generated from converting public resources into commodities and money. It is trying to survive or adapt by fitting into the public resource-based system, initiating more and more "liberal laws" and lobbying the establishment of special zones (economic, recreational, industrial parks, research centers, etc.), where the public resource-based intentions are mitigated or neutralized. However, such attempts are unlikely to succeed.

---

47 Some romantic politicians intend to expand the area of capitalism and make the ruble fully convertible. This is in direct contrast with the other declared objectives of the resource-based state. Should the authorities be consistent in streamlining resource flows, the area where the ruble will be freely convertible into "conventional currency units" will shrink substantially.

Social justice and the social structure of a resource-based state

The state creates special social groups to neutralize threats, i.e. to utilize the resources allocated for this purpose. When the state recognizes an existing external military threat, the armed forces must neutralize it; where there is an internal threat, special armed forced—the internal troops—are required to neutralize it. Thus, the social structure of the Russian society-state is represented by groups formed by this very state to serve its purposes. Such groups are further referred to as post-Soviet estates.

However, the vast majority of Russian citizens have no idea to what social group they themselves or their parents currently belong. The social structure of the USSR was based on relations between the workers, peasants, and employees, but these groups no longer exist. Evidently, new social groups and new relations between them have emerged. However, it is precisely these groups and these relations that have as yet not become the subject of special analysis.

For the purposes of this work, social groups are the totality of people, whose self-definition and external definition match. The consistency of external identification with self-identification forms the social groups as participants of political and social processes. Thus, the "middle class" social group, for example, exists in the sense that there are people who consider themselves belonging to it, on the one hand, and whose self-identification is confirmed by the views and conduct of those representing the upper and lower classes, on the other hand.

The social structure is the totality of social groups, as defined above, and the relationships between them.

For the purposes of this work, social stratification includes all forms of social differentiation on property, power, corporate, and other grounds.

Of all the diversity of social groups, this work addresses only classes, estates, and corporations.

Classes herein are understood only as social groups varying by levels of consumption. We consider and review no other definition of classes.

Estates herein are understood only as social groups formed by the state to address its challenges, primarily to neutralize the threats. Estates formed by any existing state coexist with those formed by the previous state. For example, the Russian Federation has estates created over the past twenty years, such as state civil servants, and estates inherited from the Soviet Union, such as the military. We consider and review no other definition of estates.

Corporations herein are understood only as social groups formed in the market with the aim of monopolizing or maintaining a share in it. Corporations may be formed on territorial, industrial, ethnic, and many other grounds. We consider and review no other definition of corporations.

People form groups based not only on awareness of a similar property status, estate, ethnic, or clan affiliation, but, above all, on a common perception of social justice, or, more importantly, its violation, i.e., social injustice towards the social group to which they believe they belong. The desire to overcome social injustice promotes relations between the groups and drives social change.

Social justice was practically never a topic of research for sociologists, as it was in the competence of philosophers, experts on ethics, and lawyers. According to G.Yu. Kanarsh, "The classic definition of justice belongs to Aristotle: 'Justice is equality, but only for equals' (and vice versa: 'Justice is inequality, but only for those who are unequal'). In *Politics*, Aristotle also formulated the idea of "mixed constitution" (or "mixed government") as such, which resolves all social conflicts and ensures general satisfaction (the balance of interests of different social groups). This idea is central to the West European tradition. In modern history, Thomas Hobbes, debating Aristotle's social and ethical insights, lays the foundation for the contemporary (liberal) concept of justice. .....the liberal model formed the legal framework of the modern concept of justice with its prevalence of personal rights, ideas of social contract, minimal state, and secular society."[48] In one way or another, numerous concepts and opinions describe the essence of justice.[49]

---

[48] Kanarsh G.Yu. *Social justice: Philosophical concepts and the situation in Russia. Monograph* / G.Yu. Kanarsh, M.: Moscow Humanitarian University Press, 2011. - 316 p.

[49] According to Plato, justice is based on principles of goodness, which express the virtue of the state and involves appropriate relations of domination (see Plato. *The Republic.* 557-562 // Plato. *The Republic.* SPb.: Nauka, 2005). Aristotle implies the essence of justice to be equality for equals and inequality for those who are unequal. (see Aristotle. *Politics.* III, V, 8 // Aristotle. *Politics. Constitution of the Athenians.* M.: Mysl', 1997) (see also Aristotle. *Nicomachean ethics.* / translated by N. Braginskaya. M.: Publishing house Exmo-Press, 1997). For Thomas Hobbes, a just society is a patrimonial one based on the liberal premise that the rights of individuals are primary and inalienable (see Hobbes, T. *Leviathan, or the matter, forme, and power of a common wealth, ecclesiasticall and civil.* Chapter. XV // Hobbes, T. *Leviathan.* M.: Mysl', 2001). John Locke sees justice in equal rights to liberty and the exercise of jurisdiction (see Locke, J. *Two treatises of government.* Book II Chapter 2 // Locke, J. *Two treatises of government.* Translation from English; edited and compiled by A.L. Subbotin, with introduction and comments of the editor. M.: Kanon+ ROOI Reabilitatsiya, 2009). Jean-Jacques Rousseau believes that the only legitimate source of legislation is the general will (see Rousseau, J-J. *Of the social contract, or principles of political right.* Chapter. I // Rousseau, J-J. *Of the social contract. Treatises:* Translation from French M.: Kanon Press, Kuchkovo Pole, 1998). Immanuel Kant believes the rule of law over any ideas of good to be just, and supports the idea of a patrimonial state (see Kant, I. *On the old saw: That may be right in theory, but it won't work in practice //* Kant, Immanuel. Collected works: In 4 volumes, in the German and Russian languages. Volume 1: Treatises and articles (1784-1796). Prepared for publication by N. Motroshilova (Moscow) and B. Tuschling (Marburg). M.: Publishing House JSC Kami, 1993); Robert Nozick believes that justice involves an absolute supremacy of individual rights with a minimal interference of the state (see Nozick, R. *Anarchy, State, and Utopia.* New York. Basic Books, 1974). John Rawls defends the concept of justice as fairness (all social values should be equally distributed, except when inequality benefits everyone, and the greatest benefit goes to the least advantaged members of society) (see Rawls, J. *A theory of justice* / Translator and science editor: Tselishchev V.V. Novosibirsk: Novosibirsk University Press, 1995). Ronald Dworkin sees justice in an equal right of everyone to care and respect (see Dworkin, R. *Liberalism // Modern liberalism:* Rawls, Berlin, Dworkin, Kymlicka, Sandel, Taylor, Waldron / Translated from English by L.B. Makeeva. M.: Dom intellektual'noi knigi, Progress. Traditsiya, 1998). Alasdair MacIntyre appeals to the concept of virtues and implies strict regulation of individual benefits within the society for the sake of the common good (see MacIntyre, A. *After virtue: a study in moral theory* / Translated from English by V.V. Tselishchev. M.: Akademicheskiy Proekt; Ekaterinburg: Delovaya Kniga, 2000). Amartya Sen and Martha Nussbaum believe that social justice lies in developing the basic human functional capabilities (see Sen. A. *Development as freedom.* Translation from English; edited by R.M. Nureev; with afterword by the editor. M.:

In this work, we rely on Aristotle's distinction between corrective and distributive justice.[50]

Corrective justice implies equality before the law, whereas inequality (and corresponding injustice) emerges as a result of the people's market activity, their success or failure in the market. An enormous number of studies substantiating the political practices of a state of law are based on the philosophical analysis of corrective justice. In particular, the very notion of private law originates from the ideas of corrective justice.

Distributive justice implies equality of all people before the authorities (the superior, the sovereign) that distribute the resources. Injustice arises when people are deprived of their share of resources in the course of distribution. The welfare state theory is based on the philosophy of distributive justice. Moreover, the very notion of public law originates from the ideas of distributive justice.

Although the basic philosophical and legal definitions of justice appear to be logical, their empirical (in the sociological sense of the word) interpretation raises many questions. In particular, both classical and recent writings on social justice imply that social groups and the relations between them, i.e. the social structure, are somehow involved in implementing its principles. However, we found no studies describing this involvement with an exactitude that would allow switching from philosophical constructs to social research and measurement.

To make the philosophical and legal concepts operational, we will introduce the notion of levels on which justice is realized, that is, justice "in reality" as opposed to justice "in fact".[51] We interpret "reality" as a set of laws and other statutory regulations, and life according to these laws and statutory regulations.

In social practice, however, along with "reality" (and with it), "another life" exists, which laws determine indirectly rather than directly, if

---

Novoye Izdatel'stvo, 2004; Nussbaum, M. Aristotelian Social Democracy // Liberalism and the Good / R. B. Douglas et al. (eds.). N.Y., 1990), etc.

50 There is also a distinction between justice focusing on the individual and the society, and a distinction between natural and conventional justice.

51 The logic of such a distinction is provided in the work of S. Kordonsky *In reality and in fact*.

at all. This other life can be illegal or neutral with regard to law, but in any case, it takes place in a social space other than that governed by the legal framework. We determine "other life" as something that exists "in fact".

"In reality", <u>corrective justice</u> implies equality before the law, whereas "in fact", this principle is implemented according "to notions of justice", where people are actually unequal due to their affiliation to various corporations, religious denominations, ethnic groups, and so forth.

"Ideal capitalism" with its predominance of written law, civil society institutions, and democracy can serve as the ideological model of <u>corrective justice "in reality"</u>. In this case, the social structure has a class nature, where the dominating groups are classified by level of consumption: the upper, middle, and lower classes. Inequalities in consumption in this model are considered to be just.

An "ideal corporate state", where social stability is based on a rigid political (or religious, ethnic, etc.) social group hierarchy, and intergroup relations are built on "notions of justice" (ensured by a fuehrer, duce, president, or other charismatic leader) rather than written law, can serve as the ideological model of <u>corrective justice "in fact"</u>. In this case, ranked clans, corporations, and ethnic groups dominate in the social structure. Inequality in access to resources associated with belonging to different corporations (those belonging to "St. Petersburg" and "Gazprom", for example, are entitled to more resources than those belonging to "Altai" or the "Doctors") is also considered to be just in this case.

<u>Distributive justice</u> "in reality" manifests itself in specific relations of regulated distribution of resources according to the "importance" that one or another social group has for the authorities, i.e., in a welfare state, or in the extreme case under socialism. "In fact", distributive justice is realized through redistribution of resources according to "notions of justice" (in Russia—in line with the generally accepted maxim "to be near water and not quench one's thirst?"), and in the extreme case—in line with communist practice, i.e., forceful redistribution of resources in favor of various "proletarians".

We believe that the welfare state differs from the socialist one primarily by its priorities in distributing resources. The welfare state grants certain priorities to disadvantaged groups, namely, people with physical or other disabilities, unemployed, etc., whereas the socialist state favors groups it has established to neutralize threats.

On the one hand, an "ideal socialist state" distributing all consolidated resources between social groups-estates that it has created and resisting by force any redistribution, diversion, or plundering of resources can serve as the ideological model of distributive justice "in reality". In this case, estates, such as workers, peasants, and employees of the USSR, where social justice ("from each according to his ability, to each according to his labor") was the principal postulate of social policy, dominate in the social structure. The inequality in access to resources, associated with belonging to different estates (workers of defense enterprises were "entitled" to more resources than workers of state farms, for example) is also considered to be just.

On the other hand, this model can be partially represented by an ideal welfare state, where the class structure somehow co-exists with the estate one introduced by the state for the purpose of fair distribution.

A mythical "communist society", where all people are equally free and live by their own fully internalized "notions of justice", can serve as an ideal model of distributive justice "in fact". This ideal social system does not and cannot have any laws or institutions to implement them (the state), since they would be considered as restricting freedom. There is no social structure in the classical sense of the term, and social groups are formed as needed in the course of direct interaction between free people. The formula of justice in this case is "from each according to his ability, to each according to his needs".

Table 2 shows the relationship between reality levels and social justice principles underlying the above reasons for social stratification—class, estate, corporate, and communist.

These reasons for social stratification are individually not self-sufficient. Moreover, they are generally inextricably connected, and the politicians' attempts to justify the domination of a purely class-based stratification fail, because irrespective of the politicians' wishes, government practice reproduces also the estate, corporate, and anarchist and communist features of social reality. The interaction of groups driven by their own ideals of justice brings to life state systems where power relies primarily on classes (capitalist states of the early—middle 20th century); estates (Soviet socialism); corporations and clans (corporate states in Italy and Spain in the 20th century); on a combination of classes and estates (contemporary European welfare states); and on communist ideals (embodied in the social practices of utopia, such as Soviet Russia in the period from 1918 to 1922).[52]

Besides substantive i.e., related to social reality, reasons for stratification, which emanate from ideas of social justice, attributive grounds based on statistical and innate characteristics of people, such as gender, age, education, place of residence and citizenship, and employment (occupation) are also applied. These attributes are often almost the only basis for social stratification, especially in the works of "empirical" sociologists, demographers and statisticians.[53] However,

---

52 These individual reasons are never isolated. As mentioned above, capitalist states include elements of the estate system (for example, in the social security system, when the disadvantaged are classified into groups and provided access to resources by non-market methods). Over time, the role of estate-based stratification increases there, where the mythologem of the "welfare state" prevails.
   The corporate-clan system dominates and reproduces itself in institutions training senior executives, such as higher education, where holders of MBA diplomas issued by prestigious universities, as well as members of various elite educational clubs, form the governing elite.
   The system creating cultural values and scientific knowledge reproduces anarchist and communist trends, which facilitates breaking the mould and generating scientific, technical, and cultural innovations.
   A socialist state inevitably generates stratification by level of consumption (latent class structure), various corporations, including territorial, professional, religious, ethnic, etc. To ensure innovations, the socialist state has to establish "zones" with special resource allocation conditions imitating (according to the officials) anarchist and communist relations of freedom and equality.
   A corporate state generates estates, i.e., groups distinguished by the state and provided for in a particular way. Besides, intra-corporate stratification by level of consumptions - a counterpart of the class structure - emerges.
   The experience of building communist societies has demonstrated that any attempt to implement this social system outside the local communities inevitably results in stratification by level of consumption, and the emergence of groups usurping special resource management rights.
53 Tikhonova N.E. *Social stratification in modern Russia. Empirical analysis.* - M.: Institut sotsiologii RAN, 2007. - 320 p.

gender, age, occupational, and other statistical groups actually exist only when they are related to class, estate, or corporate groups.

The diverse reasons for social stratification are presented in Table 3, where the rows are stratification principles from Table 2 and the columns—groups of professionals advocating specific social stratification reasons. The professionals (e.g., statisticians, demographers, sociologists—column 2 of the table) perforce refer to other reasons for stratification when studying the estate, class, and corporate-clan structures, highlighting their subjects and their notions of social reality.

Table 3 demonstrates the diversity of social stratification forms based on different principles of social justice.

Of all the possible (according to the proposed logics) ways of presenting the social structure, we consider herein primarily the estatist society, but only in the part (highlighted in Table 3) limited to the intersection of "Statisticians" and "Officials" columns with the "social-statistical level" and "estate level" rows. Our research and modeling focus only on the estate social structure as the embodiment—"in reality"—of the distributive social justice principle. We consider the corporate-clan aspects of the current social structure, i.e., non-public resource flow arrangements and the corresponding social structure only as and when required.

Table 2 Relationship between the principles of justice and reality levels

Types of justice / Levels of being	Corrective justice	Distributive justice
In reality (according to law, to rules)	Equality before statute law or formalized rules. Inequality (class structure) and the corresponding "injustice" appear in the market because of stratification by level of consumption. Class-based social stratification. Model - ideal capitalism.	Equality before the superior, the authorities. The superiors determine the volume of resources that a person is "entitled to" based on his affiliation with a certain group - estate and his status therein. "Injustice" in this case is regulatory deprivation in resources. Estate-based social stratification. Model - ideal socialism.
In fact (by notions of justice)	Equality "by notions of justice", i.e., to each depending on his/her affiliation with ranked groups. Inequality (of ethnic, religious, corporate, clan, kin, community, or other origin) and the respective "injustice" emerge, when groups (clans, religious denominations, etc.) monopolize resources and are ranked in terms of importance and the amount of available resources. Corporate (ethnic, religious, clan) basis for social stratification. Model - ideal corporate state.	Equality "by notions of justice", i.e., to all equally. Inequality and "injustice" emerge because the superiors and the authorities privatize the resources they are distributing. Power-based social stratification. Model - anarchy, communism.

Table 3 Relationship between the reasons for social stratification

Professionals Grouping principles	Statisticians, demographers, sociologists	Experts on estates, officials	Economists	Ethnographers, criminologists, and others	Anarchist-communist ideologists and practitioners
Socio-statistical (used for statistical analysis)	**"Objective" characteristics of people—gender, age, education, place of residence, citizenship, employment**	"Statistical" composition of estates	"Statistical" composition of classes	Statistical composition of clans, ethnic and other groups	Statistics of social inequalities (differentiation by income, poverty, level and quality of life)
Estate (introduced by the state or exists by tradition)	Estates by "objective" social characteristics ("youth", "elderly", "women", "men", and others)	**Estates - titular (according to law) and non-titular (according to tradition or custom)**	Class differentiation within estates: e.g., rich officials and poor public sector workers	Estates by clan (ethnic, religious) characteristics (e.g., estate of Armenians)	Estate inequality

Class (emerges in the market as a result of differentiation by level and volume of consumption)	Classes based on "objective" characteristics (rich and poor men, rich and poor Muscovites, poor single mothers, etc.)	Estate differentiation within classes: hereditary rich and the nouveau riche, rich and poor pensioners, etc.	**Classes: upper, middle, and lower**	Classes by clan (ethnic, religious, and other characteristics) (e.g., "poor Tajiks)	Class inequality, proletariat and capitalists
Corporate and clan based (ethnic, religious) emerges due to ethnic, religious or other factors	Clans (ethnic groups, religious denominations, communities, etc.) by "objective" features: "we are Orthodox", "we are classmates", "we belong to the same corporation", etc.	Clans based on estate features: e.g., "officials belonging to one ethnic group"	Clans (ethnic groups, religious denominations, communities, etc.) by class features: e.g., "Jewish oligarchs"	**Corporations, clans, ethnic groups, religious groups, etc.**	Clan, ethnic and other inequality
Anarchist (communist)	Groups without differentiation by gender, age, or other statistical features	Groups without estate differentiation	Groups without property differentiation or differences in consumption levels	Groups without ethnic or clan differentiation	**Communist groups with absolute equality**

Social stratification as a specific task of the theory of classification

A resource-based state must have its own specific social structure. Under the existing social structure research tradition, any social system can be depicted in terms of any applicable classification theory.[54] Some of these theories serve quite practical purposes, such as predicting the consumer or electoral behavior of social groups classified on their basis. The others are largely speculative, and their logics sometimes resemble Borges's famous taxonomy[55]. Theoretical constructs sometimes become political facts and serve, in particular, to justify claims to power or to redistribution of property. I believe that in the nineteenth and twentieth centuries such were Karl Marx's stratification concepts, which the communists imposed by force on the domestic reality. Despite their internal inconsistencies, the "class" features of social stratification invented by interpreters of Marxism were for decades the basis of social life in a huge state.

Based on purely internal academic procedures, sociological classification theories are an individual case of the general classification issue arising whenever it is necessary to determine what objectively exists in any field of scientific knowledge. No scientific discipline can exist without a respective operational and generally accepted description of objects specific for it. In biology, for example, the binomial nomenclature introduced by Carl Linnaeus has been serving this purpose for almost three centuries. The algorithm developed by Linnaeus allowed systemizing the diversity of forms of life by applying various determinants—keys based on consecutive identification of similarities and differences between individual animals or plants.[56] Modern analyt-

---

54 See Radaev V.V., Shkaratan O.I. *Social stratification*. M., 1996.
55 "...the animals are divided into a) belonging to the Emperor, b) embalmed, c) tame, d) suckling pigs, e) sirens, f) fabulous, g) stray dogs, h) included in the present classification, i) frenzied, j) innumerable, k) drawn with a very fine camelhair brush, l) others, m) having just broken the water pitcher, n) that from a long way off look like flies." Borges J. L. The analytical language of John Wilkins //Prose of different periods. M., 1989.
56 Since then, only what has been identified (captured in the determinants-keys) and assigned a specific genus and species name exists in biology. The "keys" serve to map any analytical (experimental) knowledge to a particular biological species

ical biology is impossible without defining exactly what animal, plant, or microorganism species is being experimented on. Moreover, a substantial part of social practice indirectly assumes that all living beings have been classified, named, and can be clearly determined. The names of species, genera, and families with their specific features have become part of everyday life and help to structure it. Due to the classification efforts of the previous generations of taxonomists, we see birds rather than "flying, feathery, and chirping". Moreover, not just birds, but crows, jackdaws, and sparrows.[57]

Human beings are as diverse as biological phenomena. However, the classification of human beings (and social realities in the broad sense) is still on the level of pre-Linnaean biology. Modern social sciences have no algorithm that would allow ranking the observable differences and similarities between people by characteristics substantial for these sciences. Moreover, contrary to the guidance of the founders of sociology, contemporary sociological methodologists do not even

---

(taxon of the lowest rank). (Based on a rather non-trivial procedure, every biological taxon receives its own name, which all researchers must use. The determinants are designed in a way allowing other researchers to test, and if needed to contest, the reasonableness of attributing an individual item to a specific species (genus, family, etc.). Thus, many generations of taxonomists are involved in systemizing the diversity of forms of life; this activity occupies a special place in the social division of scientific labor.) Any expansion of knowledge beyond a specific species (to the genus, family, class) must be additionally substantiated and tested. In order to apply any knowledge, for example, about the chemical, genetic, physiological, and ethological features of some pubic louse to all taxa of the louse genus, it is necessary to conduct experiments on the representatives of all (in the ideal) species of this genus.

[57] There is no doubt about the practical usefulness of such determinants; however, "experts in theoretical biology" do not consider them self-sufficient. For the past hundred and fifty years, they have been trying to interpret the hierarchies of biological taxa in terms of different theories of evolution, and regard similarities (when taxa are introduced) as a result of relationship and shared descent. The experts in theoretical biology have introduced a distinction between natural and artificial systems of classification, primarily to symbolically subordinate empirical classification studies to their fantasies. They consider that there are natural features inherent in the classified reality as opposed to external features of classification practices. However, the artificial (according to them) Linnaean distinctions more often than not turn out to be operational, whereas the "natural phylogenetic" ones—speculative and useless, as is often the case when genetic and immunological characteristics are used as classification characteristics. Should similarities based on such features signify relationship and shared descent, then people, for example, would be related to swine, and sturgeons could not be classified as fish.

set the task of scientific systematization in their field of knowledge. Way back, Pitirim Sorokin quoting Emile Durkheim indicated the need to develop sociological systematics. "Just as for botany and zoology rational systematics of plants and animals are essential to address certain major issues of biology, for sociology the systematics of complex social aggregates...is an indispensable and pressing matter that requires action ... The concept of species reconciles the scientific requirement of unity with factual diversity, since all individuals within a species always retain common properties, but species differ among themselves... Thus, the recognition of social species does not allow a sociologist to study only Pascals' man and formulate the laws of his development that would be applicable to all times and people. On the other hand, it spares us purely descriptive work of historians and provides the opportunity to explore the phenomena characteristic of several social groups belonging to the same species".[58]

I believe Sorokin's attempt at sociological systematics failed largely because he relied on the tradition of "theoretical biology" already popular in his time, and instead of working out an algorithm for classification, which other scientists could contribute to, as was the case in biology, he tried to develop phylogenetic social systematics. Besides, sociological systematics is much more complicated than the biological one, probably because it must include such a procedure as human self-identification, i.e., people should agree to be classified within one or another taxon. Continuing this tradition, for many decades sociologists have been looking at Pascal's man—the "thinking reed"—and introducing representations, non-verifiable by classification logics, about the existence of various social groups (conceptual counterparts to species, genera, and families of biological systematics) in order to establish a "natural historical relationship" between them.

In modern sociology, statistical processing of research findings and the so-called mathematical methods occupy the functional place of systematics. Analytical sociology recognizes as existing either the results of statistical processing of primary information, or constructs born in the minds of pointlessly philosophizing scientists. Statistically

---

[58] Sorokin P.A. *A system of general sociology.* V. 2. M., 1993. pp. 395–396.

proven existence serves as a basis for mathematical modeling of its relationships. The problem is that such existence and such model relationships exist only in the special speculative space of mathematized sociology, which has little in common with what a field sociologist observes and describes. Statistics and mathematical methods generally create only an illusion of proving the existence, and statistical groups (factors, clusters, etc.) remain suspended in an objective space filled with speculative substances unique for every researcher or school of research.[59]

Due to the absence of determinants, it is impossible to verify statistical, or mathematized, sociological knowledge, i.e. to check on what grounds the researcher decided that the obtained results refer to a certain social group, primarily because no systematics of such groups are available. Statistics and mathematical methods create their own universe, which can be hardly matched to social empiricism. Only skilled craftsmen can tackle this insoluble problem. Therefore, in sociology one can hardly clearly state the existence of anything but "Pascal's people" and statistical "groups"; moreover, it is impossible to verify the statements of existence made by other researchers.[60]

These seemingly specific sociological classification issues are far from specific. Many classifications are "built into" everyday life and underlie group behavior. I already emphasized that the classification constructs of Karl Marx and his interpreters remain the ideological basis of various social revolutions, and Stalin's definitions and classification of nations, widely accepted by the Soviet people, still manifest themselves in the form of inter-ethnic conflicts.

Estates and classes: concept operationality

In general, the object domain of sociology lacks system; however, it still has structured fields with more or less verifiable concepts of the existent. They emerged where the ideas about the existence (names)

---

59 Sometimes this space is unified by formal constructions, such as Talcott Parsons' theory with its speculative categories related to Hegel's distinctions. The result is a substantially empty but meaningful unity of mathematized and philosophical speculations, which many sociologists consider high theory.
60 Details are provided in the work of S. Kordonsky *In reality and in fact*.

of social groups introduced by the researchers matched to a certain extent the self-identification of the groups' members. Such concepts include the upper, middle, and lower classes.[61] Similarly operational is the concept of estates, where identifying "oneself" as belonging to the estate of doctors, for example, quite matches the researchers' classification of doctors as a social group. In a sense, the concepts of classes and estates (castes) have an advantage over other sociological classifiers because of simple procedures for verifying the classification quality. One can just ask the people what class or estate they belong to and on what grounds. One can also classify people based on directly observable characteristics of affiliation with a certain class or estate, such as appearance, vocabulary, material symbols of belonging to a certain estate, behavior, place of residence, etc.

Classes and estates are concepts used to analyze the social structure; they are introduced to describe or explain apparent (directly observable) differences in the people's consumer or legal status. The concept of classes depicts social hierarchies with regard to consumption,[62] whereas the concept of estates describes the hierarchies of serving or providing services, rights and privileges.

Initially, the notions of both classes and estates were no more than theoretical or axiological intuitions. These "mental entities" turned into social realities only when they "hit home", i.e., coincided with the "self-evident" but not previously articulated division into social groups. After that, they became a point of reference for group self-identification, when a sufficient number of people recognizes their affiliation with a certain group and quite rationally adopts its standards and stereotypes.[63]

---

61 See Warner, W. L. *The social class and social structure.* Yankee City // Rubezh. 1999. V. 10–11.

62 The concepts of the modern class stratification theory have nothing to do with the concepts of Marxist class theory. Marx introduced classes to depict the differences between people in terms of ownership of the means of production, whereas contemporary classes describe the difference in consumption. The division into upper, middle, and lower classes distinguished by the level and forms of consumption that Warner introduced analytically in the 1930s, has currently become a part of social practice and largely determines the everyday behavior in contemporary societies.

63 The possibility to introduce the notions of social stratification and scientific research of the estate structure appear only in a heterogeneous class society after

Classes and estates ceased to be purely theoretical constructs and transformed into everyday distinctions of social practice, into the reality of social order.[64] They exist "objectively", but this objectivity is not brought in from without; it is reproduced only in the activity of the classified people, by their very life. Notions of class stratification are captured in customs and common law,[65] whereas notions of the estate system are set forth in special laws or tradition having the force of law. Due to such recording, every new generation enters an already stratified world where it has to find its place in the established class or estate system.

In the modern market society, the upper, middle and lower classes exist and reproduce themselves because the people who have more or less rationally determined their class affiliation constantly confirm it. They work and earn like representatives of their class; they buy the same goods; reside in the same area; marry representatives of their class; and have as many children as is customary for families of this class. They behave "as expected" in order to stay in their class, and, if lucky, to move a step higher in the consumer hierarchy.

If the notions of contemporary classes are conceptually relatively clear,[66] the situation with estates is not as transparent. Moreover, it is considered a priori that the estate system is archaic and does not specify the current social reality, and it is for historians and legal scholars to study it rather than for sociologists. On the contrary, I believe that modern estate stratification—particularly in Russia—is as (if not more) relevant than the class one, and that the unconscious affiliation with estates determines social behavior far more than commonly believed.

---

it develops different social reference systems. In a syncretic social order, reflection is mythological rather than scientific.

64 I wrote about the criteria of the existence of analytical objects and the related social practice in *Cycles of activity and ideal objects*, M., 2000.

65 For example, representatives of the middle class react negatively when lower class people appear in their residential area. The custom is such that it promotes territorial class isolation, although statute law does not stipulate it.

66 Discussions about the existence of classes as "objective realities" are philosophical rather than substantive and seem to indicate that substantive representations about existence are underdeveloped. See, e.g., Bauman E. *Individualized society*. M., 2002.

According to widespread assumptions, as the market economy and democracy developed, the estate principles of social order were replaced by class ones characterized by equality before the law and prevalence of economic relations; therefore, studying estates is of purely historic interest. However, estate forms of social life arrangement (aristocracy, for example) still flourish in modern societies and coexist with the class structure, democracies, and market relations. The contemporary institutions of professions and professional associations are largely functional relics of estate stratification.

An estate is a social group that occupies a certain position in the hierarchical structure of the society in accordance with its rights, obligations, and privileges set forth by law and/or transmitted by heredity. This definition of estate—with different variations—has been migrating from text to text for many years, and it is generally accepted. An estate-based society implies inequality before law, either traditional or introduced from without. Inequality primarily means that the estates have different rights and obligations to the state and perform different public duties. The ranked (explicitly or implicitly) estates relate with each other through service or tax (tribute, dues, taxes, rent, etc.) arrangements and form the social structure of an estate-based society. Estate affiliation is often inherited—sometimes the archaic way (by right of birth), and sometimes quite modernly, when children of military officers or doctors become officers or doctors themselves through training. In modern societies, social estates are not rigid in terms of the hereditary principle, and anyone can join an estate by occupying a certain position, purchasing a respective social status, receiving it as a gift from the sovereign, etc.

Estates are reproduced, in particular, because from birth people socialize in the system of mutual serving and services, either traditional, or rationally introduced by the state. They cannot imagine a different social arrangement. Not only do they serve somebody in an unreflective way, they also consider it natural for others to serve them. Faithful service is rewarded (by the sovereign), and the amount of the reward (allowance) must be proportional to the importance of the service as generally perceived by the specific society. Anything else would be unjust in an estate-based society.[67] For members of such a society, market behavior (not serving and providing services, but working for the sake of consumption) is beyond their worldview, and they perceive it as marginal. According to the underlying principles, there can be no rich or poor (in the modern sense of these notions) people in an estate-based society, as all resources are distributed based on "service" to the sovereign or according to "custom". Pursuit of wealth (profit) or demonstration of prosperity inconsistent with the social status is usually considered immoral and negatively sanctioned, whereas self-restraint in consumption is sometimes cultivated as ideal behavior.

The very notion of working for a living is alien to the estate society, where institutions of allowances, salaries, annuity, fees, pensions, rations, and other forms of resource allocation according to estate affiliation and status within the estate prevail over market compensation for labor or business income. The higher the status of the estate and a person's status within the estate, the more resources he is "entitled to" according to estate-based social justice principles. In an estate society, sale of labor and income from market transactions-speculations, unlike rent from social status, cannot be considered a legitimate resource belonging to the owner due to circumstances or as a result of labor. This resource "must be shared" with all members of the estate society, with the proportions determined by estate (social) justice criteria. Dividing resources is the essence of social life in an estate society as opposed to a class society where the economy is based on conversion of resources into capital and their expanded reproduction.

The external attributes of belonging to a contemporary estate often include various symbols, such as identity cards, special decorations, awards and insignia, watches of a particular brand, uniforms or, contrariwise, designer clothes, hairstyle, means of travel (in particular car brands and license plate numbers), and areas of compact settle-

---

67 Further on it is not stipulated every time, but: The concept of justice is fundamental for the estate world order and seems to have no referents in a class society. Social justice in an estate society means that resources are distributed among the estates in proportion to their position in the estate hierarchy.

ment. Besides, estates have their own specific rules of conduct—estate morality (moral code) and institutions monitoring compliance with the established rules and procedures.

Class stratification into the rich and the poor (with the middle class in between) generally correlates little with the division of estates into higher/lower or servicemen/servitors. In non-estate societies, it is quite common for aristocrats to be poor and for the rich to be of humble origin. In societies where the estate world order prevails, members of the higher estates are better provided with resources than those of the lower estates, although by definition such societies have no poor and rich people (in the class sense of the word).

***

In an archaic estate system (proceeding from its simplest model), the society cannot be considered as opposed to the state, since that system has neither state nor society in the modern sense of the term. It is a certain syncretic unity, in which a contemporary researcher can only analytically distinguish proto-state and proto-social institutions.

A person's social status in this system can be determined more or less explicitly by reference to his estate by birth, occupation, or some other substantial characteristic. Members of the higher estates are usually wealthy, whereas the deprived ones belong to the lower estates or are without kith or kin. Syncretism disappears with the differentiation of social relations and the emergence of a proper state and a proper society. Then, to determine a person's status, it is no longer sufficient to indicate his or her origin or occupation. In particular, in a stratified society, nobles can be poor and commoners can be rich. In such a society, its class structure (stratification into the rich and the poor) becomes as significant as origin and kinship. In a differentiated society, social institutions of education and employment form the estates, inter alia. The ambiguous and multidimensional social stratification promotes the development of proper political institutions and ideologies required to coordinate the interests of estate groups and property owners. Power splits into branches, elections emerge as an institution, and different conflicting ideologies appear.[68]

It seems that in pre-capitalist societies, the prevailing (if not the only) stratification was estate-based (sometimes caste-based, which differs from the estate one by status inheritance principles). As markets develop, the estate system is replaced by class stratification (not completely, of course). Thus, the estate socialization system loses functionality and by inertia continues to produce members of estates that are no more. As a result, many people have skills and knowledge for which there is no demand and no way to satisfy their ambitions. When people cannot determine their place (class or estate-based) in the social structure, this results in anomie, a social pathology first described by E. Durkheim. Anomie manifests itself primarily in the fact that people, lacking the concepts to guide them in the new class structure, fail to identify themselves with any of the existing social groups. Deprived of group identity, they marginalize. They have no idea what they want and, therefore, remain in a state of social and psychological depression fraught with auto aggression or simply aggression. People well socialized in an estate world order, but unwilling to fit into class distinctions and unprepared to work for the sake of higher consumption, are doomed to marginality in a class society, if only they do not belong to an estate that retains an important place in the social hierarchy due to a monopoly on resources. Those individuals, who in spite of the circumstances retain their estate identity, believe that they languish because they have been deprived of something they are "entitled" to as members of the estate (probably already extinct). They often focus their efforts on asserting the right of their estate to resources. These efforts sometimes transform into political actions, into a struggle for social equality and fair distribution of resources. Such social actors are most susceptible to Marxist and similar social classification theories.

---

68   Without fail, one ideology would appeal to the wonderful past where there had been no ambiguity in determining a person's social status and, therefore, no injustice in distributing resources. Such ideology is embodied, in particular, in theories of the corporate state, communism and fascism.

In estate-based systems with their mythologized perceptions about the social order, either estates exist on their own, or they are God-given, established by an epic hero or by the will of the sovereign. Such societies are bound to have ideological institutions (usually the main religious denomination), which invent myths to justify the social inequality of the estates by alleging that such inequality is natural, consistent with the nature of things, created by God or, contrariwise, is a plot of the "enemies of the people". In Imperial Russia, the Orthodox clergy played this role; in the USSR—the CPSU officials in charge of ideology and their attendants—the Soviet creative elite, which using methods of socialist realism substantiated the need for unequal but fair distribution of resources among the estates for the sake of a bright future where everyone would have the same rations. Contemporary Russia is still in the process of forming such an institution of estate ideologists who would be in charge of constitutionalizing "sovereign democracy" as a mythological justification of the emerging social inequality.

In class societies, social inequality is substantiated more rationally using scientific methodology, mass media, and telecommunications. Economics, sociology and political science (in their numerous specializations) focus, inter alia, on studying social inequality and theoretically validating or refuting it. The mass media fictionalizes and replicates the findings and translates them into mass culture images that form patterns of behavior in a class society.

Modern estates, while maintaining to a certain degree their corporate and closed nature, are integrated into the class structure of the nation states and the democratic social order, and secure preferences in an alien market by virtue of a traditional or legal right to the exclusive use of resources from a source specific for the estate. Estate members obtain these resources "by inheritance", by law, by training, or by coincidence. Thus, modern physicians "by law" monopolized the right to provide medical treatment, and the scientists by tradition—the right to obtain new knowledge. Capitalizing on these resources, members of the estates enter the existing markets and become rich, poor or middle-class.

Most often estates are "tailored" to use a particular resource, and switching to a resource other than the customary one is akin to social disaster for them. In general, the estate system is also adapted to the pool of resources specific for its constituent estates. The emergence of a new resource generates an estate specializing in it, and the depletion of a resource (including abolition of estate monopoly) leads to the degradation of the respective estate. Therefore, the estates rigorously protect their corporate interests and resource opportunities, develop systems of political and economic lobbying and, thus, participate in political life. Depletion of resources by many estates within a certain world order results in its degradation or phased transformation into a new estate-based social order, as happened with the Russian Empire and the USSR.

The estate order and class structure are not alternatives—neither as theoretic constructs, nor as their behavioral implementation. In modern societies, they coexist relatively peacefully, with the main difference being which system and to what extent prevails. In nation states, the modernized estate system coexists with the class one, with the terms of such coexistence specific for each state. By trial and error, such states have worked out the most effective combinations of the estate and class systems that ensure market dynamics and political stability at the lowest possible anomie. Thus, modern European countries with their undoubtedly market and democratic systems differ, inter alia, by the way their democratic institutions associate with traditional social relations, primarily with the estate structure.

In such societies, many remaining estates are now closely linked with multinational corporations rather than the state. This, for example, is the case with doctors. Their estate communities have practically merged with pharmaceutical giants, becoming elements of the global monopoly on disease diagnostics, treatment, and prevention.

The multinationals interact forming a specific globalized market environment, of which the estates of the nation states, regardless of their internal structure, are just an element. Currently, corporations are based on the estate principles of social stratification (in domestic social practice largely replaced by class distinctions). Their numerous employees scattered around the world are linked by inter-estate corporate relations as stringently as estate members in feudal societies used to be.

Such corporations have a rigid social hierarchy substantiated by internal corporate mythologies; formalized resource distribution systems according to the estate status; a corporate understanding of social justice; corporate law and law enforcement, including courts; and meticulously cultivated corporate ethics. Administrative market principles govern the relations between the estates within a corporation and between employees of different corporations belonging to the same estate. Corporations have no place for values of free market and democracy. Such values are extra-corporate; they exist in the political systems of the nation states.

***

If we consider classes and estates as concepts of ideal social organization types, we can say that the class society corresponds to a capitalist economy, comprehensive market with its goods and money, and democracy. The estate society corresponds to a resource-based economy, local markets-bazaars, and coordination of interests through estate assemblies and councils.

Summarizing the above, methodologically we can distinguish at least two ideal types of correlation between class and estate stratifications. Ideal in the sense that they are not realized per se. The first type is the absolute domination of the estate order. It is characterized by the absence of goods, money, market, and production in the economic sense of these notions. Everything tangible and intangible is a resource. The sovereign (whoever or whatever it may be) fully controls all resources and distributes/shares them among the estates according to the formally generally accepted social justice principles. Resources are added, alienated—deducted and divided, but not increased. The sovereign cares about the people—the totality of the estates,—by distributing the resources in a way to curb the appetites of the privileged estates and keep the tax paying ones from starving to death. He considers the opinions of the estates, which reach him in the form of workers' letters, complaints, denunciations, petitions, and so forth. That was more or less the case in Imperial Russia, where such estate institutions as nobility assemblies quite significantly contributed to social stability until the end of the nineteenth century. The USSR was close to an ideal estate system. We should not underestimate the role of CPSU congresses and plenums, and the Party, Komsomol, and trade union meetings. Neither should we ignore the significance of such institutions as "complaints and letters of the working people" addressed to the authorities or published in the newspapers, as well as denunciations of "thieving officials", neighbors, and colleagues. In such a society, there can be no political relations between the estates or politics as a separate form of activity, as there is no law in the conventional sense of the word.[69] Different sorts of administrative markets where resources are distributed exist instead of politics; and the will of the sovereign (the Soviet people in the USSR), resource "management procedures", estate ethics, and various "codes of honor" in a sense play the role of law.

Such an estate-based society has no institutionalized rich or poor people. It has estates, which are more or less provided with resources. Nevertheless, propertied and propertyless categories exist, but they have no legal institutions to lobby their property interests, although such interests exist, and they realize them in their own way. The propertyless do it through complaints, denunciations and social protests—uprisings and riots. The propertied buy preferences and give bribes paying off estate social justice supervisors.

Naturally, this system of relations needs no democracy to coordinate interests. It also recognizes no individual outside a determined estate. When the estate order dominates totally, it is impossible even analytically to distinguish economy and politics, the state and the society. Such an estate system represents a syncretic unity—corporation, fief, or state of the whole people.

An unconditionally class-dominated social order completely separates economy and politics, on the one side, and the state and the society, on the other side. Goods production and monetary circulation determine economic growth; the society is split into the rich and the poor (in their various options), and their interests are coordinated by

---

69 Pastukhov V.B. *Sombre age. Post-communism as a "black hole" of Russian history //* Polis. 2007. No. 3.

political institutions through legislation. Human rights and identity are defined regardless of class, estate, or political affiliation. The functions of the authorities are limited to legislation, law enforcement, and security.

The above types are ideal because they do not exist in their pure form. In practice, communities represent a certain combination of estate and class features with one or the other form dominating, this being reflected in the government system. When the class system prevails, the political role of the estates is limited to lobbying their resource interests, and relations between the rich and the poor, whose interests are represented by various political parties, ultimately determine the political climate. This is how the modern Western society is organized. When the estate system prevails, politics and political institutions are on the fringes of the social order, the regime is considered authoritarian and undemocratic, and identity and freedom are realized mainly within the framework of estate institutions. That was the arrangement in Imperial Russia and the Soviet Union.

Russian classes and Russian estates

According to the logic herein, modern Russia is specific in the sense that the Russian society has interiorized neither the class nor the estate stratification sufficiently enough for these notions to become routine distinctions of social practice as happens in class societies or was the case in Imperial Russia and the USSR where estate identity largely determined everyday behavior. Thus, O.I. Shkaratan and G.A. Yastrebov believe that "... modern Russia has developed a specific type of social stratification where the estate hierarchy intertwines with elements of the class structure, and this type has been reproducing itself in recent years".[70]

Features specific for class societies are distinguishable in the Russian society; however, Russian citizens, even though admitting the distinction between the rich and the poor as regards their compatriots, find it difficult to determine their own place in the class structure. Generally, it is difficult to operationalize the notions of wealth and poverty in the empirical research of our social order. To all outward appearances, a person, for example, is poor, but he does not consider himself as such.[71] Moreover, many people, wealthy by Russian standards, do not consider themselves rich either. According to the respondents, most of them "live normally" and belong to the middle class. No less problematic is the estate identification based mostly on Soviet principles. Thus, a person can continue considering himself a worker although he is engaged in small business, or a scientist in spite of being professionally involved in politics.

The situation is somewhat paradoxical—it is well known that any society is stratified, including ours. This stratification is obvious even to ordinary people unaware of scientific concepts. However, the way in

---

[70] Shkaratan O.I., Yastrebov G.A. *The social and occupational structure of Russia's population. Theoretical background, methods, and selected results of repeated surveys of 1994, 2002, and 2006.* Mir Rossii. // Sotsiologiya I etnologiya. 2007. V. XVI, No.3.

[71] Research project report on poverty. The Khamovniki Foundation. Unpublished. Provided by D. Aleksandrov.

which the society is stratified remains unclear. The differences in well-being and consumption levels are striking, but they do not allow identifying the upper, middle, and lower classes. Inequality before the law stipulated by laws on public service has not become a generally accepted fact. Nevertheless, researchers relying on imported theories attempt to regard Russia as a class society and analyze the occupational and symbolic stratification using theoretic distinctions quite adequate for other social systems. However, their results provide the impression that they pertain to another society rather than the Russian one. The conceptual mirror appears either crooked, or dull, and sometimes deliberately defective as in a "house of mirrors". The imported theoretical distinctions in fact turn out to be artificial and suitable for the theory advocated by the researchers rather than the everyday practice of those they are trying to stratify.

In this work, I am somewhat opposing the existing tradition by trying to depict the imperial, Soviet, and modern Russian society using the estate notion of social stratification. I want to demonstrate that estates rather than classes were, are, and in the foreseeable future will remain the principal elements of the existing social structure in Russia. The estates in Imperial Russia, the USSR, and modern Russia differed. Transition from one Russia to another is in a fact a change in the estate framework. The times when new estates replace the existing ones are called times of trouble, reforms or revolutions. During such periods, short-term (from the historic perspective) class stratification into the rich and the poor emerges, which poorly correlates with the estate order due to the "unjust" nature of the latter. Subsequently, in the course of establishing post-revolutionary estates, class stratification is eliminated. Unlike other social systems, the estate and class structures in Russia exist in diachrony rather than in synchrony successively replacing each other.

I believe that Russia is a country where the estate world order based on inequality of citizens before the law and different rights and obligations to the state dominates in times of stability, when there are no revolutions or reforms. It was and still is a resource-based state where the resources are not increased but distributed—shared between the estates. Resource growth is achieved by an "expansion of the resource base" rather than through production of goods and turnover of capital. As soon as the resources are depleted and the resource base can be expanded no further, the estate structure experiences phased transformations, i.e. revolutions of various scale, when certain estates disappear and others appear but on a different resource base. To describe the Russian social system, Olga Bessonova introduced the notion of distributive economy, which fundamentally differs from market economy.[72] She showed that aggregate "collections" (in-kind and financial levies, duties, public service, military service, etc.) combined with aggregate "distributions"—wages, pensions, benefits, and privileges formed the base structure of the state-society, which was continuously adjusted by complaints of the estate members regarding violations of resource collection and resource distribution standards. According to O. Bessonova, the "collection-distribution-complaint (denunciation)" cycle formed the basis of the social system in Muscovy, in the Russian Empire, and in the USSR. It remains the basic social reality in post-soviet Russia as well. A disruption of the cycle (inability to collect the resources or their unjust allocation and respective failure to fulfill social obligations—distributions) results in a transformation of complaints-denunciations into riots and revolutions—reforms, collapse of the estate system and its subsequent re-emergence, only this time with new estates, as is happening now.

Consequently, a class structure appeared in Russia only before revolutions, which aimed to destroy both the remaining old estate structure and the emerging new class one. It appears that the class-forming process in our country suffered several disruptions by social revolutions, when the old estates were delegitimized and members of the estates that used to be privileged were sometimes physically eliminated. The class structure in Russia has been unsuccessfully trying to establish itself for over 100 years. It is being swept away by waves of estatist yearning for social justice, after which new estates spring up like weeds in the social field burnt out by revolutions. The underdeveloped market structures and democratic institutions of the early 20th century, which appeared on the ruins of the resource-based order and

---

72 Bessonova O. *Russia's distributive economy*. M. 2007.

estate structure of Imperial Russia, were eliminated by the socialist revolution, as was the emerging social class stratification. Instead of the imperial estate structure, the USSR introduced a socialist estate world order, which, in turn, was destroyed by the collapse of the USSR. Just as at the beginning of the twenty-first century, the underdeveloped classes of the rich and the poor are purposefully eliminated and replaced by privileged service estates and the implicitly inferior support estates.

The entire twentieth century, the country experienced the implications of the Bolshevik approach to social order, which completely eliminated the class structure in favor of the estate one. It is still not clear how the country can overcome the syncretic economic-social-political depression without restoring in full the resource-based economy and estate order—to the detriment of the market and democracy. Or how will it be able to interact with multinational corporations and be an agent of global economic processes without developing a full-scale domestic market.[73] The development of domestic markets is incompatible with overall distribution of resources, and democratic procedures cannot function when social relations are based on estate principles. There can be no market without democracy to coordinate interests in a class society, and there can be no estate order without alienating resources from the market, distributing them according to social justice criteria, and applying repressions against resource plunderers, who violate this justice.

Internally, Russia is currently organizing itself as a huge corporation,[74] but it seeks to interact with agents of the global market as a nation state, an agent of the traditional rather than globalized market,

---

73 Obviously, adequate interaction with corporations is impossible without introducing highly specialized domestic estates into their structures. Russian occupational estates are still resisting this with full support of the state. They are withdrawn into themselves, this being clearly visible on the example of domestic scientists and doctors. This results in the reproduction of "Russian science" and "Russian medicine" that are largely isolated from the world scientific and medical thought and practice, and, consequently, from their findings. Science is becoming increasingly scholastic, and medicine at the least remains "not state of the art".

74 Central election Commission Chairman Vladimir Churov, speaking in September 2007 on [Russian] NTV, said that we have already built a corporate state, and the Russian President Vladimir Putin has repeatedly stressed that the government and business should build their relations as intra-corporate ones.

an exporter and importer. It is thus in antiphase to the world order, where the markets appear to be within the states and the corporations—outside them. Consequently, other nation states perceive it as a country with a non-market corporate economy and authoritarian government, and global corporations—as a market agent not playing by the rules of inter-corporate relations.

In my work *The resource-based state*,[75] I attempted to demonstrate that in recent years Russia had been reinstating its national (resource-based) economy. This process is mistakenly interpreted as economic growth. The reinstatement of the national economy is accompanied by the reestablishment of the estate structure, contrary to the opinion on the evolution of democracy. At the same time, the post-perestroika inertia of creating fundamentally non-estate—market—relations and the tendency toward class stratification into the rich and the poor remains on a minimum scale.[76]

There are no straightforward relations between the currently forming estate and class stratifications, and a priori we cannot say that affiliation with post-Soviet service estates automatically leads to membership in the upper class by level of consumption. We can of course assume that any increase in estate coherence and administrative market allocation of resources curbs market and democracy, and vice versa. However, Russia's social structure is extremely complicated and does not fit into the standard logic of social science; therefore, such statements would be premature.

Since neither the estate, nor the class structure are definitely in place yet, universal anomie is typical for Russia's population. There are no groups in the current reality with which people can clearly identify themselves. They can neither define themselves as rich or poor (to say nothing of belonging to the middle class), nor as members of an estate society (servicemen and taxpayers, for example). The marginality of our society is all-encompassing and manifests itself in the weakening of family and socialization institutions, increasing drug and

---

75 Kordonsky S. *The resource-based state*. M. Regnum 2007.
76 This hypothesis may well explain why modern sociologists fail to locate the middle class in our social system—simply because it still does not exist; neither do the lower and upper classes. Rather than classes, more or less privileged estates are being established, the rights and duties of which are set forth by law.

alcohol abuse, as well as rampant diversion and plundering of resources, i.e. stealing anything that isn't nailed down. The current government is trying to overcome anomie, creating a new estate structure. This means that the estate system ideology, having survived revolutions and reforms, remains the basis of the domestic social order. In everyday life, estate inequality embodied in a framework of laws on various service and services is gradually becoming more important than the formal constitutional equality of citizens of the Russian Federation.

The estate system in Imperial Russia

The history of the estate structure in Muscovy and in Imperial Russia is substantially understudied, possibly because this topic was politicized in Soviet times. There are very few studies dedicated to the estate structure as such. N.A. Ivanova and V.P. Zheltova, authors of a rare work of this sort, indicate, "... domestic and foreign literature is mostly devoted to particular estates and classes, to various, often quite limited chronological periods, and many private, although significant issues".[77] Among modern historians, there is no consensus either on the principles of the estate structure, or on their empirical implementation. Gregory Freeze writes, "Pre-Petrine Russia knew neither soslovie (in the sense of estate) nor its equivalent, for the social structure consisted of numerous groups... One lexicon for the period records nearly five hundred separate social categories to denote different ranks and statuses... the modern notion of soslovie arose only in the early nineteenth century... the estate system was dynamic and still actively developing (not disintegrating) in the nineteenth century".[78]

According to the concept of B.N. Mironov, "...Muscovy was a non-estate state: social groups were open for entry and exit and their most important distinctive features were property status, types of assets, and occupation. The main categories of the population were not estates in the

---

[77] Ivanova N.A., Zheltova V.P. *The estate and class structure of Russia in the late nineteenth–early twentieth centuries.* M. 2004.

[78] Freeze G. *The soslovian (estate) paradigm in Russian social history*// American Historical Review. 1986.

European sense of the term, but they were also not fully consistent with the modern concept of "class", as origin played an important (and in the case of the elite, crucial) role for social identification.

...By the end of the eighteenth century, Russia...had established estates, which possessed the principal features of a true estate: (1) their estate rights were enshrined in law; (2) the rights were hereditary and unconditional; (3) they had their own estate organizations (nobility assemblies, municipal councils, merchant, townsfolk, craftsmen, and peasant societies, etc.) and their own estate court independent of the crown administration; (4) enjoyed the right to self-government; (5) had an estate consciousness and mentality; and (6) had the outward signs of estate affiliation... Estates in Russia were formed... under West-European influence.

...Due to this important reason, the estate system, which emerged in Russia by the end of the eighteenth century, resembled the disintegrating European estate system of the eighteenth century rather than the flourishing one of the thirteenth–fifteenth centuries.

....Important reforms of the late nineteenth–early twentieth centuries, such as abolishing poll tax and mutual responsibility among rural inhabitants; including nobility in the list of taxpayers; abolishing the passport regime; abolishing redemption payments for land; obtaining the right (in 1907) to withdraw from the commune; and, finally, introducing representative institutions and granting civil and political rights to the entire population in 1905 resulted in the fact that by 1917 all estates had legally lost their specific estate rights.

By 1917, ...the estate paradigm, although abolished de jure, de facto and psychologically had not been completely eliminated...".[79]

At the same time N.A. Ivanova and V.P. Zheltova write, "...for us, B.N. Mironov's general approach to studying estates proved unacceptable. The author considers Russia developed along the same lines as Western Europe only with slight delay... We believe it is more appropriate to study the estate order of the Russian Empire, as well as the emer-

---

79 Mironov B.N. *The social history of Russia at the times of the empire (18th–early 20th centuries): Genesis of the individual, democratic family, civil society and the rule of law*. SPb. 1999. Quoted from the author's abstract. http://bmironov.spb.ru/book.php?mn=6&lm=1&lc=nn.

gence of classes, based on the immanent development of the society in Russia itself...".[80]

The resource base of the estate system is beyond the scope of interest for historians. Olga Bessonova's studies[81] demonstrate that historically Russia's economy was not a market one and was based on collection-distribution relations (distribution of resources and their alienation), which prevailed in Muscovy, in Imperial Russia, and the USSR. Such relations are specific for an estate structure, which O. Bessonova does not analyze expressly.

I am inclined to agree with N.A. Ivanova and V.P. Zheltova in that social development in Europe and in Russia evolved in different ways. As markets developed, the estate structure in European countries lost its dominating positions and gave way to the class one, whereas in Russia, during the cataclysms of the nineteenth, twentieth, and now the twenty-first centuries, the then-existing estates were delegitimized and new estates emerged and replaced the "old" ones in the country's social structure.

The collapse of estate distribution systems was accompanied by the appearance of historically short-lived markets and associated abundance of goods and services, which were then eliminated in the course of social revolutions and replaced by new post-revolutionary distributions of resources according to estate social justice with their indispensable rationing and shortages as a consequence of rationing. Revolutions can also be considered, in particular, as a mass protest of raznochintsy (people of miscellaneous ranks, who appeared due to the collapse of traditional estates) against inequality in consumption levels and social injustice—inevitable consequences of the primitive accumulation of capital. After the revolutions, another estate society with new estates was created, social homogeneity was established (by eliminating the old estates and classes), and new social justice (estate-based distribution of resources) was introduced. Thus, the Great October Socialist Revolution resulted in the emergence of classes-estates of Soviet workers, peasants, and employees that participated in the distribution of national resources and had nothing in common with classes in contemporary capitalist societies.

---

80 Ivanova N.A., Zheltova V.P. *The estate and class structure of Russia in the late nineteenth–early twentieth centuries*. M., 2004.
81 O. Bessonova. *The distributive economy // Russia*. M., 1997.

Soviet estates

I did not succeed in finding studies dedicated to the estate structure of the USSR in general. In a sense, a series of works by German sociologist Wolfgang Teckenberg is an exception, however, they are more of a philosophical rather than sociological nature.[82] There are studies that depict the social position of certain Soviet estates, usually limited in rights;[83] however, the authors present such estates separately, without reference to the system as a whole. Numerous Soviet-period texts focus on workers, peasants, and employees. However, due to their ideological emphasis and (in most cases) lack of empirical data, these papers can be regarded as the product of Soviet estate mythmakers/ideologists rather than scientific research.[84]

One can only conclude that the imperial system of inter-estate relations, regardless of what it had been, had disappeared during the February 1917 revolution. In the course of socialist construction, the representatives of the Imperial estates, which were within the reach of Soviet power, were destroyed "as a class". Almost up to the end of the twentieth century, all personal data forms for Soviet citizens contained an "origin" field. An entry to the effect "from the nobility" automatically meant a restriction in rights, i.e. the inability to transfer to any other full-fledged estate of the Soviet society. There were such institutions as "disfranchisement" (as a practice of socialist law enforcement) that resulted in the emergence of "lishentsy" ("disenfranchised") as a special Soviet estate stripped of civil rights[85] and restriction in rights of

---

82　Teckenberg W. *The social structure of the Soviet working class. Toward an estatist society?* // International Journal of Sociology. 1981–1982. Vol. 11. No. 4.
83　Deportees (Spetsposelentsy). (Berdinsky V. *Deportees*. M. 2005), nepmen (people who engaged briefly in private enterprise during the New Economic Policy (NEP) of the 1920s) (Pakhomov I. B., Orlov S.A. *Capitalists in disguise at the NEP feast of life*. M., 2007), hired labor (Borisova L.I. *Labor relations in Soviet Russia (1918–1924)*. M., 2006), lishentsy (disenfranchised), nepmen, "specialists", exiled, deportees, labor army members (*Marginalized in the community. Marginalized as a community. Siberia - the 1920s-1930s*. Novosibirsk, 2007).
84　Exceptions include, for example, the following work: Gordon L.A., Klopov E.V. *Man after work*. M., 1972, and some others.
85　A *lishenets* is a citizen of the USSR who under the first Soviet Constitution was deprived of voting rights in the period from 1918 to 1936. Not only were *lishentsy* disallowed to vote, they could also not occupy any governmental position, or receive higher and technical education. *Lishentsy* received no food stamps, which

those who happened to be "on occupied territories" or were noticed to have habits or relationships "discrediting a Soviet person".

Due to the efforts of the CPSU (Bolsheviks)—CPSU, classes—the estates of workers, peasants, and employees, whose forerunners Marxist historians so diligently constructed in the imperial past— became the basis of the Soviet social structure. The entry "from workers", "from peasants", or "from employees" stated in the personal record determined the estate status of the Soviet person based on his/her social origin. Alain Blum and Martine Mespoulet describe the formation of the Soviet estate structure as follows, "The increasingly frequent use of identity for political purposes did not follow a unified and logical pattern... there were three conflicting trends in designing individual identities. The first of these related to categories created by various agencies that subsequently entailed discriminatory (and often repressive) measures or acts of positive discrimination... It was necessary to identify precisely the "genuine" Germans or "genuine" Greeks and thus reveal those who failed to state their nationality clearly. The second trend... was autobiographic identification, which emerged and became mandatory when joining the [communist] party... Finally, the trials and repressions of the 1930s brought affiliation with a certain network or community to the forefront and drew attention to relations between people".[86]

According to S.A. Krasil'nikov, "...when the estate system was formally destroyed (abolished by decrees), it re-emerged and re-established itself in modified forms as a new Soviet estate stratification under the guise of classes. In other words, the society as such went back to feudalism. This assertion is based on the fact that the principal feature of estate stratification—the scope of rights, privileges, and duties to the state—became even more prominent and obvious,

---

in times of famine often led to death from starvation. The 1936 Constitution restored *lishentsy* in their voting rights. The list of disenfranchised included former army and police officers, people using hired labor, those with unearned income (interest on capital, etc.), merchants and middlemen, clergy and monks, persons convicted, insane, or under wardship. Their family members also automatically became *lishentsy* // Wikipedia: http://ru.wikipedia.org/wiki/%D0%9B%D0%B8%D1%88%D0%B5%D0%BD%D0%B5%D1%86.

86 Blum A., Mespoulet M. *Bureaucratic anarchy: Statistics and power under Stalin.* M., 2006.

since after the revolution the role of the state increased manifold rather than diminished.

...five estate-type categories are distinguishable in the Soviet society:

1. The nomenklatura. By analogy with the pre-revolutionary estate, Stalin's nomenklatura can be defined as "service nobility", since it received rights and privileges only for service and did not possess property and inheritance rights.
2. Workers as a quasi-privileged estate. Most of their rights were a declaration only, but certain features distinguished workers from the rest of the population. Top performers—Stakhanovites—had extensive rights.
3. Professionals and employees. Two privileged groups are discernible within this stratum: the elite, whose representatives had certain privileges similar to those enjoyed by "Honorary Citizens" before the revolution, and trade executives holding key positions in the distribution system.
4. The peasantry. This group retained its estate features to the utmost until the beginning of collectivization, which was accompanied and followed by widespread de-peasantification of the village.
5. Marginal groups including the remnants of the former privileged estates—clergy, merchants, nobility as well as "innovations" of the Stalin era—deportees, military logistics support personnel (*tyloopolchentsy*), etc."[87]

In his classification, S. Krasil'nikov captures what he considers the basic principles of the USSR estate order, but he fails to cover all the diversity of the Soviet estate stratification, which I believe has still not been depicted. Without claiming to provide an exhaustive analysis, I will nevertheless try to determine the logic of Soviet estate stratification and describe some aspects of its practice.

If in the Russian Empire the estates were determined based on a combination of tradition and law, in the USSR the principal estate

---

[87] *At the ruptures of the social structure: Marginalized in the Russian post-revolutionary society (1917 – late 1930s)* // http://www.zaimka.ru/soviet/krasiln1.shtml

distinctions were first introduced ideologically (as part of the communist utopia myth), and then—in 1936—constitutionally. Three ideologically designed estates—the classes of workers, peasants, and employees—formed the foundation of the social structure. These groups were equally important for the process of socialist construction, the ultimate goal of which was to create a socially homogeneous Soviet people—a single super estate, where all Soviet people would have the same rights and responsibilities.

Socialist classes were ideological constructs designated in accordance with their function in building the future communist society: the workers created resources for the peasants, the peasants—for the workers, and the employees (working intelligentsia, in Stalin's definition of the social structure[88]) coordinated the resource flows between the workers and peasants. Since 1936 (since the adoption of Stalin's Constitution), these ideal estates have become fundamental constitutional entities, and all other relevant social distinctions—functional,

---

88 "What does Article 1 of the Draft Constitution speak of? It speaks of the class composition of Soviet society. Can we Marxists ignore the question of the class composition of our society in the Constitution? No, we cannot. As we know, Soviet society consists of two classes, workers and peasants. And it is of this that Article 1 of the Draft Constitution speaks. Consequently, Article 1 of the Draft Constitution properly reflects the class composition of our society. One may ask: What about the working intelligentsia? The intelligentsia has never been a class, and can never be a class - it was and remains a stratum, which recruits its members from all classes of the society. In the old days, the intelligentsia recruited its members from the ranks of the nobility, of the bourgeoisie, partly from the ranks of the peasantry, and only to a very inconsiderable extent from the ranks of the workers. In our day, under the Soviets, the intelligentsia recruits its members mainly from the ranks of the workers and peasants. But no matter where it may recruit its members, and what character it may bear, the intelligentsia is nevertheless a stratum and not a class.
Does this circumstance infringe upon the rights of the working intelligentsia? Not in the least! Article 1 of the Draft Constitution deals not with the rights of the various strata of Soviet society, but with the class composition of that society. The rights of the various strata of Soviet society, including the rights of the working intelligentsia, are dealt with mainly in Chapters X and XI of the Draft Constitution. It is evident from these chapters that the workers, the peasants, and the working intelligentsia enjoy entirely equal rights in all spheres of the economic, political, social, and cultural life of the country. Consequently, there can be no question of an infringement upon the rights of the working intelligentsia."
J.V. Stalin, *On the Draft Constitution of the USSR. Report Delivered at the Extraordinary Eighth Congress of Soviets of the USSR.* // Collected Works. Vol. 14. M., 1997.

sectoral, and territorial—were aligned with them. A Soviet person had to be of worker, peasant or employee origin. This enabled vertical mobility within the estate while maintaining the initial social status. Members of the Politburo of the CPSU Central Committee and its earlier equivalents until death were considered mostly workers, and family members of enemies of the people died as family members of traitors of the Motherland.

Using B. Mironov's criteria for determining Soviet estates cited earlier, we can say that the rights of Soviet estates were secured by socialist law and order and were unconditional. For example, "we are miners, therefore, we are entitled to..." was an accepted motivation for asserting one's rights. Legally, affiliation with an estate was not hereditary, however it was assumed following the logic of a Soviet joke that the Russian President sincerely enjoys: "The son of a general can become a general, but cannot become a marshal, because the marshal also has a son".

The estates had their own organizations such as party cells at the workplace, and trade union and Komsomol organizations. Where appropriate, their meetings acted as "courts of honor". It was common matter to discuss the misbehavior of estate members at a party or trade union meeting.

Members of Soviet estates identified themselves with the estate and had respective mentality ("we are the military", "we are the security forces", "we are peasants", "we are workers", etc.). The estates had no self-government rights; however, there was a certain independence in the decisions taken by estate assemblies (CPSU, trade union, and Komsomol meetings). Uniform was mandatory for a substantial number of estates, therefore, their members had outward signs of estate affiliation. Extremely idealized outward signs of estate affiliation were "introduced into the masses" in the form of relevant cultural archetypes, such as, for example, Vera Mukhina's sculpture *The Worker and the Kolkhoz Woman*. Formal portraits of war and labor heroes, their cinematic and theatrical images formed a gallery of acceptable appearance and public behavior. In everyday life, the builders of socialism adhered to these stereotypes imposed by the all-pervading "propaganda and agitation". For parades and demonstrations symbolizing the general rejoicing over "the unity of the Party and the people", they dressed up to resemble as much as possible (as far as their supply category and ability to "procure scarce goods" allowed) the archetypes of "genuine builders of socialism". Attempts to go beyond the permitted in appearance and public behavior were firmly suppressed in special campaigns such as "opposing dandies" and other forms of "kowtowing to the West".

Relations between Soviet estates were governed by the socialist legal framework, which contained codified penalties for breaching the resource handling procedure. Besides socialist laws, there were other relation regulators (canonical for an estate society), such as socialist morality, ultimately codified in *The Moral Code of the Builder of Communism*. The institutions of party, trade union, and Komsomol meetings served primarily as regulators of estate morality. They were a platform for discussing and condemning violations of the moral standards of socialist construction.

In addition to being ideological institutions, Soviet estates were also nominal social groups formed by the socialist state to address specific matters of labor resource concentration and distribution based on gender, age, nationality, education, social origin, place of residence, and employment in sectors of the socialist resource-based economy. In fact, every parameter of the passport system (items of the Soviet passport) institutionalized a certain nominal estate with its own rights and responsibilities. Men and women, children and senior citizens, Russians, Tatars, Jews (and all other "Stalin nationalities") formed such nominal estates. Their composition was determined by the governance procedure, i.e., the totality of non-public bylaws and departmental regulations setting forth the procedure for estate members to get access to resources. In this socialist world order, occupation was to some extent equivalent to estate affiliation. Professional development meant first and foremost estate socialization, and any career change resulted in being reclassified to another registered estate.[89]

---

89   Probably that was why Soviet studies of the social structure focused mainly on occupational distinctions. *See, e.g.*, Arutyunyan, Yu.V. *The social structure of rural population in the USSR*. M., 1971.

The state created nominal social estates[90] as needed. Addressing the challenges of socialist construction, the Soviet authorities gradually became a factory for producing estates required to meet these challenges. In order to implement socialist development plans, the government established ministries and agencies that were entitled to labor resources in the form of workers, peasants, and employees with certain credentials. Labor resource management bodies satisfied socialist construction sectoral requirements. As a result, nominal estates of Virgin Land workers and cosmonauts, miners and railroaders, Soviet state farm workers and water transport personnel appeared. Upon employment with respective ministries and agencies, citizens of the socialist state received food and other resources, to which builders of socialism were entitled, and became members of estates.

Some estates turned out to be non-functional or not up to the goals of a specific socialist construction phase. The state repressed such estates and disenfranchised their members. That was the case with "repressed nationalities"—the Chechens, Kalmyks, Crimean Tatars, and many others. After completing the tasks for which they had been established, the estates were not disbanded but continued to exist; however, their status was generally lowered, which meant that they received less resources for their core activities.

Gradually, a substantial part of the population changed into uniform with shoulder boards or without, and practically every page of the official "tear-off calendar" referred to the principal holiday of one or another estate—from "November 7" as the major day for Communist Party members to "Day of the Chekist [security officer]" or "Day of the Fisherman". Because of this continuous generation of estates, by the end of the twentieth century their total number was so significant that the very notion of a socialist estate and affiliation with it became largely nominal and devoid of any sense other than access to the "feeders", which by the 1980s had become rather meager.[91]

---

90 In the works *Markets for power* and *1987–1997—per aspera in anus*, I referred to them as nominal social groups.
91 In the course of implementing the principles of social justice, too many estates received access to the "feeders", whereas distributable resources became relatively increasingly scantier - in proportion to "socialist labor" performance, which

Other nominal social estates emerged to fulfill social obligations towards participants of socialist construction generated by the national significance of the challenges they had met. This was the case with the estates of Chernobyl nuclear disaster liquidators and war veterans.

Rigid differentiation existed within an estate depending on the significance of its core tasks. The worker estate, for example, was divided into groups—sub-estates depending on the registered place of residence, sector of the economy, gender, age, education, and social origin. A worker at a defense plant in Moscow and a state farm worker in a village near Kyzyl [capital city of the Tuva Republic] belonged to different groups. Defense industry workers of the highest categories were entitled to a completely different freedom of movement and goods supply than collective farmers. The latter (as an estate) until the 1960s were deprived of the right to remuneration in cash and the right to change their place of work and residence simply because they did not have (and could not have, according to the governance procedure) passports and labor books—documents required to participate in free socialist construction. By far not everyone could join the ranks of the privileged estate "workers of the defense sector of the national economy". The ethnic background of a grandparent, relatives who had lived on occupied territories during the war, a criminal record of a family member, or their aristocratic roots could become an obstacle.

People classified into "inferior estates", such as convicts, exiled, deported, family members of enemies of the people and those who had records of belonging to "repressed nationalities" for a certain period had no right to freedom of movement and until the middle of the twentieth century had to report regularly to local penitentiary authorities. Prisoners were dressed in uniforms, varying according to the alleged severity of the committed crimes. They were also divided into special estates, such as the "socially close" (i.e., ordinary criminals) and "enemies of the people".

Some estates that were important for socialist construction received the right to special and strictly rationed benefits, such as ac-

---

consisted in utilizing the allocated resources. The more resources an estate utilized, the more it became entitled to.

cess to foreign information or travel abroad. Besides uniforms, badges, chevrons and shoulder boards, a system of ranks (honorary and meritorious), as well as various awards and commendations served to distinguish the special status and merits of certain estate members. Lenin Prize and State Prize winners and Heroes of the Soviet Union and of Socialist Labor formed the super-elite of the Soviet estate society.

Documents mandatory for a Soviet citizen indicated his or her position in the multidimensional estate universe. Passport, labor book (employment record), diploma or other certificate of education, military ID or service card, CPSU, Komsomol and trade union membership cards, pension certificate, handwritten CV, and award documents captured in their entirety a person's social origin, his/her occupational—estate status and career, educational level, military service record, and some other characteristics facilitating or, vice versa, hindering social mobility. An individual Soviet citizen was identified by the unique combination of his documented credentials, and, depending on the situation, could be attributed to different nominal estates. Certain combinations were prohibited. Thus, representatives of "repressed nationalities" (with a respective entry in "item five" [ethnicity] of the passport), those who had relatives abroad or who had happened to be on occupied territories during the Great Patriotic War were banned from employment in specific sectors of the economy.

Affiliation with an estate primarily gave (at least at the outset of estate construction) access to resources, which were often limited to plain food and barrack bunks. A person devoid of estate affiliation had no legal right to resources, therefore, the government machine started by assigning members of the socialist society to different estates, including that of prisoners. Such assignment was the main expression of how the "CPSU cared about the well-being of the people". The Party's other concern was to provide resources to the people assigned to estates according to the standards of social justice—the estates most important for socialist construction received incomparably more resources than the relatively less significant ones. Certain people were entitled to tangerines, beefsteak, and imported instant coffee; the others—to bread rations; and some had to be grateful to the Party and government for the opportunity to survive off subsistence farming. A large part of the population belonging to low-ranking estates bought essential goods in shops. However, a relatively small share of resources was released into "free trade", and the retail chain was generally used to "sell" rationed goods, which members of the socialist society "entitled" to nothing else could "purchase" for food stamps or coupons, waiting for their turn in long lines.[92]

The privileged estates were taken care of by Workers' Supply Departments (ORS) with their distribution outlets—"feeders", where the "shopping" took place, i.e., where estate members received the resources they were entitled to in the form of consumer goods and foodstuffs. It was forbidden to use other (belonging to another estate) feeders, although Soviet people considered it a matter of honor to "find a way" and get access to an outlet for geologists, atomic scientists or, with a stroke of fortune, to that of a CPSU district, regional or central committee.[93] The assignment of the population to different estates—nominal social groups resulted in stratification based on consumption levels guaranteed by the state, which outwardly resembled class stratification into the rich and the poor. Members of the upper estates had a high, albeit rationed level of guaranteed consumption, whereas members of the lowest estates had no consumption guarantees whatsoever and often lived in misery, barely surviving on potatoes, onions, and kvass. That was the case for collective farmers from the onset of collectivization until the mid-1950s.

***

---

[92] Osokina E.A. *The hierarchy of consumption. Life under Stalin's supply system. 1928-1935.* M., 1993; Idem: BEHIND THE FACADE OF "STALIN'S ABUNDANCE". *The role of distribution and the market in consumer supplies during industrialization 1927–1941.* M., 1995.

[93] In 1983, a sociological expedition for the first time got permission to conduct empirical research of CPSU's leading role in a rural administrative district. When a petty party official offered the hungry junior research fellows the opportunity to purchase goods in a trade outlet of the CPSU district committee, the head of the expedition, an academician and prominent scientist, was filled with indignation. She believed that would violate the principles of social justice. Stories told by experienced people about the food they ate at the buffet of the CPSU Central Committee, and, more importantly, how much it had cost them, are an evidence that for an ordinary person the mere fact of visiting a "feeder" was an adventure, a trip to another social world.

The pursuit of social justice in distribution of resources made the USSR estate structure extremely complicated. Besides the evident groups, it also included specific ones. Both the Communist Party and the Komsomol (Young Communist League) had apparent estate features. Members of the CPSU formed a sort of super estate. The worthiest (in terms of their nominal credentials) representatives of all other estates became members of the CPSU. As a result, the CPSU structure reflected the country's estate system, with the exception of deprived groups. The CPSU represented an acting model of inter-estate relations.[94] Not every Soviet citizen could become a member of the CPSU. Internal party regulations established bans and restrictions on admitting new members depending on the actual political situation.

Members of the CPSU formed the dominant estate opposed to an extent to the remaining "non-party" population (as the vanguard of the builders of communism), but composed by selection from the other estates. Quotas for membership in the CPSU were distributed more or less similarly[95] to other benefits. A person could apply for CPSU membership only if he or she had a combination of acceptable social origin and nominal credentials—gender, age, education, ethnicity, place of residence, and occupation. Membership in the Young Communist League was a mandatory intermediary stage before joining the CPSU. Therefore, the estate of Komsomol members was also a very significant element of the estate structure formed, in turn, from Young Pioneers. The procedures of estate initiation, such as joining the Little Octobrists (Oktyabryata), Young Pioneers, Komsomol, and the CPSU were rather important events in the private life of members of the Soviet estate world order that symbolized their successive (as they grew older) approach to the status of a full-fledged builder of the communist society.

CPSU membership, manifested by a respective membership card, secured preferential access to various social benefits, including executive positions. Without such membership, any transfer from the

---

94 "The unity of the party and the people" consisted in the exact correspondence between the registered social composition of the CPSU and the population. Naturally, such an approach did not consider the inferior estates.

95 Considering the ideal model of the Soviet social system, where there was no place for social groups worthless for the bright future.

lower registered social groups upwards was virtually impossible, be it industrially or regionally. For a CPSU member, the party membership card meant more than the passport. Its loss, under aggravating circumstances, resulted in the loss of social status and transfer to the lowest estates. Expulsion from the party was the worst punishment for its members—it symbolized their social death.

Within the estate of CPSU members, the party nomenklatura formed a separate group—a super estate of the second order, which, in turn, was a quota sample from CPSU members. The nomenklatura was formed from CPSU members on grounds of gender, age, education, occupation, ethnic and social origin, as well as regional and sectoral criteria. All estates had their talent pools, i.e. lists of CPSU members, who qualified for membership in the nomenklatura based on their nominal credentials.

According to government ideologists, quota representation of CPSU members in the nomenklatura served to coordinate the tactical and strategic interests of the Soviet estates during the construction of socialism, i.e., in overcoming the differences (estate) between the city and the village, between workers, peasants, and employees, between Stalin's nationalities, between physical and mental labor, and so on. Based on the idea of "the leading role of the Communist Party", decisions rolled out at party meetings, plenary sessions, conferences and congresses should have satisfied and guided all estates of the society, since statistically all their principal interests were represented in the CPSU and its nomenklatura.

Trade unions were another form of uniting members of Soviet estates into an integrated Soviet people. The All-Union Central Council of Trade Unions and the industrial trade unions it united provided their members with various resources (from foodstuffs and vouchers to resorts and holiday homes to payment for medical treatment and establishment of mutual aid funds) according to effective social justice criteria. Trade union meetings were an important element of estate integration. When their agenda included debates regarding violations of the moral standards of builders of communism, such meetings became significant events in the life of labor collectives.

The trade unions (along with sectoral Workers' Supply Departments) controlled the distribution of enormous amounts of consumer resources (housing, vouchers to medical and health institutions, places at childcare facilities, etc.). Not being a trade union member actually meant being deprived of access to social benefits, which were in very short supply. Russian humorists of the 1930s captured the slogan of the estate society of that time: "Beer is served only to members of the trade union".

Earned and unearned income, administrative trade, and shadow economy

Communist estate building pursued the goal of establishing a socially homogeneous Soviet people as a single estate whose members would have equal rights and responsibilities towards the state. However, inequality in resource provisioning uncontrolled by the Communist Party constantly emerged in the course of this process. The reason was diversion of resources, their plundering, and enrichment of individual estates, i.e., the shadow economy. The CPSU was continuously concerned about the implicit and ideologically unmotivated stratification into the rich and the poor, and made efforts to eliminate it. This concern manifested itself in rigid control over the composition of estates and inter-estate mobility, i.e., in repressive and administrative regimes.

According to the logic of the administrative market, the higher-level sectoral and territorial organizations were supposed to alienate the resources from the lower-level ones and then distribute them based on the principles of social justice and national economic priorities in general. To ensure <u>minimum</u> opportunities for economic activities at each functional place and on all levels of administration, Communist Party committees and Soviet executive committees had to coordinate and control both the appropriation and distribution of resources. Diligent socialist workers had to participate in socialist emulation in order to exceed the indicators targeted by economic plans, i.e., maximize their performance in utilizing the allocated resources.[96] Fair distribution (based on the established minimum) of alienated resources constituted the principal content of Soviet governance.

The end of mass repressions and the weakening of the administrative regime that started in the 1950s and continued with varying success in the 1970s and the 1980s, led to a gradual degradation of Soviet estate stratification and its transition to the post-perestroika form. Individual estates, industries, and regional administrative entities started acting as if they had their own socio-economic goals and possessed the means to achieve them. They engaged in collecting illegitimate (for the official system) estate rent, using it to adjust the official perceptions of social justice. These fragments of the socialist world order developed their own perceptions of social justice different from those of "the party and the government". Industries, regional administrative entities, enterprises, and individuals found ways to re-distribute in their favor the products alienated by the state and turn them into the resources they needed.

The regulatory logic of socialist construction was inverted in the social practice of the "Brezhnev-era stagnation". Republican, regional, and district committees of the Communist Party began influencing the process of determining which industries were most important for their areas, so that the development of a specific industry in the area within their jurisdiction would generate maximum benefits in the form of housing, infrastructure, social and cultural facilities, and other resources. Adjustment of priorities consisted in exchange relations between the party committees and industry leadership, when, for example, in exchange for the opportunity to build an enterprise in a specific region, the industry leadership provided additional assets to the region, territory or republic, thus allowing their administration to cope

---

[96] Socialist labor consisted in utilizing the resources allocated for a certain activity and in fulfilling plans for supplying other participants of socialist construction with resources. Socialist emulation presumed that given an equal amount of allocated resources, "labor enthusiasm" would allow diligent workers to produce more resources than initially planned. This mythological component imposed by propaganda and agitation was supposed to be the main driver of the "socialist economy". I fully agree with Evgeny Dobrenko, who introduced the concept of "political economy of socialist realism" and demonstrated that "socialist art mobilizing for valorous labor" was a key element of the socialist economy.

with shortages. It was impossible to obtain quotas for cars, raise purchase prices, increase supply standards for foodstuffs, consumer goods, and other resources beyond the framework of exchange relations. The totality of methods used to bypass public mechanisms of alienation and distribution received (in the government's reflection) the name of shadow economy.

The existence of labor not attached to a fixed place of work was a precondition for the existence of the shadow economy. Such labor became common after the 1960s and consisted of non-estate teams of construction workers, bums (bichi), tramps, and other categories of laborers who performed odd jobs on a lump-sum or contractual basis and were not bound by social guarantees, benefits and privileges provided by estate affiliation. Local authorities needed respective executive bodies to utilize the resources resulting from exchange relations. Generally, this role was performed by local offices of communist party committees and Soviet executive committees that could assign "informal" jobs to staff personnel of local enterprises and organizations or engage mobile labor through shadow agents for certain operations or for permanent work in the shadow economy segment. Thus, the shadow economy gradually undermined the foundation of the estate world order.

The shadow economy was a necessary structural (but not formalized) component of the existing resource-based activities. It could be criminal—when government bodies were directly linked with the shadow agents who redistributed the materials and resulting products among the actual producers and party and Soviet functionaries. It could also be non-criminal—when such links did not exist and the shadow agents were coordinated only by enterprise and entity directors or line managers in the course of routinely meeting or exceeding socialist economic targets.

The shadow economy had a specific feature. To redistribute the products alienated by the state in their favor, enterprises, organizations, industries, and territorial bodies used the existing institutions of the administrative market since its arrangement and operation blocked or hindered the establishment of new organizational forms. Without exception, all elements of the administrative market became actors of the shadow economy, but naturally, its institutions varied depending on the organizational level. The shadow redistribution of resources was based on "tit for tat" exchange relations with unfair (in terms of socialist social justice) distribution of consumer resources becoming the visible result.

Analytically, it is possible to split the population of the former Soviet Union in two groups, keeping in mind that such a rigid division is purely nominal. It is logical to include those members of the estate world order into the first group, whose only source of income were their "wages", i.e., earned income in the socialist sense of the word, including resources they were "entitled to" as members of one or another estate, i.e. estate rent. Even at the lowest levels of the estate hierarchy, official estate rent included housing on a "first come, first served" basis, vouchers to resorts and holiday homes, pioneer camps and a lot more. In addition to the guaranteed minimum, members of privileged estates were supplied with high quality foodstuffs, imported clothing and household appliances; they had the opportunity, for example, to buy a car or spend their vacation abroad—in socialist-camp countries. We can say that this part of the population lived under real socialism (from each according to his status ability, to each according to his labor, i.e. the fulfillment of his status duties). The state established and maintained the status system, determined status abilities and measured the labor "performance".

For the overwhelming majority of Soviet citizens, working time "remunerated" by the state was the main source of income. However, the total amount of resources, ways of spending and consumer goods that a Soviet citizen could afford depended on his position in various socio-economic hierarchies, which were largely (but not fully) determined by party-nomenklatura regulations.

Power was the second main source of resources. Power was measured by a specific resource—administrative currency at the disposal of an individual executive. The very fact of authoritative alienation of resources with their further distribution (irrespective whether legitimate or illegitimate, legal or illegal from the official standpoint) meant that the citizen possessed administrative currency. Administrative currency could be in cash or non-cash form (the currency of a direct order or indirect instruction resulting from coordination of interests), different nominal value (documents on CPSU letterheads had higher value than those on the letterheads of Soviet bodies), etc. All resources and administrative currencies were partly inter-convertible. Rubles could "buy" membership in minimally privileged estates. For example, one could obtain "registration" in Moscow and become a member of the Muscovite estate. At the same time, certain statuses and related administrative currencies allowed "making money", i.e., deriving rubles from one's power status and connections. Status features determined the type and amount of administrative currency available to the status holder. Administrative currency was a specific and only partially legitimate type of estate rent, which allowed alienating resources from lower-level estates. It was a direct result of the estate hierarchy as such and was a poorly controlled by-product of the estate order established by the CPSU.

The total amount of resources consisting of earned income plus income derived from the opportunity to use administrative currency ranked people in estate relations. The sources and the amount of resources received by citizens of lower status, by definition should have been completely "transparent" for holders of higher status. The lower estates had no right to collect estate rent outside the relations controlled by the authorities. When the amount of resources at the disposal of relatively low-status citizens exceeded a certain standard level, such resources were declared "unearned income", i.e. not corresponding to the predetermined position of the person in the estate system.

Incomes of those affiliated with privileged estates were "not transparent" for members of the lower estates. In the public opinion of the lower strata, all income of the upper strata appeared to be "unearned", since the regulations on the hierarchies of estate governance, available to the lower strata, contained no indication as to the sources of income—conversion of administrative currency into other resources and estate rent. The "public opinion" about social injustice in the distribution of resources was driven by the upper estates' non-transparent incomes.

Let us go back to the initial distinctions. Earned income (in the socialist sense of the term) was fixed by the state and determined by the specified position of an individual in the public governance and distribution hierarchies. Earned income also included estate-specific rent as far as it was related to the individual's status (specified by the state) in the distribution and power system. Estate rent was nominally included in the definition of the estates' status and manifested itself in formal privileges, including the amount and quality of consumer resources a specific estate was entitled to.

Unearned income is generated not by the possession of administrative currency as such, but by its unregulated conversion into other resources, i.e. it results from using one's power status in the process of distributing resources and collecting additional estate rent. Unearned income meant primarily income from converting administrative currency into other resources, including money. People derived unearned income from their position in the power hierarchies and in the process of collecting estate rent. Therefore, such income received by the lower strata of the population could indicate the existence of an illegal form of administrative currency and concealed hierarchies of power, certain positions in which enable unauthorized (by the state) disposal of resources. For the upper strata, the very fact that the lower strata could receive unearned income evidenced breaches in the system of government power, therefore, the state permanently opposed this.

People that possessed administrative currency did not content themselves with earned income that included standard estate rent. Being involved in resource distribution, they received additional revenue from their social status. Such revenue was the main origin of resources, which breached the principles of social justice. Resources were distributed through tough administrative bargaining, which embraced, without exception, everyone holding any position of authority whatsoever.[97] People regarded their involvement in administrative bargaining and the ability to charge illegitimate rent due to their status as a natural aspect of social reality indispensable for life. As the say-

---

[97] Kordonsky S. *Markets for power. Administrative markets of the USSR and Russia.* M., 2006.

ing goes: it is impossible to "be near water and not quench one's thirst", i.e. to have the opportunity to dispose of resources and not to take advantage of it.

At the last stages of the socialist state's existence, administrative trade when allocating resources was the first and only reality. Public institutions, governance hierarchies, and relations within them were perceived as auxiliary, dependent elements underpinning bargaining positions. At its initial stages, perestroika was actually an attempt to eliminate or limit exchange relations and the associated shadow economy. Unregulated estate rent was declared illegal. Perestroika took the form of government efforts, namely, undertaken by its repressive bodies, to eliminate exchange relations and resource redistribution. It started by trying to put a stop to shadow relations at the lowest levels of the administrative market hierarchy—by "struggling against unearned income" and restricting the activities of all types of "teams" and other mobile labor formations. Subsequently, perestroika took the form of fighting illegal entrepreneurs (*tsekhoviki*). The third stage of perestroika dealt with investigating shadow activities "covered up" by functionaries of the CPSU and Soviet administrative bodies. The struggle consisted in eliminating individual people occupying certain functional places in the administrative market relationship hierarchy: first, work "teams" and subsistence farmers; then, organized semi-legal and illegal producers (tsekhoviki); and finally, CPSU and Soviet officials, who controlled such businesses. The ideology of the struggle assumed that the essence of the problem was the abnormal behavior of individual persons rather than the resource-based estate system of relations. Thus, the USSR leadership betrayed the core principle of regulating resource-based relations—resorting to mass repressions of members of the "estates that had been caught stealing". The desire to localize and neutralize certain tensions in the system backfired. It resulted in the shadow economy becoming a general phenomenon and made possible mass protest actions of the lower estates, which by the late 1980s took the form of labor conflicts—walkouts and strikes. At that time, CPSU and repressive bodies, as well as the editorial offices of CPSU publications were flooded with complaints and denunciations regarding unfair distribution of resources. This torrent transformed into riots against the governance procedure.

Repression as a form of regulating inter-estate relations in the USSR

Supplying resources to estates based on social justice criteria is fraught with a phenomenon, which since time immemorial has been referred to as bribery—now we call it corruption.[98] Distributing resources according to the predefined significance of the estates, the estate order strives for justice. However, on the way to fair distribution the resources undergo transformations described in the previous chapter. As a result, a substantial part of them never reaches those for whom they are intended. Resources are diverted, in particular, because of estate rent levied on them, since every member of an estate society possesses what he is in charge of and what he distributes. Resources are also plundered by people "not entitled" to them, who nevertheless want to eat, like millions of our compatriots convicted and sent to prison camps under decrees of 1932 and 1947, popularly known as the "seven/eight" decree (it was issued on the 7th of August) or the "law of spikelets".[99]

---

[98] I believe the term corruption is in principle not applicable to inter-estate relations. Corruption is specific for a class society and can be defined as the abuse of power by an official for personal gain. In an estate system, members of the upper estates collect estate rent from members of the lower estates, which is similar to corruption only in appearance. Estate rent is a constituent aspect of the estate order rather than abuse of power by individual officials.

[99] The Decree of the Central Executive Committee and the Council of People's Commissars of the USSR dated 7 August 1932 *On protecting the property of state enterprises, kolkhozes, and cooperatives and consolidating public (socialist) property* explicitly stipulated that "those guilty of theft of goods on rail and water transport... embezzlement (theft) of kolkhoz and cooperative property... be sentenced to capital punishment with confiscation of all personal property; in the event of mitigating circumstances, execution shall be replaced by a prison term of no less than ten years with confiscation of all personal property". People convicted for such crimes were not subject to amnesty... "In order to prevent theft of beetroot during harvesting... the Decree of the Central Executive Committee and the Council of People's Commissars of the USSR dated 7 August 1932 shall be applied to thieves of beetroot" (Decree of the Council of People's Commissars of the USSR dated 17 September 1932). "Individuals found guilty of committing sabotage in the course of agricultural operations, stealing seeds by harmfully understating seeding rates, ploughing and sowing in a way that is damaging for the fields and results in reduced harvests, intentionally breaking down tractors and vehicles, and killing horses shall be treated as thieves of kolkhoz property and charged under Decree of 7 August 1932" (Decree of the Central Executive Com-

The inner life of the estate order consists in the struggle for appropriate, targeted use of resources. Estate morality condemns diversion of resources, even more so their plundering. Such actions are persecuted according to the governance procedure—a form of regulating relations on collecting, storing and distributing resources specific for the estate system. Over centuries of estate-related history, vast experience (including repressive one) in combating violations in the procedure of using resources has built up. This experience shows that even individual impaling hardly curbs the thieves' appetites. The institute of mass repressions proved to be much more effective. It was fully applied during the construction of socialism in one particular country and, albeit on a lower scale, it was used by all rulers of the country when "restoring order". During mass repressions, the state impales total estates rather than their individual representatives. Repression of total estates that had learned to divert resources or proved to be inadequate for new goals at a specific stage in the construction of a new society had made collectivization and industrialization in the USSR possible. The national economy developed at soaring rates due to this method of regulating inter-estate relations, which relied

---

mittee of the USSR dated 30 January 1933); cit. ex Maksudov S. Population loss in the USSR. - M., 1989. pp. 292-293.

In 1947, the Decree on criminal liability for theft of state and public property was adopted. "In order to establish consistent laws on criminal liability for theft of state and public property and enhance measures on combating such crimes, the Presidium of The Supreme Soviet of the USSR hereby decrees:

1. Theft, appropriation, embezzlement or other plundering of state property shall be punished by imprisonment in a corrective labor camp for a term of seven to ten years with or without confiscation of personal property.
2. Repeated plundering of state property, as well as that committed by an organized group (gang) or on a large scale shall be punished by imprisonment in a corrective labor camp for a term of ten to twenty-five years with confiscation of personal property.
3. Theft, appropriation, embezzlement or other plundering of kolkhoz, cooperative or other public property shall be punished by imprisonment in a corrective labor camp for a term of five to eight years with or without confiscation of personal property.
4. Repeated plundering of kolkhoz, cooperative or other public property, as well as that committed by an organized group (gang) or on a large scale shall be punished by imprisonment in a corrective labor camp for a term of eight to twenty years with confiscation of personal property.
5. Failure to report to the authorities a certain case of planned or committed plundering of state or public property, stipulated by Articles 2 and 4 hereof shall be punished by a prison term of two to three years or exile for a period of five to seven years".

on using forced labor of members of repressed groups. Members of the "fat cat" (excessively active in collecting estate rent) estates "were put before a firing squad" en masse, as was the case with several generations of high-ranking security officers, or transferred to the estate of prisoners working at socialist construction sites. At the command of the Communist Party, GPU-OGPU-NKVD-MVD [secret police at different stages in Soviet history] supplied these most mobile "labor resources" to the national economy. Numerous Soviet estates allowed focusing repressions on one or several of them in order to provide the economy with labor resources and simultaneously destroy the resource diversion system established by these estates. In the absence of mass repressions, resource plundering and diversion plague the estate-based society and undermine its foundation—fair distribution.

The repressive method of regulating inter-estate relations was specific for the USSR in the 1920s–1950s. Stalin's death put an end to the political will needed for large-scale repressive regulation of inter-estate relations and the estate system stagnated. Post-Stalin estates "successfully adapted" to diverting resources, stealing them and collecting illegitimate estate rent. As a result, the whole system of estate-based distribution lost its functionality. This manifested itself in the phenomenon of overall shortages formally not compensated by anything. Selective repressions of the 1960s-1980s against individual trade, catering, police and other executives only appeared to promote sophisticated methods of diverting resources, thus further undermining their fair distribution. No matter how many offenders were imprisoned, shortages remained as acute as before. Diversion of resources, their theft and illegitimate collection of estate rent became common practice during the "Brezhnev-era stagnation" in the 1960s-1980s. Moreover, "prosecutions" seemed to have an opposite effect. They promoted the development of the shadow economy and transformation of resources into goods that circulated in the black market, where everything was available that was "in scarce supply" in the public distribution system.

The collapse of Soviet inter-estate relations

The system of Soviet inter-estate relations relied on the social framework dominated by the base status of Communist Party member and the leading role of the CPSU and its nomenklatura, and on repression as a social control mechanism. Termination of mass repressions and abolition of the constitutional "leading role of the CPSU" destroyed, in particular, the foundation of the estate system and resulted in general status uncertainty—mainly because of destroying estate-based resource distribution. The collapse of the Soviet Union was primarily the collapse of inter-estate relations, i.e. the society. I would like to emphasize once again that the society in an estate-based system is inseparable from the state. CPSU membership lost its social relevance, and the nomenklatura disappeared together with Party institutions of personnel selection and placement.

The shortage of material resources[100] for distribution combined with the ideological helplessness of the Soviet authorities resulted in former Soviet Republics plundering the USSR. The collapse of the Soviet estate system accompanied this process. By then, Soviet ideology had depreciated so much that it could no longer serve to justify overall shortages, which, according to the Communist Party, were unavoidable on the way to achieving once great purposes, which had lost their appeal. In search of a new ideology, Soviet intellectuals read an reread the works of Marxist-Leninist classics and absorbed scraps of imported social order concepts, which reached them mainly as samizdat [self-published] translations of the writings of economists, polit-

---

100 Any private disposal of resources was forbidden in the USSR. Only the state, through distribution, could supply resources to members of socialist estates. Resources could also be obtained in the process of administrative bargaining, procured by pulling strings, stolen or concealed. At the outset of socialist construction, soap, fabric, needles, thread, and matches were subject to distribution, not to mention fixed assets, land or access to communications. Goods in short supply were obtained by all possible means and exchanged for whatever was at that time available. At the final stage of socialist construction, in the 1980s, the list of shortages included tobacco, alcohol, coffee and tea, footwear and clothing. Needles and thread escaped this fate, but people hoarded them just in case. They exchanged scarce goods creating a rather closely-knit network - leading a social life of "obtaining goods and services by pulling strings or using good connections".

ical scientists, sociologists, and philosophers. Undigested imported social science distinctions fundamentally not applicable to the domestic estate order ultimately formed the theoretic and axiological basis of perestroika.

The decay of the estate system (which happens when the resources for "carving up" disappear) was accompanied by the automatic appearance of markets and stratification of the population by level of consumption, i.e. by the emergence of the class structure. The class structure is like cancer for the estate organization of a society-state—it destroys estate institutions and stratifies estate members separating them into classes. Such periods reveal the social inequality previously concealed by estate-based distribution. It is expressed primarily in different access to resources. The emergence of the "black market" where resources are converted into freely circulating goods and money was a challenge for the estate system, since it disrupted the predetermined social harmony and the estate members' common approach to "carving up" resources and collecting estate rent.

After the collapse of the USSR and the establishment of the Russian Federation, after the overall shortage crisis, the Russian estates (exactly in line with estate philosophy) perceived the market, market relations, and democracy as a new source of "carvable" resources (oil was such a source in the last decades of the Soviet regime) that could be used to develop further the estate-based state-society. Post-perestroika politicians and reformers "built" the market primarily as a new system for coordinating estate interests.[101] Moreover, the most active of them identified themselves as the estate of "young reformers" with a closed membership and privileges in the privatization of "public property". However, probably against their will, the society was separating from the state and the economy was separating from the state.

---

[101] When it turned out that the market was neither a resource, nor a source of resources, but something hardly compatible with the re-emerging estate structure, the remnants of the Soviet estate-based state started instinctively opposing market expansion by restricting access to resources for entrepreneurs, in particular, by winding up privatization and revising its results.

The newborn society did not behave as the liberal reformers expected it would, and the freshly minted entrepreneurs, having privatized public resources, started acting in line with the market rather than the resource logic. Special trade outlets as well as in-house and trade union resource distribution systems disappeared, and all citizens, independent of their Soviet estate affiliation, started purchasing consumer goods at markets that immediately mushroomed. The trade unions, which used to represent estate interests, ceased distributing scarce goods and services, thus losing their respective status and the role of the estate system consolidators. The shadow economy first fully replaced estate-based socially just resource distribution and then began transforming into economy as such. Real goods and almost real money—nominally convertible currency—appeared in the country.

The collapse of the USSR destroyed the system of inter-estate relations established when building socialism (just as the February 1917 revolution destroyed the relations between imperial estates); although in a sense, the estates themselves still exist. Modern Russia is no longer stratified into workers, peasants, and employees. Therefore, their numerous ideology-driven derivatives have lost meaning. However, the nominal social derivatives of workers, peasants, and employees—the military, KGB servicemen, miners, sailors, cops, pensioners, public sector workers, etc.—remain. These groups largely preserved their Soviet estate identification and the remains of the Soviet estate morality, but their members are no longer bound by membership in the Communist Party, the Party's leading role, as well as trade union affiliation. The surviving estates have retained their claims to resources, and in spite of everything demand that the resource flows to them be resumed. Actually, they demand reinstatement of inter-estate relations—an estate society and resource-based state.

In the 1990s, people became completely confused about "where we were then, where to go, and who was who", what social group he or she belonged to and what could be expected of whom. The collapse of inter-estate relations deprived the population of social guidelines. Practically everyone, like it or not, had to draw on their past (go back to the roots) to determine their place in the present. That was the time when retrospective estate identification peaked. Dressed in uniforms that never existed and decorated from head to foot with orders and medals of all times, the "descendants" of Cossacks, nobles, clergy, and other "imperial aristocrats", as well as "successors of the socialist revolution"—new revolutionary soldiers, sailors, propagandists, agitators, and other ardent revolutionaries became an element of the everyday political landscape along with "genuine descendants" of the so-called indigenous people and "titular nations" of the USSR provinces.[102]

For a time, compiling personal genealogies and writing "histories" of provinces and ethnic groups gone into oblivion became a flourishing domestic business, and "a la antique" engravings with images of spreading family trees—pedigrees took a place of honor on the "parlour" walls of the servicemen and the new rich—the merchants. Nowadays this trend has almost exhausted itself. At the beginning of the twenty-first century, the surviving Soviet estate order that few perceive as an estate one and the extremely idealized picture of the imperial system of social relations with its service and taxable estates serve as reference points.

Unlike the October 1917 revolution, the 1991 revolution was relatively mild; it destroyed only the system of coordinating the interests of Soviet estates and estate-based resource distribution. The situation in Russia did not go so far as to physically eliminate members of Soviet estates, although some democrats and champions of justice adopted Stalin's approach to shaping the social structure and insisted not only on decommunization the denazification way but also on the elimination of "chekists and communists as a class".

The collapse of the Soviet system released an enormous amount of resources labeled "public" but actually ownerless. Until the end of the twentieth century, social processes focused on utilizing these resources, plundering them and transforming into goods and money, with the plunderers turning into market agents. The market, which emerged on the barren social land due to privatization of previously

---

[102] These "genuine descendants" - nationalists became a personification of Stalin's nationalities, i.e. people for whom their passport ethnicity—item five—used to be and remains the basis of self-identification.

all-estate—public property, rapidly developed. It did not take long for the remnants of the Soviet estate order to start resisting class stratification associated with market development. Pensioners and public sector workers, civil servants and military personnel, security officers and policemen voiced demands to "restore order", "establish social justice", and fight against "plunderers of public property", i.e. the oligarchs. Their aggregate demands paved the way for revitalizing the interest coordination system—the estate system based partly on the Imperial and partly on the Soviet model.

The desire for social justice, i.e. resource distribution according to an estate's status, diligently cultivated by the estate system, was and remains the main obstacle for class stratification. A special and rather sustainable social group specific for the estate society but not an estate in itself—the intelligentsia, passes this desire and its ideology from generation to generation.

The intelligentsia always opposes the estate-based social order, which created it. In times of stability, it debates and condemns the methods for shaping institutions of just estate-based distribution, its principles, results, and proportions, mass repressions when fighting plunderers, and the deprivation of the lower estates. In times of change (liberalizations and revolutions), when market principles start replacing estate institutions, the intellectuals, who actually constitute the self-conscious part of the estate society, first become influential authority figures. Later, as their power ambitions encounter resistance, they try to bring life back on the track predetermined by their interpretation of history and build a society where resources would be distributed fairly. For them this means primarily providing resources for education, science, culture, healthcare, etc., i.e. for principal intellectual occupations, which are mostly related to institutions for estate socialization. Intellectuals form images of external and internal enemies (wrongly managing, owning or claiming title to resources) that oppose the establishment of justice and make mythological efforts to combat them.

At times of liberalization, the intelligentsia becomes the social stratum that ensures continuity of the estate system ideology and paves the way for the emergence of authoritarian leaders, who strive to establish a strong, tough and "just" (but "progressive") state, where there would be also be a place for the intellectuals. It appears that there is a law of conservation of the intelligentsia. The premises of this law include the existence of an estate-based system, which the intelligentsia opposes, but which reproduces it as its essential element.

Contemporary service (titular) estates and state service

As I already mentioned, the Federal Assembly of the Russian Federation has adopted in recent years several laws on various state services that actually introduce a new estate-based order according to the imperial model and determine the mode of existence of service estates. Such laws include the federal law on state service and associated laws on state civil and military services, as well as laws on the status of judges, deputies, and the municipal and Cossack services.

Contemporary post-Soviet estates introduced by law (actually, also like the remnants of the Soviet ones) are still not full-fledged. According to B.N. Mironov's criteria, their rights, albeit legal, are not unconditional; estate organizations-societies and courts are lacking; they do not enjoy the right to self-government; and their members have no estate consciousness and mentality. Moreover, estate members usually have no reflection of belonging to an estate. Instead, their self-identification is occupational. Nevertheless, the legal framework of a new estate world order is virtually in place.

In contrast to the Soviet estates that were created for building a bright future, the new Russian estates are established to serve, similarly to the privileged estates of Imperial Russia, according to the researchers.

In addition to serving, bylaws introduce relations of service facilitation and service support. Some service estates serve, the other service estates facilitate services, and the non-service estates support them.

Let us consider contemporary forms of service. Federal state service is professional service activity by citizens designed to ensure administration of powers of the Russian Federation, as well as powers of federal government bodies and persons holding public office in the Russian Federation.

Pursuant to Federal Law No. 58-FZ, *On the State Service System in the Russian Federation*, the federal state service includes three types of state service:

1. Military service
2. Law enforcement service
3. State civil service.

Military service is a type of federal state service constituting professional service activity by citizens holding military positions in the Armed Forces of the Russian Federation, other troops, and military (special) units and bodies responsible for defense and security. Military service consists in protecting the state from internal and external threats and enemies using force. Since enemies and threats are different, military service is specialized along the following lines:

- Ministry of Defense of the Russian Federation (Defense Ministry)
- Federal Service for Special Construction (Spetsstroi)
- Federal Security Service (FSB)
- Federal Guard Service (FSO)
- Foreign Intelligence Service (SVR)
- Ministry of the Russian Federation for Civil Defense Matters, Emergency Situations and Managing the Consequences of Natural Disasters (MChS) including the military units of the State Fire Service (GPS)
- Ministry of Internal Affairs (internal troops)
- Main Directorate for Special Programs under the President of the Russian Federation (GUSP).

The law thus distinguishes nine subtypes of military service and, respectively, nine military sub-estates. In accordance with Federal Law *On conscription and military service* and the *Regulation on the military service procedure* (as approved by Presidential Decree No. 1237 of 16 September 1999), military personnel are assigned military ranks.

Law enforcement service is a type of federal state service constituting professional service activity by citizens holding law enforcement positions in government bodies, services, and agencies responsible for security, law and order, combating crime, and protecting human and civil rights and freedoms. Law enforcement personnel are assigned special ranks and titles. Similarly to the military service system, law enforcement and administration is specialized according to law violation types and forms. Persons serving in law enforcement bodies and bearing special ranks assigned under Russian law can be staff members of the following bodies:

- Ministry of Internal Affairs of the Russian Federation (MVD)
- Federal Migration Service (FMS)
- State Courier Service of the Russian Federation (GFS)
- Federal Penitentiary Service of the Russian Federation (FSIN)
- Federal Customs Service of the Russian Federation (FTS)
- Federal Drug Control Service (FSKN)
- Federal Bailiff Service (FSSP)
- State Fire Service subordinated to the MChS (GPS MChS).

Thus, the state law enforcement service is divided into eight subestates. It is noteworthy that the law on law enforcement service, similar in status to the laws on military and state civil service, has not been enacted yet—it is at the stage of coordination.

FSIN and GPS MChS personnel are assigned special internal service ranks. Employees of the Russian GFS belong to the personnel of the Ministry of Internal Affairs. They are assigned special internal service officer ranks. FMS employees also belong to MVD personnel. They are assigned special police and internal service officer ranks.

Newly recruited and effective personnel of the Federal Drug Control Service are assigned special police ranks, obviously, because FSKN was established on the basis of the disbanded Tax Police.

Public prosecution officers (prosecutors, investigators, and some other categories of federal state employees) within the Prosecution Service of the Russian Federation are assigned class rankings. State civil employees of the prosecution, who are not prosecution officers, are assigned qualification levels (class ranks of the state civil service). Prosecutors and investigators of the military prosecutor's office serve in the Armed Forces of the Russian Federation, Federal Security Service border troops, other troops, and military units and bodies pursuant to the federal law *On conscription and military service* and have the rights and social guarantees stipulated by federal laws *On the status of military personnel* and *On the Prosecution Service of the Russian Federation*. They are assigned officer military ranks. Pursuant to Article 48 of the law *On the Prosecution Service of the Russian Federation*, the military ranks of military prosecution officers correspond to the class rankings of public prosecution officers on the regional level.

Thus, prosecution work is not a separate service but an aggregate of all types of state service—state civil service, military service, and law enforcement service.

Investigators within the judiciary system are governed by regulations and legal framework similar to those of the prosecution.

State civil service is a type of state service constituting the professional service activity by citizens holding state civil service positions designed to ensure the administration of powers of federal government bodies and government bodies of the constituent entities of the Russian Federation.

In accordance with the federal law *On the State Civil Service in the Russian Federation* and Presidential Decree *On the procedure of assigning and retaining state civil service class rankings*, federal state civil servants holding federal public offices are assigned civil service class rankings and diplomatic ranks.

The law on the state civil service provides for three sub-estates:

- Federal state civil servants
- Regional state civil servants
- Diplomats.

The characteristics of the services as defined in the above laws and regulations fully conform to the dictionary definition of estates. For example, the law *On the Prosecution Service of the Russian Federa-*

tion explicitly determines the estate privileges of prosecutors, who as a sub-estate enjoy the privileges of all three types of state service.

The result is the following. Under the law on state service, the state distinguishes three types of service and, respectively, three estates (state civil servants, military personnel, and law enforcers) and twenty sub-estates within them—federal state civil servants, regional state civil servants, diplomats, Russian army personnel, Federal security service personnel, Foreign Intelligence Service personnel, Federal Guard Service personnel, police force, etc.

In addition to the general law on state service, certain sub-estates are also governed by separate laws—on the Federal Security Service, Ministry of the Interior, Federal Guard Service, Foreign Intelligence Service, and the Prosecution Service.

Further, the law on the status of deputies determines deputy activity as a <u>law-making service</u>. The law determines the responsibilities of deputies to the state and their privileges, including immunity from prosecution. Therefore, there is every reason to classify deputies as a separate estate divided into sub-estates:

- Deputies of the State Duma [lower chamber of parliament]
- Members of the Council of the Federation [upper chamber of parliament]
- Deputies of regional legislative assemblies.

"On 7 February 2007, the State Duma passed the federal law *On municipal service in the Russian Federation*. The law governs relations arising in connection with enrollment of citizens of the Russian Federation for municipal service, its discharge and termination, and the definition of the legal standing (status) of municipal employees.

...Pursuant to this federal law, the fundamental distinction between the status of municipal employees and that of state civil servants of the Russian Federation is employment on the basis of an employment agreement rather than a service contract as provided for state civil servants of the Russian Federation. The federal law specifies the basic rights, responsibilities, and guarantees of municipal employees, as well as restrictions and prohibitions related to municipal service".[103] Thus, comments to the Presidential Decree published on the official website of the President of the Russian Federation define municipal service and the estate of municipal employees. Moreover, the law also includes into this estate deputies of local legislative assemblies—persons, who hold municipal office, but are not municipal employees.

The law on Cossacks introduces the notion of Cossack service and defines the estate status of Cossacks and their relation to state civil, military, and law enforcement services. The Cossack estate is in the process of forming sub-estates—regional Cossack hosts (armies).

According to the law *On the status of judges*, judges constitute a separate estate, and federal judges down to the district level are appointed by personal decree of the President of the Russian Federation. Nevertheless, their status is fundamentally uncertain. Judging presumes serving the law rather than the state, and in this sense it does not qualify as state service. The judges are operating within the state service system; however, their status is unique to a certain extent. It is difficult to define this status under the estate world order, since such a world order provides for no other service than the state one.[104] In a sense, judges belong to the law enforcement service; however, this is not specified in the law on their status. Judges receive their salaries from the state, but their activity (judicial proceedings) is financed by the Supreme Court of the Russian Federation through its judicial department. Judges are divided in at least three sub-estates differing by the scope of their rights and privileges:

- Federal judges
- Constitutional judges
- Justices of the peace.

I believe there is also fundamental uncertainty in the definition of such law enforcement service as penitentiary activity in what concerns the

---

103 http://www.kremlin.ru/priorities/events31001/2007.shtml.
104 To a certain extent, similar problems exist in defining the status of the clergy, who serve God rather than the state or civil law, however, it has not yet come to appointing priests by decrees or financing church service from the state budget, although the trend is there.

status of those being punished. Persons involved in the execution of punishment perform either military (internal troops) or law enforcement (Ministry of Justice and Ministry of the Interior) service. The execution of punishment is inseparable from those being punished—prisoners, persons under investigation, and persons under surveillance. The execution of punishment is a titular service; consequently, crime and subsequent punishment also have a certain titular aspect. Therefore, prisoners, persons under investigation, and persons under surveillance may also be regarded as a titular estate with its rights, responsibilities, and privileges, which exists as long as there are those, who execute the punishment and thus perform titular service. A similar uncertainty exists as to defining the status of migrants not affiliated with any of the estates, whose estate socialization is the responsibility of the Federal Migration Service. Nevertheless, in further sections I will be treating law violation and illegal migration as non-titular activities.

Thus, at present, federal laws have introduced seven basic types of service and, accordingly, to them, seven principal estates. I consider state civil servants, military personnel, law enforcers, judges, deputies, Cossacks, and municipal employees to be titular estates, because federal laws explicitly determine their rights and responsibilities, as well as privileges.

The military, law enforcers, and Cossacks have specific (for every individual service) uniforms distinguished by military or special rank, state or departmental decorations, and insignia.[105] Certain categories

---

105 According to different laws, decrees, and orders, uniformed personnel includes the following categories: military personnel (Russian Armed Forces, Federal Guard Service, Federal Security Service, Foreign Intelligence Service, Ministry for Emergency Situations, etc.); personnel of the internal affairs bodies of the Russian Federation, MChS State Fire Service, and penitentiary institutions and bodies; diplomats; employees of Rospotrebnadzor and the environmental supervision service of the Ministry of Natural Resources; tax officers; employees of supervisory authorities under the Ministry of Agriculture (quarantine, veterinary, technical, and game wardens), State Technical Control employees; departmental security staff; communications and special communications staff; transport inspectors, Ministry of justice employees (bailiffs, judges), land cadastre service employees, drug control police officers, employees of the Federal Migration Service, customs officers, Federal Agency for State Reserves (Rosrezerv) employees, Russian Shipbuilding Agency personnel, rescuers, builders, prosecutors,

of state civil servants also have special uniforms, insignia, and rankings. Senior officials of the state civil service do not have uniforms and special estate insignia, as opposed to the employees of numerous state civil branches, whose clothing allowance includes uniforms of the most exotic designs and colors, such as the crimson jackets of Rospotrebnadzor (Federal Service for Protecting Consumer Rights and Public Health) officials or dazzling white ceremonial uniforms of the senior prosecution officers.

Service-related privileges and restrictions applicable to members of titular estates are stipulated by law. The notion of work and, accordingly, work-related or performance-related payment is not applicable to members of titular estates. Servicemen serve rather than work. Members of service estates receive compensation for their service in the form of pay, the amount of which (remuneration) depends on the rank (class ranking), position, length of service, and service conditions.

Relations between titular estates

The life of titular estate members consists in mutual service, which is called service facilitation. The structure of such service can be presented in the form of a matrix table (Table 4), where the left column lists the estates established by federal laws, and the top row—corresponding estate activities. Thus, state civil servants perform state civil service, whereas law enforcers perform law enforcement service. Serving means performing corresponding activity. The intersection of similarly named activities (services) and estates corresponds to the law (diagonal element of Table 4) introducing the respective estate and the system of ranks (titles) ranking its representatives. Further, the table provides the structure of relations between the titular estates—their mutual service.

The rows of the table represent an organized list of an estate's composition. Thus, the estate of state civil servants must consist of state civil servants facilitating military service; state civil servants facili-

---

and Cossacks. The list is probably incomplete, and the number of uniformed sub-estates may be even greater.

tating law enforcement service; state civil servants facilitating municipal service; state civil servants facilitating law-making; state civil servants facilitating Cossack service; and state civil servants facilitating administration of law (judging).

Considering that the estate of state civil servants consists of the sub-estates of "federal state civil servants" and "regional state civil servants", as well as diplomats institutionalized by bylaws, the forms of state civil service are quite numerous. Thus, there must be state civil servants facilitating military service (they are, in turn, classified into those facilitating internal and external security, guards service, protection from emergency situations, etc.). There must be also state civil servants facilitating law enforcement in all its manifestations—from protecting law and order to executing punishment.

Therefore, only in relation to titular estates, federal state civil servants are split into several dozens of groups facilitating all other titular activities. The total potential number of groups involved in mutual service (facilitation) of titular estates is equal to the square number of sub-estates, i.e., amounts to several hundred. This absolutely does not mean that such an internal service framework is already in place. Rather, this is the space of logical possibilities arising from the relations between titular estates. Probably, it can be used to study empirically our inter-estate relations in order to identify the logical patterns already existing, i.e., people engaged in respective services and service facilitation.

State records of titular estate members are kept in the form of so-called registers of state civil, military, and law enforcement services, which are classified under law. Therefore, it is problematic to make a quantitative assessment of titular estates. According to Goskomstat (Federal State Statistics Service), the number of those engaged in state and municipal management (state civil and municipal employees) exceeds eight hundred thousand persons; the state military establishment employs about five million people (including military judges and prosecutors); Cossacks are about seven million strong,[106] civil

---

106 According to law, only those Cossacks are titular, who facilitate state civil, law enforcement, and military service. Therefore, the Cossack estate is classified into

judges and prosecutors total about one hundred and twenty thousand people.[107] The number of deputies on the federal level is about one thousand people. We were unable to obtain information as to the total number of deputies of regional and municipal legislative assemblies.

---

those who serve and those, who do not. The latter part is not regarded as a titular estate.
107   http://www.gks.ru/free_doc/2007/gosobr/t1.htm

Table 4 Relations between titular estates

Social functions Estates	State civil service	Military service	Administration of law	Law enforcement	Municipal service	Law-making	Cossack service
State civil servants	**State civil servant class rankings. Law on state civil service**	State civil servants facilitating military service	State civil servants facilitating administration of law	State civil servants facilitating law enforcement	State civil servants facilitating municipal service	State civil servants facilitating law-making	State civil servants facilitating Cossack service
Military personnel	Military personnel facilitating state civil service	**Military ranks. Law on military service**	Military personnel facilitating administration of law	Military personnel facilitating law enforcement	Military personnel facilitating municipal service	Military personnel facilitating law-making	Military personnel facilitating Cossack service
Judges	Judges facilitating state civil service	Judges facilitating military service	**Law on the status of judges**	Judges facilitating law enforcement	Judges facilitating municipal service	Judges facilitating law-making	Judges facilitating Cossack service

Socio-Economic Foundations of the Russian Post-Soviet Regime

Law enforcers	Law enforcers facilitating state civil service	Law enforcers facilitating military service	Law enforcers facilitating administration of law	**Special ranks. Law on the law enforcement service**	Law enforcers facilitating municipal service	Law enforcers facilitating law-making	Law enforcers facilitating Cossack service
Municipal employees	Municipal employees facilitating state civil service	Municipal employees facilitating military service	Municipal employees facilitating administration of law	Municipal employees facilitating law enforcement	**Municipal employee class rankings. Law on municipal service**	Municipal employees facilitating law-making	Municipal employees facilitating Cossack service
Deputies	Deputies facilitating state civil service	Deputies facilitating military service	Deputies facilitating administration of law	Deputies facilitating law enforcement	Deputies facilitating municipal service	**Deputy types. Law on the status of deputies**	Deputies facilitating Cossack service
Cossacks	Cossacks facilitating state civil service	Cossacks facilitating military service	Cossacks facilitating administration of law	Cossacks facilitating law enforcement	Cossacks facilitating municipal service	Cossacks facilitating law-making	**Special Cossack ranks. Law on Cossacks**

The hierarchy of titular estates and corporate relations

The columns of matrix table 4 can be regarded as specific corporations, i.e., a pool of representatives of different titular estates facilitating individual titular activities. Such facilitation mainly consists in using public funds allocated for this activity. The federal budget primarily presumes financing activities—service and services (state civil, military, and law enforcement services in their numerous variations) rather than the estates themselves. Representatives of all the estates facilitating a specific activity utilize ("carve up") the resources that the federal budget allocates for this activity.

Based on the table, we can distinguish the following (titular) corporations in contemporary Russia:

1. On facilitating—utilizing the resources allocated for the state civil service
2. On facilitating—utilizing the resources allocated for the military service
3. On facilitating—utilizing the resources allocated for the law enforcement service
4. On facilitating—utilizing the resources allocated for the administration of law
5. On facilitating—utilizing the resources allocated for the municipal service
6. On facilitating—utilizing the resources allocated for the law-making activity
7. On facilitating—utilizing the resources allocated for the Cossack service.

State civil service financing absolutely does not mean that all budget funds allocated for this titular service are used to pay civil servants. Rather, under these budget items, state civil servants (following the logic of Table 4) receive only salaries and allowances for title, rank, and special conditions of service. Budget items intended to provide resources for the state civil service are used primarily to finance members of other titular estates facilitating the state civil service.

Corporations on utilizing funds allocated for other titular activities—law enforcement, judging, law-making, military, and Cossack—are designed similarly.

The amount of resources allocated for the services is limited and subject to distribution among all members of the estates facilitating these services. This means that the distribution of such resources triggers administrative competition among members of the estates facilitating such activity.

Table 4 logically distinguishes two types of competitive relations within the estate framework. The first one is competition between representatives of all estates for resources allocated for individual titular services, i.e., distribution of resources by column of Table 4. This is competition for the allocation of funds under federal budget items, which takes the form of drafting, discussing, adopting, and adjusting the federal budget. Considering that the total amount of budget resources is limited and the proportion to which each service is entitled can vary, representatives of all estates engage in a relatively public bargaining to determine the share of every service in the federal budget. These shares are annually stipulated in the law *On the Federal Budget* passed by the Federal Assembly and signed by the President of the Russian Federation.

The second type of competition involves distributing the amount of resources allocated for a specific titular activity among all members of the corporation facilitating this activity. This means determining the share an estate receives for facilitating the titular service of another estate. The bargaining for facilitating services is as tough as the one for determining the share of resources due to an individual titular service; however, as a matter of principle, it is not public, as opposed to the bargaining for resource allocation under items of the federal budget.

Thus, we can say that bargaining for the share of resources due to an individual titular activity (Table 4 columns) determines public priorities. Judging by the share of allocated resources, state civil service, for example, turns out to be more significant than military service. Corporate bargaining for the share of resources due to members of estates facilitating the specified activity determines the status of the estates and shapes their current resource hierarchy. This hierarchy, for example, demonstrates that the share of resources due to the military (the total of the respective Table 4 row) for facilitating all other services is substantially higher than that due to state civil servants for facilitating the same services.

The resulting distribution of resources by estates may not match (and generally does not match) public priorities stipulated by the federal budget, since the share of resources utilized by a specific estate (i.e., the amount of resources received by estate members for facilitating other titular activities—row total) is significantly higher or lower than the share of resources allocated for the estate's titular service (column total). Thus, according to various estimates, total resources utilized by the military are materially higher than the amount of resources allocated for military service by the Federal Budget.[108] Therefore, the distribution of resources by type of service (Table 4 columns) in the federal budget is nominal; the actual amount of resources than an estate eventually receives is determined by what members of one estate receive for facilitating other services.

The sequence in which the estates are presented in Table 4 is largely arbitrary, since law does not stipulate it. Nevertheless, intuition indicates that the military are senior (the rank of their estate is higher) to the law enforcers, whereas the latter are senior with regard to municipal employees or Cossacks, for example. Moreover, within the military service, the status of FSB and SVR personnel is higher than that of Russian army servicemen. Uncertain mutual rankings of sub-estates comparable by the public significance of their service trigger, in particular, a struggle to raise the status, mutual "attacks", and attempts to redistribute the allocated resources. Thus, chekists fall upon the cops, the cops on the prosecutors, the prosecutors on the military, the military on the chekists, and the chekists on the judge corps accusing each other, inter alia, of corruption and incompetency. All together, they "attack" the state civil servants for not providing resource

---

[108] To determine the real estate hierarchy, it is necessary to compare the proportion of resources allocated by the budget with that received for facilitating other titular activities. In principle, this can be done using current federal budget implementation statistics.

flows from the federal budget sufficient for serving and facilitating services. Such "attacks" result in the emergence of situational estate hierarchies, which differ from region to region.

Publicly funded pay for utilizing resources allocated for a certain titular activity is not the only source of resources for members of titular estates. Besides salaries, they are entitled to monetary and in-kind allowances; however, a much more important source of resources is estate rent. In everyday life, members of high-ranking estates collect estate rent from members of low-ranking estates in the form of bribes, kickbacks, offerings, gifts and, equally significantly, in the form of opportunities to avoid additional exactions from members of other titular estates. Losing these additional sources is an extremely sensitive issue for members of titular estates, and acquiring such opportunities automatically raises an estate's status. It is one of the reasons why service estates compete for the right to perform operational-investigative activities, since they, in particular, give the opportunity to collect estate rent.

Inter-estate relations manifest themselves in a non-formalized procedure of determining whose "protection" ("krysha") is superior (it is well known that a prosecutor's "protection" means more than a cop's) and in collecting estate rent. Representatives of titular estates are much less exposed to "traffic police rent" than members of non-titular estates due to the special license-plate numbers of their cars, official IDs, and uniforms. The estates' visible insignia, such as shoulder boards, ribbon bars, badges, license-plate series and colors and many other indicators demonstrate the status of their holders to representatives of other estates and provide a reason to refuse to pay estate rent. In case of state civil servants, official IDs, expensive suits and watches (as a substitute for uniforms), as well as car models and government license-plate numbers play the same protecting role.

Law enforcers, the military, state civil servants, judges, deputies, and Cossacks—all collect estate rent. They do it less publicly than the traffic police but in no lesser scope.

One can say that the the total amount of utilized resources determine the actual importance of an estate. Such resources consist of the following:

- Resources allocated for the titular activity
- Resources received as a result of corporate distribution for the purpose of facilitating other services, and
- Estate rent.

Estate rent arises where the ranking of the estates, their order of precedence, is not clearly defined. The estate hierarchy is then dynamically determined in the process of collecting estate rent. Enshrining a definite estate hierarchy would inevitably result in stagnation of the entire system of inter-estate relations and its closing in on itself, therefore, it as at least unwise to establish the order of precedence once and for all.

Champions of market and democracy often claim that estate rent is corruption. This interpretation appears to be completely inadequate, since corruption is a market phenomenon specific for a class society, where the society is separated from the state, whereas estate rent integrates the estates into an estate-based socio-state system and is functionally indispensable. Such rent is inevitable in an estate-based society, moreover, in such a society, which is now being shaped in Russia.

The problem with estate rent is not that it exists, but that it is illegitimate. Thus, "isolated facts of corruption" are acknowledged rather than the generally known and widespread systemic manifestation of inter-estate relations. The fight against corruption in the form of revealing, exposing and prosecuting rogue cops and other rogues cannot be effective, because it applies the rule of law to extralegal conduct. The estates where the "rogues" had been either found for political reasons or by chance, perceive "the fight against corruption" as inter-estate struggle for resources, in the course of which competing estates had used non-conventional "harmful" methods. To put it mildly, "the fight against corruption" in its present form does not facilitate effective relations between the estates.

The only method that proved effective in fighting against estate rent is mass repression or its contemporary equivalent, which means eliminating as a class the estate that was overzealous in collecting estate rent. That was the case with the tax police, whose resource of collecting rent from entrepreneurs was replaced by the resource of collecting rent from drug trafficking, with themselves renamed into drug controllers.

In estate-based societies with a certain understanding of their nature (like the pre-reform Imperial Russia), non-repressive regulation of the procedures for collecting estate rent was implemented by the institution of estate morality, where violating the code of conduct of a nobleman could result in ostracism. In contemporary Russia, there is still no awareness of its estate structure and, consequently, there are no moves to establish internal regulators of intra- and inter-estate relations. Estate morality can emerge only subject to public recognition of the estate-based nature of our social order and institutionalization of intra-estate relations—various estate organizations, assemblies, and courts.

The service of titular estates

The service of titular estates consists, primarily, in neutralizing various internal and external threats identified by numerous national security concepts. In times of peace, the service of titular estates consists in revealing threats and preparing to neutralize them and in times of war or emergency—in fighting internal and external enemies.

Another aspect of service is alienating resources from non-titular estates in the form of taxes and levies and controlling the performance of various duties.[109] Such activity is also justified by the need to prepare for neutralizing threats, since this requires stockpiling sufficient resources. This activity consists in alienating all resources from other estates in excess of the amounts that an individual estate is entitled to according to social justice criteria.

Resources are alienated under a respective plan drafted for every serviceman. The alienated resources are consolidated in the budget and in stocks, material or financial. The alienated resources must be

---

[109] Duties include obligations imposed by various superior authorities on the lower-level ones and on businesses to promote sports and build sports facilities, invest resources in the development of education, science, culture, etc., as well as the implications of the "social responsibility of business" for entrepreneurs.

preserved and then distributed as required. Therefore, storage and distribution of resources (consolidated in the budget and inventory—the State Reserves) among all estates is a component of service. The functions of servicemen include observing principles of social justice when alienating and distributing resources, controlling their storage, utilization, and write-off.

Systematically checking and auditing the expenditure of resources from budgets of all levels is an essential component of serving. Federal and regional state civil servants, deputies and controlling departments of the Federal Assembly, municipal employees, law enforcers, and the military, carry out such activity. Should they reveal infringements, they issue orders or initiate proceedings against violators of the resource management procedure. Law enforcers then investigate such cases and present their findings to the judges. The judges qualify violations of the resource management procedure as breach of law and impose punishment pursuant to the Criminal Code. Since the resource management procedure is codified,[110] but not systematized, the judges can find a pretext to impose criminal sanctions on any activity, especially if this serves the interest of functionaries—raiders.

If the controllers act in strict conformity with law, virtually any producing (market-oriented) activity may be interpreted as a violation of the resource management procedure, because it results in additional (not accounted for by the state) resources that the market actor can distribute improperly, i.e., not in line with estate-based social justice principles. In such cases, the topic of socially irresponsible conduct of certain business people and the social responsibility of business in general is raised.

Because of the struggle against violations of social (estate) justice, the inspecting servicemen, whether they want it or not, literally burn out any market manifestations. However, generally, the inspected simply pay off the servicemen by paying the estate rent in one or another form and securing themselves the opportunity to continue operating in the market "under protection". Accepting "protection" most often means that an entrepreneur who used to work in the mar-

---

[110] In the Land, Water, Forestry and other Codes.

ket turns into a merchant supporting a certain budget. Operating "under protection" is often the only way to save the business. For the domestic business, searching for reliable estate "protection" has become an essential element of its market strategy. It is quite likely that consequently business will no longer be a market activity and entrepreneurs will turn into a merchant estate providing services to various budgets and public funds—similar in a sense to the imperial merchant estate. Ultimately, the guild-based imperial commerce may become a model for modern practitioners of estate stratification.

According to the head of a private agribusiness, the following logic is typical of inspectors. A fisheries inspector of the federal environmental service shows up at an agricultural enterprise, which has no trace of fish farming, and demands that the enterprise pay a fine for violating environmental standards. He motivates it as follows, "There is manure at your farms, which you have to remove. It is inevitable that during removal some of it will spill onto the ground. Through the ground, it will seep into the water reservoirs. So pay the fine, if you want to avoid trouble". And people pay, because otherwise it can get worse, sometimes really bad, up to criminal prosecution.

Service performance is judged by "slashes" and "ticks", i.e., by reported facts of preventing, disclosing or investigating violations in the procedure of collecting, storing, distributing, utilizing, and writing off resources. Every state service has a certain service plan. Failure to meet target indicators means inefficient service and is punishable by official reprimands, "incompetency" charges, and lowering in rank or position. Fulfilling the plan "on ticks" is equivalent to high performance, for which servicemen receive bonuses calculated in numbers of monthly salaries, departmental or government awards, and promotions.

Service is multi-level. At the federal level, over 40 state agencies are involved in state civil, military and law enforcement services with their functions including "accounting and control". This is besides different forms of parliamentary control. All these services are represented at the district and regional levels by respective inspections and controlling bodies. The number of such entities at these levels of the administrative-territorial structure of the estate-based state increases (as compared to the federal level), since one federal authority can have several organizations representing some services (controllers).

District, federal, and regional services are represented at the municipal level. Since accounting and control are universal, the federal services are continuously checking both the regional and municipal services, and the regional ones are controlling their employees at the municipal level, often based on the results of already performed inspections. In general, a market actor of the municipal level has to deal with anywhere from 80 to 100 inspecting and controlling bodies.

It is by accounting and control that the numerous servicemen facilitate other activities. To prove the effectiveness of such facilitation, it is vital for every service estate to demonstrate the relevance of their service and their own significance to the other estates. Therefore, the cops try to convince the other estates that criminality is on the rise; security officers—that foreign intelligence services and terrorists are becoming more active; environmental inspectors warn of pollution; and sanitary inspectors tell about horrible epidemics threatening the country if the share of resources allocated to them for facilitating other services is not increased.

Indeed, the efforts of various servicemen trigger social epidemics throughout the country and a huge number of criminals, threats, and "enemies of the people" (human and inhuman) appears. These include criminals and rapists, terrorists and grant receivers—agents of influence, migrants and exceptionally dangerous viruses that can be neutralized only if additional resources are allocated to the respective services, thus, obviously, raising the status of the estates allowed to utilize them.

Non-titular estates

Besides titular estates, there are other, non-titular, estates, where estate distinctions are determined indirectly—not through service, but by indirect laws or Soviet tradition. Non-titular estates do not serve. Rather, they support by providing services. They are established according to their social (public) function, which is not always clearly defined. Some non-titular estates, such as merchants and persons engaged in liberal professions (hereinafter, independent professionals), appeared only in post-Soviet times, whereas others—the clergy, pensioners, public sector workers, employees, and prisoners—were inherited from the Soviet era and reproduce the Soviet estate philosophy. According to the state, wage labor (employment), support of public constitutional obligations (development of education, healthcare, culture, and science), expression of interests of other estates and their informing, and commercial activity are not forms of service. Rather, they are certain support activities. Such activities are partly governed by law and financed from the federal budget, however, they do not imply providing special privileges, insignia, uniforms, etc. to employees, independent professionals (cultural figures and scientists, journalists, writers, artists, athletes, clergy), public sector workers (supporting social obligations of the state) or pensioners.

Nevertheless, pensioners, public sector workers, and employees have certain legislatively stipulated duties to the state and privileges in line with their status. The reaction of pensioners and public sector workers to the recent attempt of "monetizing social benefits", which was a way of stripping members of these estates of Soviet-era membership attributes, demonstrated the social significance of such privileges. One can say that the reaction to monetization of social benefits was a manifestation of the conflict between contemporary service estates and the surviving relics of the Soviet estate structure.

The estate nature of heterogeneous groups, which I united into the non-institutionalized estate of independent professionals (privately practicing doctors and healers, lawyers, artists and private detectives, political strategists, journalists, clergymen, etc.), is emphasized by the fact that they receive fees rather than wages, salaries or pensions for the services they provide to other estates. The social functions of this estate consist primarily in expressing publicly the interests and needs of the other estates, which those cannot explicate and satisfy themselves, and in satisfying such needs and interests.

The borders between non-titular estates are not always clear. Some groups can be attributed to several non-titular estates, for example, working pensioners or nominally employed independent professionals. Scientists actively engaged in research can be classified as independent professionals. However, they can also be public sector workers, if they only participate in utilizing public funds allocated for research and development.

There are numerous marginal groups, whose position allows classifying them as independent professionals, such as prostitutes, for example, who form a specific stratum with respective estate features and a pronounced internal hierarchy—from elite prostitutes, providing contractual services to high-ranking members of titular estates, to "street" and "road" girls providing services to employees, migrants, and prisoners.

The uncertain status of non-titular estate members triggers intra- and inter-estate conflicts, for example, between scientists representing the estate of "independent professionals", whose aim is to generate new knowledge, and scientists—public sector workers, whose principal task is to utilize budget funds allocated for research. Strictly speaking, scientists from among independent professionals should receive resources under scientific grants issued by national science foundations, whereas scientists from among public sector workers—from respective items of the federal budget. However, in practice, the resources of national science foundations have become an item of budget financing, this causing the discontent of independent professionals—"real scientists". The estate of scientists vividly demonstrates the ambiguous estate status of independent professionals also because the scientists consider themselves to be a titular estate serving Science,—similar to the clergy that serve God. The state, however, regards scientific work as a form of support and does not provide any special estate benefits to scientists other than members of the national science academies.

The situation with clergy as members of the estate of independent professionals is quite peculiar. In Imperial Russia, the clergy were a titular estate. In a country, where Orthodoxy was a state religion, the relation of clergy with the state was defined as serving God. In modern Russia, religion is separated from the state according to the Constitution, therefore, religious needs (serving God) may not be financed from the federal budget and the clergy may not form a titular estate in the literal sense of the word, since they provide support rather than serve. Currently, the clergy form a special sub-estate within the estate of independent professionals. This is emphasized by specific estate languages of communication, uniforms, insignia, and claims to a special place in the state structure. The clergy provide support to the military, law enforcement, and state civil services without becoming a separate titular estate in spite of striving for it. Their activity is partially financed by fees paid from the budgets of state titular services. An example is the Russian army, where Orthodox priests formally (under the existing military hierarchies and regulations) hold church services in military units and garrisons.

The clergy, artists, scientists, journalists, prostitutes, and other representatives of the estate of independent professionals communicate in their specific languages; they have a special manner of dressing, which allows identifying them—distinguishing them from members of other estates and capturing the distinctions within their own estate.

Public sector workers, that is, people engaged in fulfilling social obligations of the state in healthcare, education, culture, and science, are much less inclined to bear outward signs of their estate affiliation than independent professionals. Distinctive features, common in the past, such as "spectacles and a hat", have largely lost their diagnostic force. By their conduct, public sector workers are currently almost indistinguishable from employees and pensioners, who have no apparent tradition of demonstrating their estate affiliation. Their way of life is what distinguishes them from other estates. Thus, public sector workers, employees, and pensioners use public transport rather than private cars; they buy food in low-cost retail chains rather than expensive supermarkets and food boutiques; and they purchase clothes at clothing markets. Public sector workers are ranked according to hierarchies of honorary titles and other tables of rank specific only for them (honored and people's workers of culture, education, and science; academicians and corresponding members; "outstanding" and just "prominent" figures of science and culture; candidates and doctors of science; medical doctors of the highest, first, and second categories, and so forth). Public sector workers receive salaries, and the Labor Code governs their work.

Wage laborers (employees) are paid according to their "labor input" based on performance standards and productivity criteria, and taking into account their skills and length of service. The Labor Code defines the employees' estate status, and numerous wage rate scales and skill levels determine their ranking within the estate. This estate is quite ideology-driven largely due to the inertia of the Soviet estate order, where "the working people" were the positive "proletarian" pole as opposed to the "non-workers", who were associated with exploiters.

According to statistics, pensioners constitute a substantial part of Russia's population. Pensioners receive pensions; their estate status is determined by numerous pension laws and enormous benefits and privileges partly inherited from Soviet times, and partly established already in the post-perestroika era. This estate is quite heterogeneous; it includes pensioners due to age, hazardous labor conditions, or disability, retired military civil servants, and law enforcers—differing by pension levels and by their rights and privileges.

The Soviet Union had no merchant estate. Its imperial prototype were the merchants, and in Soviet times—"tolkachi" ["fixers" or "pushers"]—supply agents who traveled across the country searching for scarce supplies. To an extent, the federal law on public procurement defines the social function of merchants. The law stipulates that all services be provided to state bodies and agencies only under public contracts. This law triggered the emergence of an estate, whose members, having passed various inspections, are participating in auctions and tenders for the procurement of everything necessary for state service. In contrast to entrepreneurs, who are orthogonal to the estate structure, merchants are engaged in a specific administrative business with its bribes, "kickbacks" and "carve-ups" of budgetary resources allocated for facilitating services. Merchants operate in the administrative market, as opposed to entrepreneurs, who operate in the ordinary market. They are involved in all types of bargaining—in determining the share of resources for a specific service, in corporate relations on "carving up" resources, and in collecting estate rent. There is still no formal hierarchy within the merchant estate and, as I already mentioned, it is quite likely that such a hierarchy will eventually follow the imperial model, when merchants were divided into guilds. The division of merchants by membership in the Russian Union of Industrialists and Entrepreneurs (the first guild), "Delovaya Rossiya" (the second guild) and "Opora" (the third guild) can serve as a prototype of a guild-based organization. The fact that the state introduced Entrepreneur's Day as a public holiday may be a step forward in formalizing the estate structure of commerce.

Persons convicted of offenses, on remand, or otherwise limited in rights such as mentally ill people represent a special estate category. Their status, like that of the titular estates, is determined by law, but in a negative way, through deprivation or restriction of rights and the imposition of additional duties according to the gravity of the offense. Membership in this estate is forced. It is the cumulative result of the activity of titular estates, in particular, their service on controlling resource flows. To a certain extent, conscripts serving in the state's military organization (drafted into the army) have to be included in the category of persons with limited rights.

Members of different estates may lose their status and join the estate of persons with limited rights if servicemen decide that they are violating the procedure of utilizing resources. However, members of different estates have different chances of being convicted. Members of non-titular estates are more likely to become prisoners than those of the titular ones, because the latter are either immune from prosecution, or the coordinated efforts of their colleagues neutralize charges against them. Such estate frankpledge and specific morality have found no public explication yet.

The estate identification of convicted prisoners, individuals with a criminal record, and others limited in rights is quite clear. When imprisoned, they have obvious distinctive features, such as clothing. In the course of estate socialization in prisons and colonies, they acquire other distinctions, such as a specific dialect, tattoos, and gait. Out of prison, they demonstrate the acquired skills and dress in a specific manner. Prisoners and other persons with limited rights receive rations.

People not integrated into the estate framework—migrants, for example,—are also negatively determined through deprivation of civil rights. Due to the specific Russian attitude, foreign migrants form a separate estate. Rather, members of Russian titular and non-titular estates treat foreign migrants in such a way that these people—with their uncertain estate status and specific appearance—are virtually automatically classified as migrants without estate affiliation and, therefore, subject to estate socialization. This sometimes takes forms similar to prison camp initialization, humiliation, and affiliation with the lowest possible stratum in the estate framework. The Federal Migration Service was established precisely to protect persons not affiliated with any estate and facilitate their lawful socialization-estatization.

Table 5 demonstrates the composition of non-titular estates.

The composition of the "independent professionals" (IPs) estate is listed as follows: "IPs supporting state social obligations", "IPs supporting employment", "IPs supporting social protection", "IPs supporting commerce", "IPs supporting execution of punishment", and "IPs supporting state estatization".

The relations between non-titular estates are not as clear as in the case of titular estates, where mutual service—facilitation—is specified by the state. Here, we can speak only about support. It is quite possible that some non-titular estates exist if not virtually, then only in those periods when the state starts providing resources for the respective activity. Thus, the estate of public sector workers appears when the state is concerned with fulfilling constitutional obligations in education, healthcare, science, and culture.

When the state provides no resources for science, education, healthcare, and culture, the estate of public sector workers breaks up into those who can more or less successfully earn a living in the free market and those who are incapable of doing it and demand that the state resume providing resources for their existence. As soon as there are resources to be distributed, the procedure for "carving them up" is launched, and the activity on utilizing budget resources emerges from nowhere. The more resources the state allocates for various good deeds like the development of science, education, culture and healthcare, the more consolidated are the ranks of relevant public sector workers and the fewer are the people who are willing to risk for the sake of deriving profit in the market for educational services, medical treatment, new knowledge, and production of cultural values.

Table 5 Relations between non-titular estates

Estate activity	Expression of estate interests	Supporting social obligations of the state	Employment	Social protection	Commerce	Execution of punishment	Estatization
Independent professionals	**No hierarchy. No law**	Independent professionals supporting fulfillment of social obligations	Independent professionals supporting employees	Independent professionals supporting social protection	Independent professionals supporting commerce	Independent professionals supporting execution of punishment	Independent professionals supporting estatization
Public sector workers	Public sector workers supporting expression of estate interests	**Hierarchy of honorary titles: honored, people's. No law**	Public sector workers supporting employment	Public sector workers supporting social protection	Public sector workers supporting commerce	Public sector workers supporting execution of punishment	Public sector workers supporting estatization
Employees	Employees supporting expression of estate interests	Employees supporting fulfillment of social obligations	**No hierarchy. Labor legislation**	Employees supporting social protection	Employees supporting commerce	Employees supporting execution of punishment	Employees supporting estatization

	Merchants supporting expression of estate interests	Merchants supporting fulfillment of social obligations	Merchants supporting employment	**Laws on commerce and entrepreneurship. No hierarchy.**	Merchants supporting social protection	Merchants supporting execution of punishment	Merchants supporting estatization
Merchants							
Pensioners	Retired independent professionals	Retired public sector workers	Retired employees	Retired merchants	**Pension hierarchy (personal pensioners). Pension legislation**	Retired penitentiary personnel	Non-estate pensioners
Persons convicted and limited in rights	Convicted independent professionals	Convicted former employees	Convicted employees	Convicted pensioners	Convicted merchants	Classification according to the Criminal Code and the Criminal Procedure Code	Non-estate convicts
Non-estate persons	Non-estate persons supporting expression of estate interests	Non-estate persons supporting fulfillment of social obligations	Non-estate persons supporting employment	Non-estate persons supporting social protection	Non-estate persons supporting execution of punishment	Non-estate persons supporting convicts and those limited in rights	**Migration laws. Classified into compatriots and others**

The situation with pensioners and employees is more or less similar to the one mentioned above. If the state pays no pensions, the estate of pensioners breaks up into those who sink into social coma and focus on subsistence farming or crafts, those who enter local markets trading in whatever they can find, and those who demand that the state pay the pensions "due" to them.

When guaranteed rights to work are no longer observed and the labor distribution system collapses, the employee estate splits up into those who successfully enter the labor market and those who without any inflow of resources continue simulating participation in their distribution and demand that this inflow be resumed. They simply "go to work". Where there is a labor market free from state intervention and regulation, there is no employee estate.

Where the state takes no measures to control migration, there are no persons without estate affiliation that require special official control. Where the state does not control the very existence of those who arrive from the CIS and other countries, the newcomers somehow merge with the core population and eventually either socialize or form local communities of the china-town type. When the state eases its repressive policy, the number of prisoners and people with limited rights decreases.

The federal budget and extra-budgetary funds allocate resources for the support of respective activities: coordination of estate interests and information (mass media, propaganda and agitation, culture, and arts); public procurement; fulfillment of the state's social obligations; payment of pensions and social benefits; payment of wages and salaries; estatization of migrants and persons without estate affiliaition; and maintenance of penitentiary institutions. Budget resources allocated, for example, for the state's constitutional obligations in education, culture, and science (Table 5 column) are "carved up" by representatives of all estates supporting these activities. Thus, resources allocated for science and science support are distributed in the course of administrative bargaining among the following estates: independent professionals—scientists; merchants dealing with science budget allocations; retired scientists; public sector workers—scientists; and support personnel, i.e., people employed in science and science support.

As a result, just as in the case of titular estates and their services, the total amount of resources received by the representatives of a given estate does not correspond to the share of resources allocated from state budgets and funds for the respective activities. It can be bigger or smaller, but the actual distribution of resources among the estates (and, therefore, their significance, rank) is determined in the course of administrative bargaining between all non-titular estates.

The institution of estate rent, i.e., mutual rankings and "collections" from lower-ranking estates, functions here as well, just as in relations between the titular estates. This includes fee-based medicine, when a salaried doctor charges additional fees for his official duties; and the teachers' demands to pay for standard educational procedures; and the parents' "financial assistance" to the school where their children study. The estate rent collected by non-titular estates also includes contributions from individual grants to the research organizations, the institution of gifts to tutors and doctors (flowers, wine, chocolate, or milk-and-eggs that a poor pensioner feels obliged to offer the medical assistant at a rural health post in gratitude for the consultation as to her state of health).[111]

The actual amount of resources received by each estate group comprises the share of budget financing allocated for its activity, the share obtained in the course of administrative bargaining under corporate relations on "carving up" resources allocated for this activity, and the share of estate rent arising from relations with the supported estate groups.

In general, we can say that interaction between non-titular estates appears only subject to budget financing of respective activities. If the budget allocates no resources for public procurement, development of science, education, culture and arts, payment of pensions and salaries to employees, no corporations on "carving up" these resources emerge.

---

[111] Not for treatment, since paramedics at the rural health posts get virtually no resources for treatment - medical drugs, equipment or professional skills.

When there are no resources to be distributed, the system of relations between the estates falls apart and those estate members who had retained their estate identification go public demanding that financing of respective activities be resumed. They want to restore inter-estate relations and social justice in resource distribution.

The remaining estate members learn to deal with educational, healthcare and other matters in the markets for respective services. This is unacceptable for the people with estate identification and only urges them to address claims both to the state for not fulfilling its social and other commitments and to their former colleagues for becoming bloodsuckers, capitalists, and oligarchs.

Only a rough assessment of the total number of people belonging to individual non-titular estates is possible. Thus, the Pension Fund of the Russian Federation gives the figure of about forty million pensioners. The public sector employs about fifteen million people. The number of employees is difficult to assess, since the method of recording them is not clear. According to unofficial data of the Russian Federal Migration Service, the number of migrants (persons without estate affiliation) is anywhere between ten and fifteen million; convicted prisoners, remand prisoners, and other persons with limited rights exceed a million people (without drafted conscripts serving in military organizations). The total number of merchants is difficult to assess. The same is true for independent professionals. It is quite problematic to keep a social record of people affiliated with non-titular estates. There is no state register for members of non-titular estates—they are not subject to state registration.

Relations between titular and non-titular estates

The space of estate stratification is continuous and integral—it bears no emptiness and no external, primarily market, inclusions. The fact that law stipulates some estates, and the status of the others is not so strictly codified does not hamper inter-estate corporate relations and does not stop from collecting estate rent, if the state allocates respective resources. I attempted to present the general environment of inter-estate relations—titular and non-titular—in Table 6.

Table 6   Relations between titular and non-titular estates

Social functions / Estates	State civil service	Military service	Law enforcement	Municipal service	Law-making	Cossack service	Expression of estate interests	Support of state social obligations	Employment	Social protection	Commerce	Execution of punishment	State socialization - "estatization"
State civil servants	State civil servant class rankings. Law on state civil service	State civil servants facilitating military service	State civil servants facilitating law enforcement	State civil servants facilitating municipal service	State civil servants facilitating law-making	State civil servants facilitating Cossack service	State civil servants facilitating expression of estate interests	State civil servants facilitating fulfilment of social obligations	State civil servants facilitating employment	State civil servants controlling social protection	State civil servants facilitating commerce	State civil servants facilitating execution of punishment	State civil servants facilitating estatization
Military personnel	Military personnel facilitating state civil service	Military ranks. Law on military service	Military personnel facilitating law enforcement	Military personnel facilitating municipal service	Military personnel facilitating law-making	Military personnel facilitating Cossack service	Military personnel facilitating expression of estate interests	Military personnel facilitating fulfilment of social obligations	Military personnel facilitating employment	Military personnel facilitating social protection	Military personnel facilitating commerce	Military personnel facilitating execution of punishment	Military personnel facilitating estatization
Law enforcers	Law enforcers facilitating state civil service	Law enforcers facilitating military service	Special ranks. Law on law enforcement service	Law enforcers facilitating municipal service	Law enforcers facilitating law-making	Law enforcers facilitating Cossack service	Law enforcers facilitating expression of estate interests	Law enforcers facilitating fulfilment of social obligations	Law enforcers facilitating employment	Law enforcers facilitating social protection	Law enforcers facilitating commerce	Law enforcers facilitating execution of punishment	Law enforcers facilitating estatization
Municipal employees	Municipal employees facilitating state civil service	Municipal employees facilitating military service	Municipal employees facilitating law enforcement	Municipal employee class rankings. Law on municipal service	Municipal employees facilitating law-making	Municipal employees facilitating Cossack service	Municipal employees facilitating expression of estate interests	Municipal employees facilitating fulfilment of social obligations	Municipal employees facilitating employment	Municipal employees facilitating social protection	Municipal employees facilitating commerce	Municipal employees facilitating execution of punishment	Municipal employees facilitating estatization
Deputies	Deputies facilitating state civil service	Deputies facilitating military service	Deputies facilitating law enforcement	Deputies representing municipal employees	Deputy types. Law on the status of deputies	Deputies facilitating Cossack service	Deputies facilitating expression of estate interests	Deputies facilitating fulfilment of social obligations	Deputies facilitating employment	Deputies facilitating social protection	Deputies facilitating commerce	Deputies facilitating execution of punishment	Deputies facilitating estatization
Cossacks	Cossacks facilitating state civil service	Cossacks facilitating military service	Cossacks facilitating law enforcement	Cossacks facilitating municipal service	Cossacks facilitating law-making	Special Cossack ranks. Law on Cossacks	Cossacks facilitating expression of estate interests	Cossacks facilitating fulfilment of social obligations	Cossacks facilitating employment	Cossacks facilitating social protection	Cossacks facilitating commerce	Cossacks controlling execution of punishment	Cossacks facilitating estatization

Socio-Economic Foundations of the Russian Post-Soviet Regime

	IPs supporting state civil service	IPs supporting military service	IPs supporting law enforcement	IPs supporting municipal employees	IPs supporting law-making	IPs supporting Cossack service	Honorary titles—honored, people's. No law	IPs supporting fulfillment of social obligations	IPs supporting employment	IPs supporting social protection	IPs supporting commerce	IPs supporting execution of punishment	IPs supporting estatization
Independent professionals (IPs)													
Public sector workers (fulfilling social obligations)	Public sector workers supporting state civil service	Public sector workers in military service	Public sector workers in law enforcement	Public sector workers in the municipal service	Public sector workers supporting law-making	Public sector workers supporting Cossack service	Public sector workers supporting expression of estate interests	Honorary titles—honored, people's. No law	Public sector workers supporting employment	Public sector workers supporting social protection	Public sector workers supporting commerce	Public sector workers supporting execution of punishment	Public sector workers supporting estatization
Employees	Employees supporting state civil service	Employees in military service, including contract soldiers	Employees supporting law enforcement	Employees supporting municipal service	Employees supporting law-making	Employees supporting Cossack service	Employees supporting expression of estate interests	Employees supporting fulfillment of social obligations	No hierarchy. Labor legislation	Employees supporting social protection	Employees supporting commerce	Employees supporting execution of punishment	Employees supporting estatization
Merchants	Merchants supporting state civil service	Merchants supporting military service	Merchants supporting law enforcement	Merchants supporting municipal service	Merchants supporting law-making	Merchants supporting Cossack service	Merchants supporting expression of estate interests	Merchants supporting fulfillment of social obligations	Merchants supporting employment	Laws on commerce and entrepreneurship. No hierarchy.	Merchants supporting social protection	Merchants supporting execution of punishment	Merchants supporting estatization
Pensioners	Pensioners of the state civil service	Pensioners supporting military service	Pensioners of the law enforcement service	Pensioners of the municipal service	Pensioners of the law-making service	Pensioners of the Cossack service	Retired independent professionals	Retired public sector workers	Retired employees	Retired merchants	Pension hierarchy (personal pensioners). Pension legislation	Retired penitentiary personnel	Non-estate pensioners
Persons convicted, imprisoned, with a criminal record, and otherwise limited in rights	State civil servants convicted and limited in rights	Military personnel convicted and limited in rights, including drafted conscripts	Law enforcers convicted and limited in rights	Convicted municipal employees	Convicted law-makers	Convicted Cossacks	Convicted independent professionals	Convicted public sector workers	Convicted employees	Convicted pensioners	Convicted merchants	Classification according to the Criminal Code and the Criminal Procedure Code	Non-estate convicts
Not affiliated with any estate (migrants)	Non-estate persons supporting state civil service	Non-estate persons supporting military service	Non-estate persons supporting law enforcers	Non-estate persons supporting municipal service	Non-estate persons supporting law-making	Non-estate persons supporting Cossack service	Non-estate persons supporting expression of estate interests	Non-estate persons supporting fulfillment of social obligations	Non-estate persons supporting employment	Non-estate persons supporting social protection	Non-estate persons supporting execution of punishment	Non-estate persons supporting convicts and those limited in rights	Migration laws. Classified into compatriots and others

The table is split into quadrants:

- The upper left corresponds to the titular estates Table 4
- The lower right corresponds to the non-titular estates Table 5
- The lower left demonstrates how non-titular estates support titular activities, i.e., how they participate in "carving up" the resources allocated by the state for state service, and
- The upper right demonstrates how service estates control the resources allocated by the state for public procurement, coordination and expression of estate interests, fulfillment of social obligations, social protection, execution of punishment, and other non-titular activities.

Earlier, we have considered the upper-left and lower-right quadrants. Let us now examine the lower-left quadrant.

Like all other services, the state civil service needs creative support. It is for that reason that independent professionals take part in utilizing the resources allocated for the state civil service—support it by working in state-controlled mass media, participate (for a fee) in drafting laws, "raise the status of public services" by playing respective roles in TV serials, and otherwise provide cultural, scientific, and educational support. Political strategists, artists, lawyers, and others supporting state services receive fees from the financial resources allocated to the respective service. Similarly, independent professionals support the military, law enforcement, judicial, law-making, and Cossack services by taking their part of the resource "pie" allocated for the respective titular service.

There is a large group of public sector workers supporting the state civil service: doctors and skilled personnel of specialized treatment and therapeutic institutions; teachers of educational institutions training staff for state civil, military, law enforcement, and other services. Support is covered from the resources allocated for the respective service. The military, law enforcement, law-making, and Cossack services have similar social commitments. The budgets of the state civil, military and law enforcement services contain expense items for departmental health services, education, science, and culture. Doctors, scientists, teachers, and culture workers supporting titular activities are significantly better provided with resources than ordinary public sector workers are.

Employees supporting the state civil service constitute a stratum-estate of people employed in various government establishments and organizations. This includes the service and technical staff of numerous buildings and facilities, catering, transport, domestic and other life-support systems providing services to state civil servants. The military and law enforcement services budget expenses for hiring support and maintenance staff.

Merchants supporting public procurement for the state civil, military and law enforcement services are in an exceptional position as related to other types of merchants. Generally, they pass all kinds of controls, get access to special information, and are in confidential relations with those, whom they support. The procedures for "carving up" the budgets of respective titular services are codified rather clearly, although they are not public.

Pensioners of the state civil service constitute a separate category. They are under the care of special inspectorates of the Pension Fund, in the same way as retired military personnel and law enforcers, whose ultimate pensions are substantially higher than ordinary labor pensions.

Prisoners, individuals with criminal records, and others limited in rights, who prior to the court sentence had the status of state civil servants, military personnel, law enforcers, judges, and deputies, constitute a particular category with a distinctive correction regime. They serve their sentences in special establishments, such as the [Nizhniy] Tagil prison camps. Drafted conscripts can be regarded as persons with limited rights similar to those sentenced by court.

Judging by the scarce information available, persons without estate affiliation engaged in providing services to titular state services are also ranked, in particular, by their ethnic origin (compatriots, migrants from the CIS, and others).

Let us now study the upper right quadrant of Table 6 representing the relation of titular estates to the resources allocated by the state for non-titular activities. This quadrant demonstrates the specific nature of the services, when their principal function is control over resource distribution, storage, utilization, and write-off. State civil servants, just as the military, law enforcers, and deputies, are involved in determining the share of the budget allocated for fulfilling social obligations—science, education, culture, healthcare, pensions, wages and salaries, etc.

In line with their professional duties, they facilitate the fulfillment of these obligations by controlling the use of the allocated resources and capturing violations in their receipt, utilization, storage, and write-off. State civil servants, the military, and law enforcers are required to control the use of resources and apply sanctions to those members of non-titular estates—independent professionals, public sector workers, merchants, pensioners, employees and others,—who violate the resource management procedure. Such sanctions include administrative and criminal procedures, investigations, litigation, and enforcement of court sentences, including execution of punishment in respective institutions.

Ultimately, the army of civil servants—controllers is supposed to ensure the "correct" utilization of resources allocated by the state for non-titular activities and prosecute those, who divert or plunder resources, i.e., reinforce the ranks of prisoners, convicts, and persons with limited rights. However, in fact, their activity results in ousting the market and market relations from the fabric of life and replacing them by utilization of budget resources, administrative bargaining, and collection of estate rent from any forms of independent economic activities—in the event that the member of the inspected estate engages in productive labor besides utilizing budget resources.

Considering the structure of the estate system in general, we can state that the official allocation of budget resources for titular activities does not correspond at all to the real share of resources received by members of the estate engaged in this activity. Thus, pensions paid from the budget of the Pension Fund of the Russian Federation are only one aspect of social protection monitored by various servicemen. We can estimate the actual supply of resources to pensioners by adding up the shares indicated in the *Pensioners* row of Table 6: payments to retired state civil servants, retired military personnel, retired law enforcers, retired judges, retired deputies, retired Cossacks, and others from the budgets of the respective services.

Another example. The share of budget expenses allocated for the coordination of estate interests and their information is minuscule, but the amount of resources received by independent professionals from the budgets of all other services is quite substantial. Every service deems necessary to protect its interests in the public space, which television creates. The high fees of involved independent professionals and the expensive TV time are covered from the budgets of the respective services. Thus, total expenses for the modern equivalent of "propaganda and agitation" are significantly higher than the budget resources allocated for this activity.

Estate stratification with regard to service, facilitation, and support

In this logical structure of relations, a person's estate status is determined by the service he is directly engaged in and the service he facilitates or supports. An individual's position in this system is determined in a two-dimensional grid, where one axis is the affiliation with an estate, and the second axis is participation in utilizing resources allocated for a certain service or support activity. However, the status is more or less formalized only with regard to service. It is defined by state civil servant rankings and military and special ranks. As for facilitation and support, the participants' status is determined dynamically in the course of specific procedures accompanying the distribution of resources for the services.

In such a system, the social status of estate members is determined by the superposition of the respective rows and columns of Table 6. However, this status is more or less clear only in the case of servicemen who are not engaged in research or teaching. In the event that besides their main occupation the servicemen also teach or research something (based on permissive law), their estate status is additionally determined as that of an independent professional supporting one of the state services. The situation can be even more complex for support estates. For example, an individual is a pensioner by age, but he is still a public sector worker engaged in supporting the state civil service, since he is teaching at a higher educational establishment, which trains "specialists" for this service. At the same time, this individual is engaged in publicly financed research, i.e., he is an independent professional supporting the state civil service. In spite of the certain formal estate affiliation, in practice there is always ambiguity and multi-dimensionality mostly because the currently emerging system is a hybrid of Soviet and post-Soviet estate stratification.

Let us consider the aspect of facilitation, when civil servants (for example) are divided into informally ranked groups. Conflicts around the distribution of resources result in the ranking of various military services, when some of them for a specific period become more important—senior (receive relatively more resources), and some—junior. This triggers the hierarchy of the related civil servants—those who facilitate the activity of the "senior" services receive informal status preferences as compared to those who deal with the "junior" services. State civil servants facilitating military service are streamlined according to the military service hierarchy. As a result of bargaining, for example, the Foreign Intelligence Service personnel turns out to be "senior" to the army or internal forces servicemen.

All other facilitating and supporting groups are ranked similarly—depending on the situational, currently relevant significance of the services. For example, political strategists (independent professionals) supporting the state civil service are significantly "more important" than the political strategists supporting, for example, the fulfillment of social obligations in education, science, culture, and healthcare. A Cossack facilitating military service is fundamentally different from a Cossack supporting employees.

Knowledge of such situational hierarchies is not formalized; it is taken for granted and exists in the form of rumors, gossip, speculation, and guesswork, resulting, in particular, from the functionaries' interpretation of internal documents, mailing lists for approval, and schedules of the executives' personal meetings.

However, the internal structure of informal hierarchies is even more complex and concealed to make any objectivation or research possible. To get at least a rough understanding of the complexity of estate hierarchies, it is necessary to take into account that their members are ranked either according to the table of ranks or by other less rigid acts, such as regulations about honorary, scientific, academic titles, awards, etc. Every estate member has a title, degree, or ranking attributed for the length of service, special merits or for other reasons. He occupies a certain position in the power structure, and advancing in the system of ranks and titles is no less important for his personal career than promotion. Especially since regulations generally clearly map ranks and positions. A major general may not be appointed commander of a military district or a service arm of the armed forces, just as a council of the third class may not head a department of the Presidential Administration.

When it comes to facilitation and support, the real status of an individual is determined by the rank, title, and position of the official whose activity he is facilitating or supporting. A political strategist supporting a federal state civil servant has a much higher status than a political strategist supporting regional state civil servants does. A municipal employee facilitating the activity of an army general (whose official summer residence is located within his municipal district) is much more influential than a formally similar municipal employee facilitating the holidaymaking of a colonel is. He is generally believed to be able "to settle matters" in the course of routine facilitation of military service and through contacts and connections with top-ranking officials required for such facilitation.

A full list of the top state service positions determining which service people are entitled to use the Lounges for official delegations in Russia's transport network is provided in the order issued by the Administrative Directorate of the President of the Russian Federation (Appendix 2).[112]

Administrative bargaining as a way of social life

The share of resources allocated for a certain service is proportional to the status of the similarly named estate, i.e. its position with regard to the other estates. There are high-status estates, such as the mili-

---

112 http://www.rg.ru/2010/08/24/aerozal-dok.html

tary, that receive more resources for their service as a result of administrative bargaining and collection of estate rent. And there are low-status estates that receive substantially less resources for their service. The opposite is also true—the more resources an estate manages to secure in the course of administrative bargaining with the other estates, the higher the status of its members. Therefore, in an estate-based society, the estates are continuously fighting each other for resources. This is the substance of social life, which is opposed to the state to the extent that a specific estate feels that it did not get its fair share. There can be no other social life in an estate-based state. The ultimate distribution of resources is always at odds with the estate members' perception of "fair" distribution. Resources are always scarce, and the estate members are never satisfied. Therefore, social life manifests itself in the overall negative attitude toward the mechanisms and results of resource distribution, that is, to the state in general. It appears that dissatisfaction with resource allocation mechanisms in an estate-based system binds the society and the state stronger than a surplus of goods in a market economy and democracy. The need to "secure resources", "procure scarce goods", design strategies for utilizing and writing them off, and form alliances for these purposes generates a very dense structure of personified social relations, which in Soviet times were called "blat" (string-pulling) and "znakomstva" (profitable connections). This system of relations actually is the estate society, which is inseparable from the state and forms with it a rather conflicting unity. Such a system is stable as long as there is a flow of distributable resources and becomes disastrously conflict-prone as soon as the resources are depleted or their amount shrinks. When it turns out that the treasury is empty and there is nothing to divide, routine inter-estate conflicts aggravate and can even result in civil war. Then the unity of the state and the estates can fall apart, just as it happened in Russia in 1917 and 1991. Generalized shortage crises emerge when the system of coordinating estate interests collapses or the underlying resources are depleted.

The system of connections—string-pulling—corruption generated by the fundamentally insurmountable shortage of resources is functionally similar to the "bourgeois society"—a society separated from the state. However, unlike the bourgeois society, which is complementary to the state, it is always opposed to it and at the same time fully integrated in it. We can also say that the state is fully integrated into the estate-based society. In order to allocate resources, it is first necessary to consolidate them.[113] Consolidation implies alienating the resources from their current holders. Alienating resources from enemies and distributing them among numerous Soviet estates was the essence of the syncretic social-political-public life of the USSR. Consolidation of resources is by no means a peaceful procedure since it represents their redistribution—an estate-based society can only divide; it is incapable of multiplying. Any repartition implies coercion against "the enemies" that had usurped control over the resources. Therefore, enemy identification, personification, and objectivation is an essential element of the resource-and-estate-based world order, its "ideology". The enemies are always "appointed", i.e., identified in the course of administrative bargaining between contenders to the resources, because when the enemy has been identified, relevant resources must be allocated to a particular estate to fight this enemy. When the enemy is external, the military and diplomats receive such resources, when it is internal—the law enforcers, and if it is natural—the personnel of the Ministry for Emergency Situations. Enemy identification is the public result of the inter-estate conflict over the distribution of resources.

The mythology of coercive alienation of resources, struggle and victories over the enemies constitutes the "ideological" component of estate social life, explaining shortages by the fact that certain enemies are withholding resources, plundering them, and keeping their rightful

---

113 Most often, resources are consolidated by the state monopolizing access to them. Thus, Peter the Great introduced at a certain point a monopoly on salt, and in the USSR, all resources without exception were public (national/all-estate) property. The Soviet authorities consolidated resources through dekulakization (liquidation of the kulaks as a class-estate) and the prior nationalization of the property of all Imperial estates accompanied by disenfranchisement of some of the estate members. Currently, the state is consolidating energy resources. Moreover, every governor and mayor strives to concentrate all resources at his or her disposal in the regional or local budget in order to distribute them fairly as opposed to what is happening in the market. Any shortage is attributed to enemy plots with subsequent search for these enemies and alienation of their resources to have something to distribute fairly and control the distribution.

owners from dividing them. Alternatively, through environmentally harmful activities, such enemies withdraw the resources from circulation. Due to this, estate mythology focuses on depicting wars with enemies and victories over them. Peaceful life and estate building are only short periods between wars and repartition of resources, and public holidays commemorating victories over the enemies are the core of the estate society's publicity.

Thus, war with the oligarchs, or alienation of resources from those who had appropriated them due to the collapse of the Soviet estates, was the substance of social life at the turn of the twenty-first century. As a result, in the past several years, the processes of denationalization and privatization were aligned with estate resource distribution principles. This means that those estates obtained access to resources, whose service the state deemed to be the most significant— state civil servants, the military, and law enforcers. Some resources, privatized earlier, were re-nationalized, however not in favor of the state in general, but rather in favor of particular high-ranking estates, whose members got the name of "siloviki" ("strongmen"). As a result, the markets shrank, accumulated capitals emigrated or retreated into the shadow, and a shortage of resources (mainly, financial and power, and to a lesser extent material) re-emerged signifying the restoration of inter-estate relations. Gradually, shortages trigger further consolidation of resources—their withdrawal from the market because of "revising privatization" of finances, power, and raw materials using mainly coercive methods. However, establishment of the vertical of power, monopolization of currency circulation, and nationalization of mineral companies create significantly more problems than they solve.

The market is "unfair" to estate values, therefore, the contemporary estate-based state-society establishes social justice and does everything it can to withdraw resources from the market and pump them into the state budget and reserves to be "carved up" by various services according to the established consensus—conflict-prone, but intuitively clear to members of different estates.

I will repeat—estate-based societies differ fundamentally from democratic-market ones, in particular, by the impossibility to draw a clear line between the state and the society. In the ultimately idealized perception, an estate-based society is identical with the state. The social structure of an estate-based society is at the same time the state structure for distributing resources. Bargaining in the administrative market is all about resource distribution among the estates. The subject of the bargaining is the share of resources due to a specific service—state civil service, military service, law enforcement service, for fulfillment of social obligations, etc.

After these shares are determined, administrative bargaining begins for the share due to a specific estate in the total amount of resources allocated for facilitating other services. When the shares are finalized, members of high-ranking estates proceed to collect estate rent from members of low-ranking estates. In the process, the established estate hierarchy is confirmed (or revised). In our state, such bargaining constitutes social life.

In the public sphere (although the very notion of public sphere is nonsense for an estate-based system; it exists only because the estate system has not yet fully ousted the class one), the liberal perception of relations between the state, society, and market currently dominates. According to this perception, the state should be "little"—no more than a regulator of relations between the society and the market. Its apparatus should employ as few people as possible and its functions should be limited to a monopoly on using force. The market (in line with liberal views) is efficient by nature—it uses minimum resources to derive the highest possible profit. Liberals believe that the society should be separated from the state and should live by its—political—laws.

However, the estate-based society-state is fundamentally different. Here, the society is not separate from the state, and the economy consists of collecting, distributing, and utilizing resources. Performance is measured by the amounts of resources raised, utilized, and stockpiled. The more resources the state controls, utilizes, and distributes, the more "efficient" it is. This primarily concerns labor resources, which according to the estate-based state should be fully included in its resource turnover. Without this, it is impossible to provide resources for individual citizens. That is why the Soviet state did not recognize such a category of its citizens as unemployed and applied the most severe sanctions to "parasites", i.e., people who had lost their estate affiliation and were not engaged in "branches of the economy".

The state must attribute all available people to estates and then provide these estates with required resources according to social justice criteria. Therefore, the more people are engaged in the estate-based state, the more socially oriented and just it is. People must serve, facilitate services, and support them. They may do nothing else. In particular, they may not just work for the sake of earning money and raising their living standards; they may not speculate in the market and derive profit from satisfying the needs of other people.

However, the process of distributing resources among the estates is not endless. With time, available resources are depleted and the transition to their other types is usually a disaster, since it implies changing the estate structure due to the emergence of estates specializing in the new resources.

Political groups as integrated estates: government, the people, active population, and the marginalized population

It is customary for the public political practice of the contemporary Russian state to classify the population of the country into the people, government, entrepreneurs, and various marginalized groups. This classification reflects the commonplace and political perception of the social structure.

Advocates of the social contract theory focus on determining the place and role of the people in relations with the government. They regard government as an institution for implementing justice in the distribution of various resources. Advocates of this theory believe that the people consciously surrender some of their rights and freedoms to the state due to their natural desire for a certain order. Essentially, the people are deemed to include those individuals who have entrusted the state to implement the principles of social justice in resource distribution. This approach considers such institutions of government as criminal and administrative law as the embodiment of the people's desire to give up personal activity in achieving justice and to transfer the relevant functions to the state for the purpose of establishing and maintaining uniformity, "order".

The desire to turn life into a routine, a sequence of non-reflective stereotypes, is natural for such people. For the people, government in the broad sense of the term is a generator of various routines—from ways to dress and undress to stereotypes of thinking. This allows them to avoid making any choice in the broadest sense of the term. Such an approach regards the people rather as a tool for legitimizing government. Government establishes new standards, templates, and stereotypes for the people, cutting short any attempts of independence and limiting to the utmost the opportunities for unconventional choice.

Such people are not subjects who actually choose the legal system, but an inactive mass whose attention contenders for power over them are seeking. In this situation, any choice will serve to realize the people's aspirations, their desire to escape from freedom, independent decisions, and the fear of unconventional procedures.

Entrepreneurs and independent professionals (the active population), as well as the marginalized groups are not part of the people by definition; they are not parties to the social contract in the above sense. They do not comply fully with the stereotypes established by the state, and they have to make independent choices to the extent allowed by the government and the people. These groups are internally stratified along the lines set by relations between the government and the people. They have their own elite similar to government and the equivalent of people—the non-elite, or the masses (the mass of entrepreneurs, professionals, and the marginalized), who abide by the standards set by the elite.

The marginalized (persons with criminal records, convicted, limited in rights, migrants, etc.) emerge as a group following the government's actions on "restoring order" and establishing social justice. By applying criminal or other sanctions for violations of distributive justice standards, the government labels individuals and assigns them a relevant status.

According to official declarations, the relations between the above groups are set out as follows:

- The government is called upon to take care of the people, and the people support the government by voting for it at elections.
- The government cares for entrepreneurs by creating conditions for the development of business, and the entrepreneurs pay taxes and, in addition, perform the social functions that the state imposes on them under social responsibility of business.
- Relations between the people and entrepreneurs are seamless; the people welcome the "market economy" and the entrepreneurs act based on the needs of the people.
- The government controls the offenders of social justice by isolating them from the society.

Outside the declarations, "in fact", these relations are often quite different:

- The government cares only about itself, and the people just survive. Mainly older-aged public sector workers, some employees, and pensioners attend elections.
- The government robs the entrepreneurs, and the entrepreneurs by all means try to evade taxes and avoid the duties that the state calls social responsibility of business.
- The people hate entrepreneurs, and the entrepreneurs seek to enrich themselves at the expense of the people.
- The government "prosecutes for no apparent reason", and those who were marginalized as a result hate the government.

The notions of people, government, entrepreneurs, and the marginalized population are not defined in written law and are not aligned with the legislative framework that the state uses to establish the estate-based social structure and to achieve distributive justice.

The social structure of Russia presented above was depicted using concepts introduced by the state in the legal framework determining the existence of social groups-estates, and, minimally, the relations between them. However, the groups formed by the state have never been a subject of socio-structural studies.

In the past ten years, the state has formed social groups of state civil servants, the military, law enforcers, judges, deputies, and municipal employees that serve it. Members of these estates must neutralize various threats and provide protection from them. The assortment of relevant estates depends on the threats that the state identifies for itself. The military are charged with neutralizing external threats, and the law enforcers—internal ones; state civil servants must neutralize threats associated with violations of distributive social justice, and so on.

Members of these estates <u>serve</u> the state and <u>facilitate</u> the service of other estates. For their service and facilitation, they receive pay, allowances, bonuses and various compensations.[114] In addition, they receive administrative rent, or income from their power status.

Besides the service estates, there are also support estates—partly inherited from the USSR, like public sector workers, pensioners, and employees, and social groups of entrepreneurs and independent professionals, new for post-Soviet Russia. The group of entrepreneurs, or individuals receiving income from market activities, is rather heterogeneous and besides registered entrepreneurs includes various internal labor migrants (otkhodniks), and independent professionals.

Members of these estates must support members of the service estates in their difficult task of neutralizing threats.

The formal and official nature of this social structure manifests itself primarily in the fact that citizens are affiliated with estates by the state, that is, externally. In most cases, this is not accompanied by the internal and reflexive self-affiliation of the individuals with the estate into which they had been placed by the state. Therefore, in the case of such groups we can speak only about protoestates rather than full-fledged estates, where the external affiliation with an estate corresponds with the self-identification of its members.

As mentioned above, marginalized individuals—with criminal records, convicted, and limited in rights—constitute a separate social group. Besides, many persons have lost or have not acquired estate identity. Primarily, this concerns migrants and then various homeless and freaks who can also be classified as marginalized individuals.

Support estates have the following types of income: pension (pensioners), salary and status-related rent[115] (public sector workers and employees), market income, gain (entrepreneurs and merchants), fee and grant (independent professionals), allowances, scholarship (dependents).

Marginalized individuals have the following types of income: share, ration, allowance, prison ration, criminal status rent.[116]

---

[114] The idea to match the type and source of income and use it as a stratification criterion belongs to Juri Plusnin.
[115] Rent from title (honored, people's teacher, actor, etc.), class (doctors), and category (employees).
[116] Such as "crime lord" ("avtoritet") or "thief in law" ("vor v zakone").

Thus, the entire population of Russia is officially[117] divided into groups-estates, and every person, regardless of whether he understands it or not, is affiliated with a particular estate or attributed to a specific group of people without estate identity or with a lost identity and, therefore, subject to forced estatization, which is carried out by customized organizations, namely, the Federal Migration Service.

We believe it is reasonable to identify the service estates with the government; some of the support estates (employees, public sector workers, pensioners, and some other groups)—with the people; various entrepreneurs and independent professionals—with the active population, or those on whom the state has imposed "the social responsibility of business"; and persons with criminal records, convicted and otherwise limited in rights—with the marginalized groups.

This procedure maps the social groups-estates (civil servants, public sector workers, pensioners, etc.) enshrined in the laws of the contemporary state, on the one hand, to the social groups, which the

---

117 In contemporary social practice, each person can be assigned to several support estates at the same time, unlike members of the service estates, where affiliation is uniquely determined. An individual can be at the same time a pensioner, public sector worker, and independent professional, or an official and part-time public sector worker (if he is engaged in teaching or scientific research). In any case, the individual does not reflect on any of the statuses indicating his estate affiliation.

From the perspective of the state, a logically coherent social structure consisting of estates and the relations between them is in place. However, from the citizens' perspective, this social structure, to put it mildly, is not transparent. They hesitate to affiliate themselves or their parents with any social group. At best, they identify themselves with groups of the Imperial or Soviet period in Russian history - merchants, entrepreneurs, nobility, officers, workers, peasants, employees, Soviet public sector workers, etc. However, these means of identification are not supported by the state and can rather be regarded as an amorphous protest of members of the estate society against the opacity of the social order. The lack of clarity in basic social relations generates anomie, or the citizens' indeterminacy in the social space-and-time and respective limitations in desinging personal strategies. Outwardly, anomie manifests itself in the latent desire to emigrate, specific for members of virtually all estates, which is expressed in the widespread comparison of living conditions "here" and "there" and in the negative assessment of everything "here" as compared to "there". Part of the population realizes these aspirations in migration. Due to anomie, it is rather difficult to get information about affiliation with a social group-estate from the person in question. This means that neither surveys, nor statistical methods, which usually capture only one, principal for the specific method, social status, can be extensively used to depict the social structure.

politicians consider to be elements of the modern social structure, on the other hand—government, the people, entrepreneurs, and the marginalized.

As already noted above, the social structure is not only and not so much a list of social groups, but, above all, the relations between them. We will assume that the basic relations uniting contemporary Russian estates into the post-Soviet social structure are mutual services (support) and facilitation, for which estate members receive their income—pay, bonuses, salaries, pensions, allowances, etc.

The combination of the income type (salary, pay, pension, etc.) with the income source (public institution, market, publicly funded organization, etc.) is the main stratification criterion in this work. The income type is further regarded as an indicator of estate affiliation, whereas the income source shows which estate the individual facilitates or supports. A public sector worker supporting the state civil service (e.g., a doctor in a specialized clinic of the Main Medical Division of the Administrative Directorate of the President of the Russian Federation) differs fundamentally from a public sector worker supporting the law enforcement service (physician in a correctional facility) or a rural doctor.

A combination of the income type (pay, salary, pension, etc.) with the income source (for what service or support the income is accrued) determines an individual's social status.

Thus, two coordinates determine the social (estate) status of Russian citizens:

- Affiliation with a specific estate
- The estate the activity of which the citizen facilitates or supports.

We believe, this significantly distinguishes the Russian estate-based society from other societies, particularly, the class-based capitalist ones, where the determining factor is the amount of the income[118] rather than its type or source.

---

[118] Thompson, William; Joseph Hickey (2005). *Society in Focus*. Boston, MA: Pearson. Stratification is based on the income level in combination with the educational attainment and the type of occupation.

Tables 8–12 present a general list of Russian estates with an indication of their approximate size[119] matched to the above groups of "government", "the people", "entrepreneurs", and the "marginalized population".

Table 7   Political groups, their estate composition, social functions, and income types of their members

Group	Government	The People	Active Population	Marginalized Population
Estates within the reference groups	State civil servants (federal and regional), diplomats, municipal employees, military personnel, law enforcers, judges, deputies, Cossacks, top executives of state corporations and companies with government participation	Public sector workers (education, culture, healthcare, social protection), employees, pensioners, the disabled, the unemployed, welfare recipients	Independent professionals (actors, musicians, writers, artists, lawyers, prostitutes, etc.) Freelancers Clergy Entrepreneurs Otkhodniks	Individuals with criminal records, convicted prisoners serving sentences, remand prisoners, persons released on parole, drafted conscripts, alcoholics and homeless, migrants, and orphans

---

119 At best, the estimated numerical strength of the estates provided in Tables 8-12 characterizes the order of magnitude. Some figures (e.g., rosters and registers of the state civil, military, and law enforcement services, and the number of persons with criminal records) are classified, therefore, we have to use expert estimates. Since the number of government employees differs significantly from source to source, we rely mainly on Rosstat (Federal State Statistics Service) data. Official statistics keeps no record of otkhodniks (internal temporary labor migrants), therefore, we rely on expert estimates and empirical research findings (Juri Plusnin), according to which every fifth Russian family has an otkhodnik. Rosstat presents all the working population as employed without distinguishing employees, entrepreneurs, etc., therefore, we estimate the number of employees based on the residual principle. There are no statistical records of independent professionals and freelancers, so we rely mainly on expert estimates.

Income type	Pay, bonuses, administrative rent, various compensations	Pensions, welfare, salaries, status rent, scholarships	Market income, fees, status rent	Ration, prison ration, alms, criminal income—share, criminal status rent, situational income from informal employment
Social function	Serving the state. Neutralizing threats, facilitating the activity of other social groups	Supporting other social groups	Supporting the state, other social groups, deriving profit	Supporting other social groups
Origination	Training in specialized educational institutions—"departmental academies" and relevant departments of state educational institutions. Selection for state service positions	General and special vocational education Training, employment, retirement	General and special education, self-education Contract for performance of work, service agreement	Education in marginal subcultures. Membership (generally) results from the state's activity on neutralizing threats and in the course of socialization in marginal subcultures

Table 8   Estates included in "Government"

Estate	Sub-estate	Approximate size
State civil servants 1,704,700	Federal civil servants	878,000 Rosstat data
	Regional civil servants	283,600 Rosstat data
	Diplomats	30,000 Expert estimate
	Municipal employees	513,100 Rosstat data
Military personnel 2,565,000	Ministry of Defense of the Russian Federation	1,700,000 According to Wikipedia.org
	Federal Service for Military and Technical Cooperation	
	Federal Service for Defense Contracts	
	Federal Agency for the Supply of Weapons, Military and Special Equipment and Material Resources	

	Federal Service for Special Construction		
	Federal Security Service (with border troops)	350,000	Expert estimate
	Internal troops	250,000	Expert estimate
	Federal Guard Service	25,000	Expert estimate
	Foreign Intelligence Service	20,000	Expert estimate
	Ministry for Emergency Situations	200,000	Expert estimate
	Main Directorate for Special Programs	20,000	Expert estimate
Law enforcers 1,931,260	Ministry of Internal Affairs	1,280,000	Data from the MVD website
	Federal Customs Service	70,000	Data from the FTS website
	Ministry for Emergency Situations	100,000	http://www.mchs.gov.ru/law/index.php?ID=29152

Ministry of Justice	4,100 Staffing according to the respective presidential Decree http://www.minjust.ru/ru/about/regulations
Federal Penitentiary Service	328,000 According to Wikipedia, which refers to http://www.fsin.su/main..phtml?cid=6
Federal Bailiff Service	45,000 Staffing according to the Decree of the President of the Russian Federation No. 1316 of 13 October 2004 http://www.rg.ru/2004/10/19/pristavy-doc.html
State Courier Service	4,600 Staffing according to the Decree of the President of the Russian Federation No. 1074 of 13 August 2004 http://www.gfs.ru/pravovaya-osnova/ukazy-prezidenta/ukaz-13-08-2004-n-1074
Federal Drug Control Service	40,000 Staffing according to the Decree of the President of the Russian Federation No. 976 of 28 July 2004 fskn.gov.ru/pages/main/info/legal_foundation/4114/4374/index.shtml
Federal Migration Service	34,260 Staffing according to the Decree of the President of the Russian Federation No. 928 of 19 July 2004 http://www.fms.gov.ru/law/861/details/37067

	Federal Registration Service	25,300 Staffing according to the Decree of the President of the Russian Federation No. 1315 of 13 October 2004 http://www.rg.ru/2004/10/19/registr-doc.html
Judges and prosecutors		93,000—212,000
Deputies	Federal, regional, and municipal	100,000 Expert estimate
Senior executives of Gazprom, Transneft, Russian Railways, Central Bank, Sberbank, VTB, Vnesheconombank, Pension Fund, etc. + Transgaz and Transneft uniformed security guards		200,000—250,000 Expert estimate
Total:		6,593,960—6,762,960

Table 9 Estates included in the "The People"

Estate	Sub-estate	Approximate size
Public sector workers	Education, culture, healthcare, and social protection workers	15,000,000 Expert estimate
Working-age employees		20,000,000 - 30,000,000. Expert estimate derived from Rosstat data
Pensioners (excluding pensioners working in government bodies and marginalized pensioners)		37,498,000 Expert estimate derived from Rosstat data
Total:		72,498,000— 82,498,000

Table 10 Estates included in "Active Population"

Estate	Sub-estate	Approximate size
Independent professionals	Actors, musicians, writers, lawyers in private practice, prostitutes, journalists, etc.	4,600,000 Expert estimate; Wikipedia, http://svpressa.ru/society/article/29911/
Sole proprietors, owners of medium-sized and major businesses		2,600,000 Rosstat data
Otkhodniks		10,000,000–15,000,000 Expert estimate
Clergy		130,000 http://svpressa.ru/society/article/29911/
Total:		17,330,000–22,330,000

Table 11 Estates included in "Marginalized Population"

Estate	Sub-estate	Approximate size
Criminals	Persons with criminal records Convicted prisoners serving sentences Remand prisoners Released on parole	10,964,000 Expert estimate derived from Rosstat data
Drafted conscripts		550,000 Total number based on the 2010 spring and autumn draft According to the following articles http://www.rg.ru/2010/04/01/alternativa-anons.html http://www.rg.ru/2011/05/06/aspurant-anons.html
Without estate identity	Migrants (who had not received any estate status)	3,410,000 Expert estimate derived from Rosstat data
	Degraded individuals - those who had lost their estate identity (homeless, drug addicts, and alcoholics)	2,354,000 Rosstat, http://svpressa.ru/society/article/29911/
Total:		17,278,000

Table 12　Groups allocated pro rata to the government, the people, active and marginalized population

Estate	Sub-estate	Approximate size
Unemployed	(allocated pro rata with at least 1,253,200 assigned to the "The People" as recipients of unemployment benefits)	5,400,000
Children	Those who have committed crimes have already been included in the "Marginalized Population" category	94,300
	Orphans (currently) in boarding schools and orphanages are included in the "Marginalized Population" category	229,300
	Benefit recipients are included in "The People" category	10,254,000
	The remaining minors are allocated proportionately among the reference groups	12,276,400
Total:		28,254,000

The "Government" group includes service estates—government and municipal employees, military personnel, law enforcers, judges, deputies, and Cossacks. Members of governing estates receive pay, bonuses, administrative rent, and various compensations for their service. These estates are integrated based on their service to the state.

"The People" group includes public sector workers, pensioners, and employees. The state cares about the people, which means that it guarantees its representatives income in the form of pensions, minimal salaries, benefits, and allowances, the amount of which, in particular, depends on the estates whose activities they used to support or facilitate (pensions) or are currently supporting. Apparently, members of all other estates are not people for the state. A specific property of the people is that its overwhelming majority constantly participates in various elections, whereas members of other non-service estates take part in elections depending on the situation.

The "Active Population" (or "Merchants") group includes entrepreneurs, independent professionals, otkhodniks, and clergy. We have united these estates because they generate their income themselves from providing services (support) to other estates. Their sources of income include market income, fees, status rent (in the case of the entrepreneurs—rent from membership in business curiae—Russian Union of Industrialists and Entrepreneurs, Delovaya Rossiya, and Opora).

The "Marginalized Population" group includes persons with criminal records, convicted, limited in rights (conscripts drafted into the army), and migrants without estate affiliation. Marginalized individuals receive income in the form of ration, prison ration, alms, criminal income-share, rent from criminal status (such as "avtoritet" or "vor v zakone"), and the source of income is determined by the estates that they deal with. Thus, thieves deriving income from the people (pensioners, public sector workers, and employees) differ significantly from thieves deriving income from "merchants", i.e., entrepreneurs and independent professionals. When incarcerated, members of this group receive income from the state (ration and prison ration), and at large, they generate income themselves (criminal income-share and rent from criminal status).

Membership in the "Marginalized Population" group partly results from the activity of the service estate members, who in the course of neutralizing various threats (or preparing to neutralize them) apply administrative and penal sanctions to those individuals who pose (or may pose) a threat to the state and citizens. Due to sanctions, individuals lose their estate identity (they cease being servicemen, part of the people or entrepreneurs) and form a marginalized part of the population.

Thus, the total estimated size of the above four categories of estates ranges from 113,699,960 to 128,868,960 people. The average total is 121,284,460 people.

The average figure for the estate category "Government" amounts to 6,678,460, "The People" - 77,498,000, "Active Population" - 19,830,000, and "Marginalized Population" - 17,278,000 people. Further, we will use average values when referring to the above categories.

Minors and unemployed have no sources of income; therefore, their estate affiliation is uncertain. We have assigned them pro rata to the previously defined groups.

We will assume that representatives of each of the four groups (government, the people, active population, and marginalized population) have on average the same number of children. Consequently, minors under the care of their parents can be assigned to the estate groups proportionately to the total population. For example, to estimate the number of minors to be attributed to the estate group "Government" we should divide 6,678,460 by 121,284,460 (average estimated total numerical strength of the government, the people, active population, and the marginalized groups) and then multiply the resulting share of the "governing" population in all four groups (0.055) by the total number of minors, with the exception of those who have committed crimes (marginalized), orphans, and benefit recipients (people).

The unemployed are distributed proportionately among the four principal estate groups. Of them, at least 1,253,200 persons belong to "The People" group, being recipients of unemployment benefits registered with state employment agencies. In accordance with the methodology the International Labor Organization, the number of unemployed persons is significantly higher than the number of persons registered as unemployed with state employment agencies.

The "Marginalized Population" category already includes 94,300 children. In this way, we allocate additionally 28,159,700 people, of whom (on average):

- 974,098 persons will supplement the "Government" category
- 21,557,605 persons will supplement "The People" category
- 2,892,339 persons will supplement the "Active Population" category, and
- 2,829,985 persons will supplement the "Marginalized Population" category.

Thus, the total average estimate of the size of the estate groups is as follows:

- "Government" includes about 7,652,558 persons
- "The People" includes about 99,055,605 persons
- "Active Population" includes about 22,722,339 persons, and
- "Marginalized Population" includes about 20,013,658 persons.

The resulting estimated total average size of the four identified groups amounts to 149,444,160 people, which approximates statistical data on the population of Russia.

Model of the estate component of Russia's social structure: reference conditions

One of the objectives of this work is numerical simulation of the social (estate) structure of Russia's population, specified by relations between the groups to which the state attributed this population. We proceed from the understanding that there are explicit and implicit state standards for facilitation and support. This means that the number of facilitators and supporters must be proportional to the number of those whose activities are facilitated and supported. Thus, the number of required public sector workers (doctors, teachers, etc.) is calculated based on regulatory demand,[120] which, in turn, is derived from the number of "served clients". The "physical" number of doctors and teachers is thus attached to an ideal model of the social structure. We will assume that similar ratios are true for the social structure in general and will try to populate it proceeding from the available figure of the total population and very approximate distribution of the population among the estate groups, as indicated in Tables 8–12.

According to our average estimates, the population of Russia is 149,444,160 people, with everyone either assigned by the state to a certain estate or considered to be not affiliated, therefore, subject to forced estatization.

---

[120] Provision standards "per 1,000; 10,000; and 100,000 people" are basic social parameters underlying virtually all public documents, planning estimations, etc. However, as far as we know, research never focused on their constituent status in shaping the social structure.

The unit of measure is a person, which means that the number of individuals assigned to an estate determine its size. According to this logic, households (and the family structure) are derivatives from the headcount. This has been done to avoid double counting, where family members belong to different estates. In order to avoid duplication, we are also ignoring the fact that a person may belong to several estates as well as facilitate and support the activity of multiple estates, i.e., we consider that each person has only one type and one source of income.[121]

The hypothesis underlying our calculations

In the social structure, the estates are bound by mutual facilitation and support. The form of the relation consists in the following: in every estate there is a part that facilitates (governing) or supports (non-governing) the activities of other estates and receives income for this—pay, salaries, fees, etc. This part is proportional to the number of members of other estates whose activity is facilitated or supported. This means that if estate A has B members and estate C has D members, the share of people belonging to A and supporting C is proportional to the share of C in the total population.

Members of service estates receive pay for facilitating the activities of other estates. Some service estate members facilitate the activity of the governing estates themselves. We have determined the number of service estate members at 7.7 million people, or 5.12 percent of the population.[122] The number of service estate members facilitating their own activity (the activity of governing estates) constitutes 5.12 percent of 5.12 percent, i.e., amounts to 0.26 percent[123] of the population. This is the actual government, i.e., the leaders and top-ranking officials. The remaining members of the governing estate facilitate the activities of the other estates, and the number of servicemen facilitating the activity of a specific estate is

---

121 In this, we follow the logic of the state. This method of estimating the structure of the population is rather awkward; however, this does not stop the state from using it in drafting its plans and programs.
122 The figures are rounded.
123 Fractions result from calculations rather than measurement.

proportional to the size of that estate. This means that of all the servicemen, 66.3 percent facilitate the activity of the people (66.3 percent of the population), 15.2 percent—of the active population, and the remaining 13.4 percent—of the marginalized groups.

The "People" category (public sector workers, pensioners, and employees), constitutes 65 percent of the population. Part of the people receive pensions, scholarships, salaries, and benefits for providing services to other members of this category. An example are teachers in the schools where children of employees and public sector workers are studying or doctors in neighborhood clinics frequented by pensioners, public sector workers, and employees. The proportion of representatives of the people providing services to the people is 66.3 percent of 66.3 percent (the share of the people in the population), or 43.9 percent of the population. This means that 66.3 percent of the people provide services to representatives of their own category. The remaining people provide services to other estates. Similarly, the number of people engaged in supporting the active population (another group of estates) is proportional to the size of the active population and constitutes 15.2 percent of the people.

Part of the active population supports (receives income from providing services) the active population itself. This is the case with professional entrepreneurs, such as financial market participants. This share is 15.2 percent of 15.2 percent (which is the share of this group of estates in the total population), or 2.3 percent. The remaining 97.7 percent of the active population support other estates.

Part of the marginalized population proportional to its share in the total population provides services to its own members. Thus, 13.4 percent of the marginalized population receives income (alms, ration, prison ration, and share) from providing services to the marginalized themselves. This means that 1.79 percent of the population are "professional" marginalized individuals and persons receiving income mainly from criminal operations.

Table 13   Structure of the model

	Estate A B members	Estate C D members	B+D
B	B*(B/(B+D))	B*(D/(B+D))	B
D	D*(B/(B+D))	D*(D/(B+D))	D
B+D	B	D	B+D

Formalized model of the social structure

Based on the above logic, we have prepared a table presenting Russia's population as an aggregate of estates supporting and facilitating the activities of other estates.

The figures show the share in the total population and the share of the parts in each group of estates that facilitate and support the activities of other estates. The calculations are based on the average estimated size of the estate groups.

Let us consider the first row of Table 14—the distribution of representatives of the governing estates by groups depending on the estates whose activities they facilitate.

<u>Members of governing estates receiving pay (and other income, including administrative rent) for facilitating activities of the government itself.</u> These are top-ranking officials who actually personify the government. They maintain the government structure. If the initial premises are correct, they constitute about 0.26 percent of Russia's population. In absolute figures, this is approximately 391,863 persons, which intuitively appears to be close to reality.

<u>Members of service estates (military personnel, state civil servants and municipal employees, law enforcers, judges, deputies, and Cossacks in government service) receiving pay for facilitating activities of the people (pensioners, public sector workers, and employees).</u> These are officials in charge of paying pensions and benefits, controlling salaries and wages, monitoring working and living conditions, and many other things. They constitute about 3.39 percent of the total

population, which in absolute figures is approximately 5,072,321 persons.

Members of service estates facilitating the activities of the active population (entrepreneurs, merchants, independent professionals)—various law enforcers, state civil servants and others who are paid to control business activities, issue licenses and other business permits, collect taxes, and prosecute those who violate the rules and procedures introduced by the state. They constitute about 0.78 % of the total population, which in absolute figures is approximately 1,163,538 persons.

Members of service estates facilitating the activities of marginalized groups (persons with criminal records, convicted, limited in rights and migrants). These are law enforcers, military personnel, state civil servants, judges, and deputies who are paid to control the behavior of various marginalized individuals. They constitute about 0.69% of the total population, which in absolute figures is approximately 1,024,836 persons.

Let us consider the second row of Table 14—the people in its relations with other estate groups.

Members of the estates comprising the people, who receive their salaries, pensions, and benefits for providing services to the governing estates. These are teachers, doctors, and employees working in government organizations and institutions. Besides, this category includes retired state, military and law enforcement personnel, as well as personal pensioners. They constitute about 3.39% of the total population, which in absolute figures is approximately 5,072,321 persons.

SOCIO-ECONOMIC FOUNDATIONS OF THE RUSSIAN POST-SOVIET REGIME 199

Table 14 Model of Russia's social structure

Social groups - estates with their sources of income / Levels of the structure + sources of income	Members of the service estates. 7.7 million or 5.1% of the population. (pay)	Pensioners, public sector workers, employees. 99 million or 66.3% of the population. (pension, benefit, salary)	Entrepreneurs, merchants, independent professionals, traders. 22.7 million or 15.2% of the population. (market income, gain, fees, grants)	Persons without estate affiliation, with criminal records and incarcerated, and limited in rights. 20 million or 13.4% of the population. (ration, prison ration, share)	TOTAL
Governing (pay, bonuses, various compensations, administrative rent)	Government—members of the service (governing) estates. About 0.26% of the population engaged in government receive pay for facilitating government activities. Approximately 391,863 persons.	Members of service estates receiving pay for facilitating the activities of the people. About 3.39% of the population—approximately 5,072,321 persons.	Members of service estates receiving pay for facilitating the activities of entrepreneurs, merchants, etc. About 0.78% of the population—approximately 1,163,538 persons.	Members of service estates receiving pay for facilitating (controlling) the activities of persons without estate affiliation, with criminal records, etc. About 0.69% of the population—approximately 1,024,836 persons.	5.12%

Popular (salaries, pensions, benefits, rent from estate status)	People receiving salaries, pensions, and benefits for supporting activities of the government. About 3.39% of the population—approximately 5,072,321 persons.	People receiving salaries, pensions, and benefits for supporting activities of the people. About 43.93% of the population—approximately 65,656,716 persons.	People receiving salaries, pensions, and benefits for supporting business activities. About 10.08% of the population—approximately 15,060,977 persons.	People receiving salaries, pensions, and benefits for providing services to criminals and by virtue of that becoming marginalized and criminalized themselves. About 8.88% of the population—approximately 13,265,590 persons.	66.28%
Market (market (trade) income, fees, grants, gain, rent from estate status)	Entrepreneurs receiving income from supporting activities of the government. About 0.78% of the population—approximately 1,163,538 persons.	Entrepreneurs receiving income from supporting activities of the people. About 10.08% of the population—approximately 15,060,977 persons.	Business people and merchants receiving income from supporting business activities. About 2.31% of the population—approximately 3,454,833 persons.	Entrepreneurs receiving income from providing services to marginalized groups and criminals. About 2.04% of the population—approximately 3,042,990 persons.	15.2%
Marginalized - criminal (ration, prison ration, share from plundering, rent from criminal status)	Marginalized individuals and criminals receiving income from supporting activities of the government. About 0.69% of the population—approximately 1,024,836 persons.	Marginalized individuals and criminals receiving income from supporting activities of the people. About 8.88% of the population—approximately 13,265,590 persons.	Marginalized individuals and criminals receiving income from supporting business activities. About 2.04% of the population—approximately 3,042,990 persons.	"Enemies of the people" - professional criminals receiving income from providing services to the marginalized and criminals. About 1.79% of the population—approximately 2,680,242 persons.	13.39%
TOTAL	5.12%	66.28%	15.2%	13.39%	100%

Members of the estates comprising the people, who receive salaries for providing services to the people. This category includes early and old age retirees, as well as dependents in the families of public sector workers, pensioners, and employees. They constitute about 43.93% of the total population, which in absolute figures is approximately 65,656,716 persons.

Members of the estates comprising the people, who receive their salaries and benefits for providing services to various entrepreneurs and independent professionals. These are persons employed by entrepreneurs and independent professionals, teachers in private schools and staff of private hospitals. In addition, this group includes early and old age retirees and persons engaged part-time in the service of entrepreneurs and independent professionals.

Members of the estates comprising the people, who receive salaries for providing services to the marginalized (such as formally unemployed persons) and criminal groups of the population. These include, for example, teachers and doctors in penitentiary institutions and migration agencies; people employed by the Ministry of Internal Affairs; and people receiving salaries for providing services to various criminalized businesses—from gambling to drug dealing. Such representatives of the people are inevitably marginalized and criminalized themselves because of dealing directly with the strata, whose activities they support.

Let us consider the third row of the table—entrepreneurs, merchants, and independent professionals in their relations with other groups of the population.

Entrepreneurs, merchants, and independent professionals, who receive their income and fees for supporting activities of the governing estates. These are contractors working under various public contracts, lawyers, media professionals, and creative professionals supporting activities of the government and thereby associated with it. The group also includes members of the clergy, who provide services to the government (e.g., in army units). This group unites both "oligarchs" with "government protection" and representatives of small and medium-sized businesses, whose activity is impracticable without government contracts or without the "protection" of members of the governing estates.

Entrepreneurs, merchants, and independent professionals, who receive income for supporting activities of the people—pensioners, public sector workers, and employees. These are owners of trade chains, stores, and small-scale production facilities targeting mass demand and providing services to people, who live off pensions, salaries, and benefits. This group also includes private tutors, privately practicing doctors and nurses, and others, who are formally employed in institutions and organizations, but sell their services to representatives of the people against fees.

Entrepreneurs, merchants, and independent professionals, who receive income from services to members of their own category. This is the elite of this social stratum focused on providing services to individuals with high and very high incomes and requirements. This group includes "expensive" lawyers, economic and financial advisors, owners of boutiques and high-end shops and retail chains, entrepreneurs providing "elite" services, bankers, "expensive" doctors and various traditional healers, and so on and so forth.

Entrepreneurs, merchants, and independent professionals, who receive income from providing services to the marginalized and criminalized segments of the population. This group includes owners of stores and retail chains supplying penal colonies and their environment, providers of illegal goods and services (prostitution, manufacturing and sale of drugs and weapons, purchase and sale of stolen goods, sale of counterfeit goods, etc.), lawyers handling criminal cases of crime lords, smugglers, etc.

Let us consider the fourth, last row of the table—the relations of the marginalized and criminalized population with the other groups of estates.

Marginalized individuals, criminals (with past criminal records and serving sentences), and persons with limited rights, who receive income from providing services to governing estates. This group includes drafted conscripts (they receive rations and allowances); migrants informally engaged in providing services to government institutions, organizations, and the officials working there (they receive a share of the income of officials who engage their services); bandits and smugglers acting "under protection" provided by members of the service estates; suppliers of illegal services and goods consumed by members of the service estates; and many other categories of individuals living off a share in criminal income.

Marginalized individuals, criminals, and persons with limited rights, who receive income from providing services to the people. These are amateur and professional thieves, and petty bandits, who rob public sector workers, pensioners, and employees. Notions about criminal subculture are associated precisely with this category of the population.

Marginalized individuals, criminals, and persons with limited rights providing services to entrepreneurs, merchants, and independent professionals. These people have a share in the income of "merchants", either providing "protection" for their business or directly participating in those commercial transactions, which cannot be carried out legally.

Marginalized individuals, criminals, and persons with limited rights supporting activities that are specific to these communities. This is the elite of the underworld, its crime lords and thieves in law, whose activity reproduces the criminal subculture. They have their interest in every illegal activity and implement principles of social justice specific for this environment: for bandits—codes of the underworld (ponyatiya), and for thieves—their code of honor (vorovskoy zakon).

Discussion of the presented model

Table 14 is not just an illustration of the presented logic; it largely serves as a graphic model of this logic. The simple premise that all estates are united by proportional relations of mutual support and facilitation leads to conclusions that are not at all obvious. The table makes navigating this logic easier. The order in which the reference groups are presented in the table is irrelevant.

First, it is necessary to understand what this table is all about, and why it tallies.

Columns split the total population (100%) into four unequal parts, thus creating four groups. Then, each group is taken as 100% and divided into four parts in the same proportion as the total—this is presented as table rows. Thus, the sum of all table cells remains equal to the initial total population. It is important to ensure that the total percentage of the initial four groups by rows and by columns amounts to 100%, otherwise part of the population will remain outside the table.

The table is thus a certain numerical model of the social structure. If the underlying hypothesis is correct, the model can be used to capture more in-depth results of estate-based social stratification. By varying the size (share in total) of the reference groups, one can see how their relative shares will change because of the government's attempts to change the size of particular estates and their groups.

Presumably, it is possible to design a more diversified model of mutual services by dividing each of the groups into smaller elements (for example, to consider interaction between different types of government employees). However, further fragmentation will increase errors due to the above-mentioned features of the national social statistics. The breakdown provided in Table 14 can be presented as follows:

Table 15   Numerical presentation of the social structure in relative values based on average group sizes

		Government	The People	Active Population	Marginalized Population	Total
		0.0512	0.6628	0.152	0.1339	1
Government	0.0512	0.0026	0.0339	0.0078	0.0069	0.0512
The People	0.6628	0.0339	0.4393	0.1008	0.0888	0.6628
Active Population	0.152	0.0078	0.1008	0.0231	0.0204	0.152
Marginalized Population	0.1339	0.0069	0.0888	0.0204	0.0179	0.1339
Total	1	0.0512	0.6628	0.152	0.1339	1

Table 16 Numerical presentation of the social structure in absolute values based on average group sizes

		Government	The People	Active Population	Marginalized Population	Total
		7,652,558	99,055,605	22,722,339	20,013,658	149,444,160
Government	7,652,558	391,863	5,072,321	1,163,538	1,024,836	7,652,558
The People	99,055,605	5,072,321	65,656,716	15,060,977	13,265,590	99,055,605
Active Population	22,722,339	1,163,538	15,060,977	3,454,833	3,042,990	22,722,339
Marginalized Population	20,013,658	1,024,836	13,265,590	3,042,990	2,680,242	20,013,658
Total	149,444,160	7,652,558	99,055,605	22,722,339	20,013,658	149,444,160

Please note that the table is symmetrical with respect to the diagonal. On the surface, this is due to the rules of multiplication—the multiplied shares simply change places (since the initial proportions in the rows and columns are identical). However, this feature is a direct consequence of the underlying hypothesis.

Thus, under this model, the groups providing mutual services (symmetric with respect to the diagonal) are equal in size, which appears plausible.

This means that the size of the "governing" population providing services to the "people" equals the number of "people" providing services to the "government"; the size of the "governing" population providing services to the "active population" equals the size of the "active population" providing services to the "government" and so forth. This does not necessarily mean that the same people are involved in mutual services of two symmetrical groups. About five million members of the governing estates provide services to the "people", but not necessarily to the same "people" that provide services to the "government", although these two populations may overlap. One way or another, it is currently impracticable to compare adequately the size of these groups, since they are not captured by the national social statistics. However, we can verify the hypothesis by using more or less accurate statistics, such as the number of civil employees in military organizations, and the number of military personnel in "civilian" organizations.

The breakdown presented in Tables 15 and 16 provides a benchmark for capturing any deviations from the estimated values in the social structures of specific municipalities and allows forming hypotheses about the reasons for such deviations, which can be empirically tested.

Besides, such a table allows modeling (within the scope of formalism) changes in the social structure by answering such questions as: if the number of "governors" is reduced by x%, the number of people can formally grow by this much and the number of the marginalized—by that much.[124]

Suppose, for example, that the political leadership of the state adopts (and implements) the decision to reduce administrative staff by 20 percent, which means that the number of members of service estates will decrease by 1,530,511 people. The dismissed servicemen will not disappear into nowhere. They will be distributed among the groups of estates in proportion to the size of these groups.[125] We will keep in mind that when the state takes such decisions it also decides what particular bodies shall be subject to downsizing, respectively, some of the dismissed employees may resume service in other bodies. Following the logic of proportional redistribution, their share will be 5.12 percent. A further 66.28 percent of the redundant personnel will join the "People" group of estates, 15.2 percent—the active population, and the remaining 13.39 percent will become marginalized.

The new distribution is presented in Table 17.

---

124 We plan to develop our own mathematical tools, which will provide more opportunities for manipulating the contents of the table.
125 Of course, in this case, the proportional redistribution hypothesis should be empirically verified. However, the proportions of the groups themselves may serve as a statistical model of social behavior. Other stereotypes of behavior may also be appropriate. In any case, the proportional redistribution hypothesis seems slightly more plausible. However, it should definitely be tested.

Table 17   Change in the size of estates given a 20% reduction in the number of servicemen

		Government	The People	Active Population	Marginalized Population	Total
		6,185,393 (-19.1%)	100,080,566 (+1%)	22,957,454 (+1%)	20,220,745 (+1%)	149,444,160
Government	6,185,393	256,009 (-34%)	4,142,267 (-18%)	950,193 (-18%)	836,923 (-18%)	6,185,393 (-19.1%)
The People	100,080,566	4,142,267 (-18%)	67,022,490 (+2%)	15,374,271 (+2%)	13,541,537 (+2%)	100,080,566 (+1%)
Active Population	22,957,454	950,193 (-18%)	15,374,271 (+2%)	3,526,700 (+2%)	3,106,289 (+2%)	22,957,454 (+1%)
Marginalized Population	20,220,745	836,923 (-18%)	13,541,537 (+2%)	3,106,289 (+2%)	2,735,995 (+2%)	20,220,745 (+1%)
Total	149,444,160	6,185,393 (-19.1%)	100,080,566 (+1%)	22,957,454 (+1%)	20,220,745 (+1%)	149,444,160

The table shows that actions aimed at changing the social structure by reducing the number of administrative staff ("Government") lead (in the model) to the far from obvious consequences, such as increasing the number of professional criminals by 2%, which is quite significant.

Limitations of the presented model

The logic of the above model is as follows: we initially distinguish four categories of estates according to income type and source. Incomes are classified based on the existing public-political practice. However, we are not sure whether this classification is exhaustive and describes all possible types and sources of income.

Further, we distinguish four categories of estates corresponding to the identified types and sources of income and match them to the groups-estates existing in the national state practice. Formally, we thus allocate state-ranked groups to the four distinguished estate categories. It is not clear to what extent this procedure is justified.

We do not know whether the list of government institutions by type of service (by the number of people engaged) is exhaustive. It is also unclear whether the distinguished groups exclude (statistically) each other or whether they can overlap, for example, like pensioners and "Government" or pensioners and "Entrepreneurs".

To simplify the classification, we ignore "dual" statuses (in the mentioned sense). However, such dualism is a social fact. At the first stage of the research, when we define the general principles of the relevant social stratification, such an assumption is needed, but in future, it should be examined in detail and taken into account in the overall logic.

The model's logic treats the identified groups as ideal types. However, empirically, not all pensioners, for example, behave politically and socially like the "People" and some of them continue working and receive pension only as "additional income". Undoubtedly, some individuals with a criminal record or migrants managed to socialize in other groups, and there are groups that combine multiple types and sources of income. Hence, the obvious limitation of the premise that all people are affiliated with one estate only and provide services to one estate.

In principle, incomplete data does not exclude the possibility of classification, but the question about the adequacy of the presented model of interaction between the groups of estates remains open. Should there be any groups by type and source of income that have not been included in the model, its presentation will change accordingly. Nevertheless, this should not affect its general underlying logic (the hypothesis of proportional mutual services).

The designed model creates sixteen new groups, which are, in fact, a new classification. There are no studies as to how the statistical groups (underlying the basic distinctions), which exist in domestic practice, correlate with the new classification. Thus, the designed model converts the existing distinctions used by politicians and officials into a new classification.

After determining the composition of the estate groups, we have to estimate their size to include in the model. These estimations generate numerous questions as to their methodology and relevance. For example, it is not clear, what positions in Gazprom, Transneft, Russian Railways, and the Central Bank can be considered executive for the purposes of this study. The methodology for estimating the number of "employees" is not fully clear, and there is no certainty as to what forms of business activity other than sole proprietorship can be included in "active population". The procedure for estimating the number of otkhodniks is also deficient. It is virtually impossible to estimate the number of people with social and legal restrictions arising from a criminal record, etc.

As mentioned in the text, the size of the groups is largely judgmental. One of the reasons is nontransparent government statistics. Another reason is that some of the groups in our classification (such as the otkhodniks, "employees" in our interpretation, independent professionals, etc.) do not exist in domestic "reality". It is almost impossible to obtain "exact values" as to the size of these groups, expert estimates may vary, and the official websites of government agencies and organizations, at best, provide data on their staff numbers.

The relevance of the figures included in the model is also problematic, be it expert estimates or official sources,—such information is valid as of the date of measurement. Due to the scarcity of more or less verifiable information, the authors used estimates made at different times, which only increases the errors.

Thus, we can only expect that the order of magnitude is correct. Fractional or extremely "exact" figures characterizing the size of the groups in the model (matrix of intra-estate relations) are a result of calculations and are only indirectly related to statistics (through the size of the initial four groups).

Obviously, the methods for estimating the size of virtually every identified group should be enhanced.

The hypothesis underlying the model of the social structure also needs experimental confirmation and verification. It is necessary to verify the findings obtained based on the depicted theory and, to the extent possible, experimentally estimate the size of the mutual services groups, compare them with the theoretical values, and based on their correlation draw conclusions about the plausibility of the model and hypothesis.

Obviously, many factors distort the hypothesis about proportional mutual services provided by groups of estates. Such imbalances may be especially pronounced when attempting to interpret the model on a regional level. For example, the overwhelming majority of the Federal Penitentiary Service personnel provide services to the marginalized population. However, the selected scale (when the Federal Penitentiary Service personnel is included in the "Government" group of estates) does not show this, whereas an empirical description of the social structure in the settlements near the correctional institutions will capture a higher proportion of such servicemen in the population, and, consequently, a larger concentration of members of the governing estates.

Evidently, the assumptions about the proportional distribution of some groups of the population among all groups of estates (Table 13) have a high margin of error. It is likely that some estates have more children, and in certain regions, unemployment is higher.

Some aspects of how the contemporary estate-based structure functions: Search for a national idea, repression and depressions

In contemporary Russia, no minimum social stability or social justice (welfare state) are currently possible without at least some certainty of who is who in this state—who has what rank or title, whom do they ultimately serve, and what they are entitled to for that service. This is hardly possible outside of the estate structure. However, estate identity is not assigned a priori; it develops in the course of administrative market bargaining and collection of estate rent, which are alternative to the market of goods and services.

At the same time, class identity (self-affiliation with the rich or the poor) is impossible without a free market and its institutions, which the administrative market is currently ousting into the "shadow economy". This generates an equally shadow, not public, and unidentifiable by research division into the well resourced (relatively rich) and poorly resourced (relatively poor). An estate-based state-society perceives wealth and poverty not as a natural status of its members, but rather as a violation of the established procedure, where well-being is not a result of labor or market opportunity, but depends on estate affiliation. However, in recent years, a market with some of its attributes, including class stratification, has emerged in Russia. Virtually all citizens of the country nominally belong to an estate, but at the same time, they are focused on consumption, and, accordingly, they need a class identity.

The coexistence of the estate and class structures (with no coherent clarifications as to how they coexist) in the same social space result in a quite peculiar form of national anomie, when a person assumes (without integrating) a priori controversial and conflicting identities of his estate and market status. For example, he can be a civil servant, trade agent, businessman, and champion for the rights of the working people (employees, public sector workers, and pensioners)—all at the same time.

The simultaneous and implicitly conflict-prone (not peaceful, as in democracies) coexistence of two basic stratification systems creates social tension, where members of an (any) estate consider that they are poor because of being under-resourced by the state, whereas the other estates enrich themselves illegally by violating social justice principles. People refer to themselves and members of their own estate in estate terms and to members of other estates—in class terms.

Due to the ambivalence of the social status, state service often transforms itself into mediation or "protection", which the actors themselves often consider faithful service. The internal conflict between the roles of an estate member and market actor manifests itself in rampant alcoholism, unexplainable by other reasons, or exorbitant and conspicuous consumption, in profound cynicism and negativism combined with an instinctive willingness to lick the ass of superiors—members of higher-ranking estates—and kick the subordinates—members of lower-ranking estates.

These phenomena demonstrate the ambivalence of the social order, its ontological dualism, which a sober person can hardly grasp. However, endless drunken "frank" conversations bring one no closer to understanding the intricacies of mutually exclusive social ties and relations. People want to be clear about their status, but this is possible only if they can assuredly affiliate themselves with the classes of a market society and with estates. However, the conditions for this are nonexistent, since class identity is impossible without a real political organization of the society, a multi party system, and the rule of law. Instead, we have certain degrading "democratic" institutions of the same name, which emerged with market development and which the estate system now mainly uses to legalize the alienation of resources and indicate the intentions for their fair distribution among the estates. Estate institutions prevail over the class ones. This domination is not public and largely illegitimate.

However, legitimization of the estates, self-identification of its members, and the establishment of estate organizations-assemblies and estate courts are prerequisites for the emergence of estate identity. The state does virtually nothing in this respect; moreover, it does not recognize the very fact of establishing an estate-based order. Rather, the contrary is true. All estate "politicians" publicly interpret their actions as measures to develop the markets, establish democracy, and protect human rights—forms of social organization that are compatible with an estate-based society only if they are subordinated to the institutions of a class society.

The national idea as justification for the need to mobilize resources

The founders of socialism formulated the idea of "achieving universal equality". In the early 1920s, their Russian followers invented innovative methods to mobilize resources for its implementation. The specific feature of Soviet socialism consists in combining the idea of universal equality with such means of achieving it as total nationalization of resources with their subsequent planned distribution. The task of building it in the USSR was largely facilitated by the fact that mobilization institutions were already in place since World War I. According to the concept formulated by Olga Bessonova, the Russian ethnic "distributive" character of production, distribution, consumption, and exchange also contributed significantly to the introduction of socialist innovations.[126]

Our experience has demonstrated that universal equality is unattainable using methods developed by Lenin, Stalin, their comrades-in-arms, and followers. The founders, however, had created a self-reproducing infrastructure of forced equalization, which is so deeply rooted in our life that we, for the most part, accept it as self-evident and natural.

This infrastructure is so well preserved that it can be generalized as soon as a motivating idea appears that will be accepted by the population craving order and unattainable equality. In line with social justice criteria, consolidation of all resources by the state and their

---

[126] To acquire its national identity, Russia needs a goal (national idea). This eternally young country does not manage to grow up and become like other states that are no longer concerned about adolescent problems. In the past, this goal used to be imperial autocracy, then global communism, followed by the construction of socialism in a single country. The magnitude of the goal must justify resource mobilization costs, including restriction of political and economic freedoms.

subsequent direct distribution can become general state practice yet again. After identifying the national idea, the state will begin "restoring order" in the use of resources mechanically destroying everything that stands in the way of building yet another bright future and turning its own population into a resource in order to implement this idea.

Public opinion polls show that the socialist people (as an aggregate of nominal social groups, which the government is currently vitalizing by "national priority projects") is hopefully expecting "order to be restored" in the use of resources. People are looking forward to the prosecution of those who privatized public resources in the confusion caused by perestroika and the construction of capitalism.[127]

For many years in a row, politically concerned citizens are trying to invent something ideological that would require "clamping down on the mess". By its driving force, this something must be comparable to the ideas of early communism.[128] Until now, they have generated only ideological miscarriages, anti-Utopian parodies, and various remakes of the first verse of *Varshavianka* [revolutionary anthem].[129] The authors are definitely no Karl Marxes; however, this does not exclude the possibility that the state may adopt some version of their products as a national ideology.

A large-scale experiment is under way, which has already tested the slogans of preserving the integrity of the country; combating terrorism, fascism, and extremism; raising living standards; increasing wag-

---

127 "Honest citizens" never miss a chance to snatch something from the "feeder" ahead of the others or simply to steal a bit. However, they hate the domestic capitalists, who have made "snatching" their principal occupation. Thus, the negative attitude of our people to socialist entrepreneurs is of the same nature as a fight in the queue for vodka (during perestroika), provoked by those who are trying to jump the queue. The programs of most contemporary political parties contain an explicit or implicit demand to "loot the looted", nationalize resources and establish one general queue for them.

128 Naishul V. *The ABC of urban Rus'. The semantic framework of the Russian socio-political language*. Lecture of 26 January 2006 // Public lectures Polit.ru: http://www.polit.ru/lectures/2006/02/03/naishul_bubu.html.

129 Leontiev M., Yuriev M., Khazin M., Utkin A. *Fortress Russia. A farewell to liberalism*. Collected works. M., 2005, and – "Project Russia" - author unknown (http://www.projectrussia.ru/text)... "Hostile whirlwinds hover above us, evil forces oppress us viciously. We have engaged in a fatal battle with our enemies, and our fate is unknown". By the way, Gleb Krzhizhanovsky, renowned theorist and practitioner of socialist construction, wrote the lyrics of the *Varshavianka*.

es in the public sector; improving the health and enhancing the educational level of the population. These particular objectives have not yet become elements of goal setting and resource distribution decision-making.

Just as 30 years ago, the nostalgically socialist procedure of drawing up social and economic development plans in various forms—from the archaic *Siberia* program[130] to more modern ones, such as packages of reformist bills from the Center for Strategic Research (CSR) under the Ministry of Economic Development[131]—became a source of livelihood for humanitarian intellectuals.

The situation is somewhat paradoxical—there is still no national idea, but there are plans on implementing it, which are being developed along the lines of universal forced equality.[132]

We cannot exclude a creative revisiting of the political economy of socialism in the near future. Further, the next stage of the administrative reform will legalize the renewed practices of socialist construction and restore state planning, distribution, and price control bodies.

Resource depressions and repression as a way of "restoring order" in the use of resources

The political economy of socialism was and remains the only positive systematic description of a state system, where, among other things, the cyclic weakening-consolidation of statehood replaced normal economic cycles. Nineteenth-century ideologists developed socialism as a theory in response to the challenges posed by the catastrophic consequences of periodic economic depressions (crises of overproduction) that accompanied the emergence of capitalism. Socialism as a reality replaced crises of overproduction by socialist shortage crises.

---

130 http://www-sbras.nsc.ru/win/sbras/pr_sib/
131 http://www.csr.ru/contact/
132 In the 1970s, I accidentally overheard a conversation between instructors of a CPSU district committee, who were discussing their visit to a factory, "You cannot imagine how bad the situation is. The workers have no idea what slogan they are currently working under...". Today, not only the workers, but also the government has no idea what slogan it is working under and for the sake of what it wants to "restore order" in the enormous resource-based economy, which is already partly beyond its control.

Practice shows that the socialist state is always experiencing a more or less deep crisis in the form of a permanent shortage of resources. The state seeks ways out of the crises by tightening control over the distribution of available resources and mobilizing new ones. However, it rarely succeeds. In the absence of repressive measures, shortage crises in a resource-based state may result in its weakening or even disintegration. The reason is (putting aside the highly scientific explanations of the "real economists") inefficient use of resources consolidated by the state. Such inefficiency generally results not from deficient planning, but because the resources are diverted or simply stolen.

Repression became the only method of combating resource diversion and plundering (besides extensive propaganda of honest labor and branding of pilferers). The state resorts to repressive actions to punish for the fact that resources intended for one purpose were used for another purpose or simply stolen.

Under Soviet socialism, repression is more or less the same tool for managing the resource organization of the state as the interest rate policy is under capitalism. Persecution can be large-scale (mass repressions) or local, depending on the tasks set by the state. What is important is that under domestic socialism it always remains a method of regulating resources flows rather than the result of applying the law, before which all are equal.[133] The state focuses all its efforts on arranging the distribution of resources in a way to avoid them being stolen. However, resources are always stolen, that is inevitable. The state is forced to prosecute both those who had distributed resources in a way that they were stolen, and those who had actually stolen

---

[133] The term "rule of law" is in principle not applicable to socialist states where there is no place for traditional law. Socialist legality, which is based on political expediency, has replaced law. In its political practice, domestic socialism has always been implementing a certain repressive technique - sometimes relatively mild (like now), at other times extremely severe. D. Feldman, for example, notes that according to Stalin's criminal law, crime is defined as a violation of order or regime rather than a violation of law. Under socialist legality, repression was (and remains) a struggle with violations of the order established by the builders of socialism, primarily with regard to the use of resources (Feldman D. *The terminology of government. Soviet political terms in the historical and cultural context*. M., 2006).

them. There is no other option, as the political writers at the time of perestroika used to say.

Using repression as a tool for shaping "labor resources" became a specific feature of Soviet socialism. In the course of repression, the socialist state uses those convicted for violating the management procedure (not the law) as "labor resources"[134] and trains people how to use the allocated resources ideologically correctly.

It is no mere chance that the times considered by apologists of Soviet socialism to be the heyday of the state chronologically coincide with the most widespread repressions. It is impossible to maintain the flow of resources mobilized by the state without periodically purging those who try to channel them elsewhere. On the other hand, in periods of depression, state repression as an institution disappears. Non-state repression replaces it, since the state loses its repressive functions along with the resources. The new resource managers engage in repression as widespread as that pursued by the state when it is fully in control of the resource flows. Non-state repression is interpreted as an increase in crime. It may be that the "law of conservation of repression" functions in a resource-based state to ensure the flow of resources.

It is well known that in the period from Stalin's death to perestroika, the Soviet Union suffered from chronic shortages (of food, fuel, consumer goods, etc.), which the socialist state tried to overcome using methods not specific for socialism—minimizing repression or combining it with "economic reforms". Reforms launched by Khrushchev and Kosygin alternated with small-scale jailing of store and factory directors, and pilferers and plunderers of socialist property initiated by Shelepin and Andropov, as well as a struggle with alcoholism as a phenomenon lowering the quality of labor resources.

Such revisionist measures only drove deeper the problem of concentrating resources and managing their distribution, demotivated the apparatus, and triggered "anti-Soviet" feelings among the public. The revisionism of the Soviet leadership, which gave up the practice of

---

134 *Forced labor. Corrective labor camps in Kuzbass (1930s—1950s)*. Vol. 1. Kemerovo, 1994. See also: Kolerov M. *Prisoners of war in the system of forced labor in the USSR (1945-1950)* // Otechestvennye Zapiski. 2003. No. 3.

widespread repressive regulation, ultimately resulted in a great depression of the resource-based organization—total shortage of resources, perestroika, and the disintegration of the Soviet Union.

Perestroika and everything that followed are generally considered as the complete collapse of Soviet socialism. However, the foundations of socialism (except the ideology, which by the end of the 1980s had lost all meaning) did not collapse. They remained intact.

Perestroika and the following period were the most profound comprehensive depression of the Soviet Union's resource-based organization (when the state lost control over resource management), which led to the disintegration of the country. Post-Soviet states preserved the socialist infrastructure, and now it serves as a basis for restoring resource flow management. The process is disguised by phenomena, which give it the appearance of a market one.

Centralized repression is currently situational and takes such forms as struggling against "unauthorized developers", for "streamlining trade areas" and "protecting water conservation zones", not to mention locking behind bars "illegal entrepreneurs", "tax evaders", and "political extremists". This has nothing to do with somebody's ill will. It just happens in the course of managing resource flows, when it turns out that no methods other than repressive ones can mobilize enough resources for a socially significant area of government work. The recently adopted law on combating extremism, which includes such a sanction as confiscation of property, can become a powerful tool for restoring state control over resource flows.[135]

Trying to explain the reality they were actually experiencing, progressive economists and politicians invented the term "transition period", during which the remains of socialism allegedly coexist with the sprouts of capitalism. However, there are no and never have been any transition periods.[136] Soviet institutions, namely, science, education, healthcare, military organization of the state, administrative and territorial division, as well as social groups in the public sector formed for the

---

[135] Federal law on combating extremist activities: http://www.hro.org/docs/rlex/duma/41/ex1.htm

[136] Orekhovsky P.A. *No more need for the transition period. Cities and reforms. Opinion of a sociologist* // http://www.polit.ru/analytics/2006/06/16/soc.html

purpose of distributing resources fairly, have remained virtually unchanged and insist that the resource flows to them be resumed. Moreover, fully intact is the resource storage system, the so-called mobilization facilities and state reserves.

Current authorities intend to meet the demands of the socialist state's basic institutions. "National priority projects" on developing education, healthcare, agriculture, construction of affordable housing, and now even culture indicate this.[137] The national projects are designed and executed as resource-based activities, familiar from Soviet times. For national project ideologists, the size of the population, its level of education and health status, the number of square meters of housing per capita, and the amount of meat and milk per the same capita are directly related to resource supplies. There are insufficient resources to meet the regulatory requirements; therefore, it is necessary to create conditions for their increase. Conditions are created by distributing budget funds (and other resources) among nominal social groups of citizens engaged in education, healthcare, agriculture, construction, and culture in proportion to the significance of these groups to the state.

However, in the absence of the great national idea and the state planning committee, resources are distributed irrationally. Socialist undertakings are stalled, various resource plunderers "carve up" the budgets allocated for the national projects, and salary increases to "certain categories of workers" trigger social tension, because they breach the principles of social justice subconsciously shared by members of the socialist society.

The "publicity" around the national projects indicates a continuing trend to increase the centralized distribution of resources. The negative experience of implementing national projects will not stop the expansion of this practice. Moreover, many difficulties in implementing them are attributed to inadequate budget and distribution systems, or the resource management procedure. Attempts to improve these systems and create a legislative equivalent of the management procedure

---

[137] *Cities and reforms* / Borisov A. M., Vasyutichev A. V., Golovnina N. V., Orekhovsky P. A., Slesarev D. A., Slesareva E. V.; Edited by P. A. Orekhovsky. Obninsk, 2002: National projects. Journal: http://rus-reform.ru/?sid=4&page=100

in the form of various Codes (Forestry, Subsoil, Land, Water, Civil, Budget, Labor and so forth)[138] will hardly produce a positive result. It is quite likely that the execution of national projects will ultimately trigger the foundation of something that can establish real order and will be similar to Soviet bodies in charge of managing resource flows—Gosplan (State Planning Committee), Gossnab (State Procurement Committee), and Goskomtsen (State Committee on Prices). The functional counterpart of Goskomtrud (State Committee for Labor and Social Problems) in the form of a law enforcement Federal Migration Service with its labor migrant quotas is already in place.

Stagnation and depression as phases of public life

Analytically, we can distinguish the following sequence of public life phases: 1) strong state—stagnation; 2) thaw, reforms, turmoil, disintegration of the state; 3) economic recovery; and 4) strong state.

In terms of resources, these phases are cardinally different. At times of stagnation, the state monopolizes the accumulation of resources, their import and export, as well as distribution among the population. The state determines who is to receive the resources, including how much and what kind, how and where to store them, and how to use-consume them. The state regulates all material flows. Any movement or possession of resources beyond state control is illegal.

The state focuses all efforts on achieving a certain goal—winning the war against an ideological enemy, building socialism, developing nuclear or missile weapons, etc. The administrative market is unified; it permeates all relations between elements of the state structure and the people, thus compensating the inevitable errors in resource planning and distribution. Redistribution of resources is common, repressive measures against those who divert resources are mild.

---

138 The management procedure is variable; it depends on the circumstances. Codification of the management procedure will give rise to numerous comments, supplements, and instructions to the Codes that will embody the procedure and serve as guidelines for the bureaucrats. In a resource-based system, laws are needed to qualify violations of the procedure, whereas the procedure itself is established by the rule of law. It is sufficient to reveal a violation of the management procedure, and a court of the "Basmanny justice" system (kangaroo court) will not hesitate to find an appropriate article in the criminal code to justify the sentence.

Periods of stability are also characterized by a fusion of economy and politics and severe restrictions on the political activity of the population. Resource plunderers are either included in the administrative-market relations (by taking positions in trade, distribution, and various security and law enforcement bodies) or forced to the sidelines of life. Potential appanage princes (at different times—heads of administrations, governors, secretaries of party committees) know their place in the administrative hierarchy and, to be on the safe side, prefer not to rock the boat.

This does not exclude princely, thievish or bandit manifestations. Jabber about regional self-determination and ethno-cultural features, inappropriate use of public funds, and administrative mugging—these shadow aspects are present in the life of both regions and capitals even in stable times.

People have access to resources only in accordance with their public status and appropriate established status requirements. Resources are distributed among social groups in a centralized manner. The social groups have a defined place in the social system of accounting and control. There are sovereign bodies that distribute resource flows. All elements of the economic order, including people, are defined in terms of social accounting and ranked according to their role in achieving the great national goal. Executives are more important than subordinates, engineers are more important than workers, and the military are more important than civil bureaucrats.

Depending on their importance, group members receive rations and get access to distribution outlets and other material benefits. The needs are reduced to the regulatory minimum and any consumption in excess thereof is punished. Resource plunderers are forced to the sidelines of socialist life; redistribution of resources in everyday life is limited to exchanging withheld or stolen trifles. Propaganda depicts shortages as sacrifices inevitable on the way to achieving the great goal.

The situation reverses during the next phase—depression. Political and economic freedoms grow, but resource plunderers seize a substantial part of the social space. The mobilizing potential of the central idea disappears into nowhere, the idea itself becomes the focus of political jokes, and the functioning of the government machine largely loses purpose. The unitary structure of the state weakens; regions gain power, express discontent, and hold back resources. Government regulation of resource policy decreases, and the population blames particular officials or the state in general for the shortages. People are no longer content to keep their requirements within the statutory levels and want more and more resources. They get those resources through "violating the management procedure" and by "unlawful means", since there are no legitimate ways of appropriating resources under a resource-based arrangement of public life. Those who can, start plundering resources. Stability remains only as a reminiscence of "order under Stalin".

The state launches a fight against crime. The very struggle against crime becomes a way of redistributing resources from one sector to another, from one group of "siloviki" to another. That was the case in the 1980s, when the Interior Ministry and the KGB clashed over the right to control resources. As a result, tens and hundreds of thousands, sometimes, millions of people are repressed, as it happened under Stalin's infamous decrees "on spikelets" of 1934 and 1947.

If times of trouble are not cut short by repression, depression aggravates, and the state actually dissolves in relations between formally defined statuses that remain statuses only because they have been included in administrative markets in the era of the state's dissolution, where resources are exchanged—bartered. The regions "cut loose" and the unitary state actually becomes a federation.

Citizens of the state, including officials, conceal their thievish ambitions no longer, claiming that they thus take the edge off overall shortages. Conditions for capitalizing resources and turning them into economic reality materialize; money and goods appear; the semblance of a market starts taking shape; illusionary exchanges, banks, and share capital adapted to the task of plundering resources emerge. The state loses its monopoly on repression. Along with resources, the new resource managers obtain the right to repress those who breach the procedure of their distribution and utilization. Repression takes the form of murdering violators of the resource management procedure.

Life brims with adventure to the point of the state's collapse. The twentieth century witnessed two such periods. Both times—at great cost—the state recovered, regained control over the appanage princes, forced some plunderers to the social sidelines, and absorbed the others providing them with an appropriate status. At times of change, a moment inevitably comes when thieves have nothing to steal, bandits have no one to rob, and appanage principalities encounter their own separatists and autonomists.

In times of trouble, quasi-political life flourishes. Great ideas are publicly denounced and ridiculed in campaigns like "glasnost" losing their remaining mobilizing role. Numerous pseudo-political organizations emerge, picking out names for themselves from the always relevant history. Legitimized resource plunderers readily finance such organizations.

Joint efforts of the plunderers and their accomplices from among the feudal intelligentsia create an illusion of political life and "real market economy". These dummies are needed, primarily, to convert the stolen resources into goods and money. In addition, the existence of the quasi-market gives plunderers the opportunity to quit the game, i.e., to settle down beyond the boundaries of the state. Appanage princes tear the country apart. Disintegration is advantageous, because it generates huge amounts of ownerless resources.

In the next phase, when the inability to mobilize resources becomes critical, a period of economic recovery sets in. The remaining government apparatus, already largely deprived of the ability to dispose of resources, has to compromise with some resource plunderers to fight the others in order to mobilize resources for localizing emergencies. This happened in Chechnya, where the feudal ambitions of the Soviet autonomy evolved into an extensive war, for which the state acutely lacked resources.

The price of such compromise is always the same. The re-emerging government security and law enforcement bodies eliminate some plunderers in favor of the others, and the state redistributes resources to the situational allies. This serves to overcome autonomist and separatist trends. The state monopolizes the right to repression and becomes unitary again. That was the case in 2000−2005.

The state embarks on a quest for a major idea-goal that would allow it to return to a consolidated state where all the resources are under control; the plunderers receive a public status and are eliminated as a class.

While the quest for the idea goes on, the state launches a redistribution of assets and partial nationalization. In the process, the resources of the most notorious individuals are turned from goods and money into resources of other individuals. Redistribution is justified by the allegation that new owners of resources are more state-minded than the previous ones. Actually, the resource plunderers receive a brief opportunity to convert the accumulated resources into a status in the new, emerging, system of resource management relations. The smartest ones manage to grab this opportunity, while the others fall victim to the self-restoring repressive system. The cycle is completed, the state is strong again, and the next stagnation begins.

***

Today we can say that the path to capitalism initiated in the 1990s by doctors of political economy of socialism has led to an impasse—to new socialism. Following the depression-perestroika, at the beginning of the twenty-first century the country entered the phase of resource growth and launched a new stage of specifically Russian socialist construction. As in Soviet times, the social stability of the resource-based state relies on the pursuit of a just distribution of resources. However, our society has neither developed, nor recognized new fairness criteria; therefore, any distribution of resources is deemed unfair by the population and generates social tension. Moreover, Soviet experience shows that every distributed resource is likely to become scarce. Shortage of money as a resource can escalate into a loss of control over inflation. A potential shortage of raw materials as a resource can become a fact if the export and domestic commitments on energy commodities taken by the state are not matched by higher production and reserve growth. Finally, status as a resource may become scarce due to the general crisis of the government system.

Each one of these shortage crises is unlikely to pose a serious risk to the resource-based state as such. By robbing the population yet again, the state will overcome inflation and ensure the required level of raw material output using repressive measures to mobilize "labor resources". If the shortage of money and raw materials stays within certain boundaries, the state will be able to stabilize the government system and retain the existing power statuses even without a state ideology and with the inevitable uncertainty when transferring power through elections. However, should shortages synchronize and the crisis of government coincide in time with the commodity and financial ones, the resource-based state may collapse in a way similar to what happened to the USSR in 1991. This will mean the end of yet another cycle in our history. Or the beginning.

Relations of the estate-based order with the external world: "forming the resource base", importing and adopting

According to the precise expression of V. M. Shironin, a resource-based system can add, subtract and divide resources. But it cannot multiply them. A resource-based system adds—"expands the resource base" through geographic (including subsoil) and geopolitical expansion, regarding foreign territories, markets, and capital as resource sources that should be appropriated and distributed according to social justice principles. Such activity is usually referred to as "work on forming the resource base". Social dynamics in a resource-based state consist primarily in expanding the resource base, in acquiring resources. The very fact of possessing resources symbolizes the power of the state, its prosperity. An estate-based society perceives even a relative decrease of resources at the state's disposal as depression. Therefore, an aggressive domestic and foreign policy is always necessary to form the resource base. Any constraint on expansion, internal or external, triggers tension in the resource-based system, increases the already acute shortages, and, respectively, aggravates conflicts between estates for the distributable resources. Expansionist ideology was at the core of the Soviet world order concept, since the world would be able to acquire features of the bright future only after the global triumph of the Soviet-style estate structure and elimination of the free market with its replacement by "fair" resource distribution.

In forming the resource base, contemporary Russia differs from the Soviet Union primarily by having to compete for resources with multinational corporations as much as with other states. To participate in such competition, Russia itself has to create such equivalents of multinational corporations as Rosneft, Gazprom, and Rosatom. Naturally, other states and corporations resist potential capitals being treated as resources. The estate system interprets this attitude as hostile towards the resources-based order, as a threat. The resource-based state is always ready to fight its enemies. Its servicemen are eager to engage in combat and prepare for it continuously—they serve and facilitate service "on neutralizing external and internal threats", especially since identifying the enemy means allocation of resources to fight it. In fact, such a struggle is the main task of the state service, which focuses primarily on alienating and utilizing resources, even if those resources are represented by the capitals of "oligarchs", other socio-economic systems, multinational corporations, or mineral deposits.

Domestic tension (triggered by unfair distribution of resources among the estates) is traditionally considered more dangerous than the international one. In order to avoid generalization of domestic conflicts or mitigate them ("feed the people"), the resource-based state has to expand outwards, all the time utilizing new resources. It is in principle insatiable. However, a time comes when such a state can no longer expand its resource base, when it encounters severe constraints. As a result, endless complaints about lack of resources evolve into social revolutions liquidating the old estates and replacing them by new ones.

For a resource-based state, permanent expansion in all directions and aspects would be ideal, provided such expansion is not restricted. Land, water, air, and outer space—everything must "serve the people" as a totality of estates. According to the principal idea of this world order, nature and society should "serve the people", however, not all of them, but those who adhere to correct ideas of rebuilding the world. The ideal was achieved after World War II, when the USSR seemed so powerful that nothing could stop its expansion in any environment. The states included in the resource base because of expansion were subjected to policies tested in the process of building socialism—mass repression aimed at eliminating the old social structure and creating new Soviet-style estates. Locally established communist parties with their staffing criteria and nomenklatura controlled by the CPSU and the KGB organized and guided this process.

However, in implementing this strategy, the Soviet estate world encountered rigid internal and external constraints to expansion, where no increase of available resources could reduce the overall shortages. Rather, vice versa, the shortages aggravated proportionately to the efforts made by the CPSU to distribute resources fairly. Finally, complaints about unfair distribution started to accelerate and developed into perestroika with its disastrous consequences for the Soviet system. As I already mentioned, the collapse of the estate system resulted in the emergence of the markets, which for a time compensated the shortages. However, the current reinstatement of the estate system and resource-based economy, associated with reduced market freedoms, demonstrates that little has changed in the logic of our country's social order.

***

Of course, not all relations with the outside world can be expansionist. Largely, they involve adoption. The estate society perceives the outside world as a source of resources—unique resources, which the estate system does not and, probably, never can have. However, the estate system needs these resources, because efficient service, especially the struggle with internal and external enemies, is impossible without them. It is primarily a question of scientific and technical developments and technologies based on scientific knowledge about the outside—not social—world.

Where the needed resources can be neither stolen nor adopted, they have to be bought. Buying, however, requires real money. The state must obtain this money (currency). In the first decade of its existence, the Soviet government simply expropriated currency from the population or made it from selling works of art collected during imperial times to the "bourgeoisie". Subsequently, the search for goods that the accursed imperialists would buy constituted a quite important activity in the resource-based state. First, the state exported grain requisitioned from the "kulaks"; then came the turn of coal and metals produced by forced labor of these same kulaks, labor army members, deportees, and prisoners. Oil and gas replaced grain, coal, and metals as export goods.

Throughout the existence of the Soviet regime, the search for resources to sell abroad in order to buy everything needed for estate building never stopped. The experience of industrialization shows that leaving the country without bread and its population starving to death is less important than exchanging requisitioned resources for imported factories, technology, equipment, technical specialists, and consumer goods for further distribution among members of the privileged estates. The servicemen of today are guided by the same logic when they enter into long-term contracts for the export of energy commodities although the requirements of the population in energy resources are rather poorly met. They believe the people will somehow get along as they have always done, although some may probably freeze to death—for the glory of an energy superpower ideology.

Importing equipment, technology, and scientific knowledge has been (and remains) a specific feature of the estate world order. The Empire, the Soviet Union, and contemporary Russia—all imported technological advances, especially in the form of weapons and household appliances. Imports and distribution of such resources is a familiar and everyday affair, and the products of the domestic "light" industry are rarely original—usually they are relatively good copies of Western or now rather Eastern goods. Crafts thrive in an estate-based society, but it never comes to technology—the "socio-economic system" is not appropriate for that. Crafts allow manufacturing unique items, shoeing a flea, but they do not promote technological development. Even organizing mass production of consumer goods has always been a state issue, most often addressed by setting up a special estate and providing it with appropriate resources based on respective decrees of the CPSU Central Committee and the USSR Council of Ministers. Besides, not every technology could be imported—there have been and there remain stringent restrictions on importing weapons, military equipment, and related technology. Such products must be manufactured domestically. However, first, it is necessary to "obtain" ideas, prototypes, drawings and layouts. This is achieved by a special activity, which consists in monitoring and evaluating foreign scientific and technical developments and, where necessary, seizing knowledge, technology, and individual products to be subsequently adopted by domestic science and industry.[139] After the service people perform their duty to the Motherland and "obtain" whatever is required, it is necessary to set up "state of the art production" in an environment where this is impossible in principle, because such production is incompatible with the resource-based organization of the state and the estate structure.

This challenging task is addressed by breaching locally the estate order principles and creating "special conditions to overcome the technological and scientific gap with potential adversaries". In the process of overcoming this gap, "P.O. Boxes", "closed cities", "industrial parks", "technopoles" ("naukograds"), and "free economic zones" emerge on the vast territory of the country, where semblances of scientific and technological centers of the capitalist economy and even elements of the capitalist lifestyle are created. These oases are partly withdrawn from the general estate jurisdiction—resource management procedure; they are governed by their own laws, including laws of distributing resources purposefully, without administrative bargaining. This targeted distribution of resources (for manufacturing a certain "product" and not for activity on utilizing the allocated resources) allowed creating domestic missiles, bombs, and radars. The social result of such activity is the establishment of an estate of scientists and design engineers, who are not fully integrated into the estate world order. They are not ordinary public sector workers; rather, in current terms, they are independent professionals supporting state services.

---

[139] The scale of such activity in the USSR is evidenced by the so-called *Farewell Dossier,* which contains data from the annual report of the Military-Industrial Commission of the USSR Council of Ministers handed over to France by an officer of the KGB scientific and technical intelligence service // The New Times 2004. 2 Feb.

Such "zones" have a special social structure, where the core service consists in manufacturing "the product" and all other services are reduced to the status of facilitating and supporting ones. Thus, administrative departments of the USSR Academy of Sciences and state research institutes controlled virtually all distribution in "Academic towns" ("akademgorodok"). However, after the special regime is lifted and ordinary utilization of budget resources takes place, the reason for which such oases had been created disappears. With time, they turn into estate-based universes with a privileged touch (sometimes separated from the rest of Russia by a barbed wire fence and security perimeter demonstrating the distinctness from the ordinary estate world order), as happened with Soviet closed administrative-territorial formations (ZATO) and academic towns.

In spite of thus sacrificing the principles of the estate world order, "implementing" inventions and, in general, any innovative technologies were and remain a headache for the estate-based system, primarily because innovations change the resource distribution structure, thus triggering substantially more problems in inter-estate relations than settling. Therefore, for an estate world order, "technical upgrading" and "introduction of scientific and technical innovations" represents primarily a social problem.

Importing worldviews and knowledge of the society— the art of imitation

I have already mentioned that the ability to formulate social stratification concepts and develop appropriate theories arises only in a class society when attempting to provide a scientific description and build a body of knowledge about this society. In contrast, the estate-based society is closed for scientific reflection about its arrangement, when the researcher is a member of this society. Myths and legends, fiction and works of art, as well as value systems, sometimes taking the form of teleology (like Marxist-Leninist and similar philosophies) serve to depict and explain how an estate society is organized. From within the estate society, its member can rationally explain neither its structure, nor his own place in it. He explains it irrationally—through a myth, story, saga, legend, or work of fiction. Intellectuals regarded by other members of the estate society as cultural and social science figures create the myths.

Historic space and time, the actual social structure and economic relations exist in intellectual myth-making only because of their artistic (literary-visual) presentation. The reasoning dominating the estate society is based on myths created by intellectuals about "true life" and about "what actually happened" in combination with the opinions of intellectual experts. This social system treats such reasoning as scientific, although that is not the case. Once again, no reflection on the social structure is possible in such a society, because the institutions of positive (verifiable and falsifiable) knowledge appear only after (or in parallel) separating politics from the economy and the state from the society, i.e., when the estate system collapses and a class one emerges.[140]

Thus, intellectual myth-making replaces social sciences in an estate-based society. Science as an activity aimed at splitting the existent into parts-concepts followed by a theoretical reconstruction of the world as a whole (or its fragments) based on experimental validation of the initially identified concepts does not, and probably, cannot exist in such a society. A special place in this pseudo-scientific myth-making is reserved for imported constructions—scientific knowledge obtained by foreign researchers and adapted to domestic mythologized realities by intellectual experts on society. The body of adopted knowledge constitutes the main content of the so-called social sciences. However, I believe that humanitarian scientific knowledge, unlike the natural scientific one, cannot be adopted, alienated from the parent—market basis and transferred to the estate world order without fundamental distortions, primarily, because its targets—people and the relations between them—differ essentially in estate and class societies. In the course of importing economic ideas and theories, groups of "progressive scientists—reformers and patriots" emerge.

---

140   It is no mere chance that "outbreaks" of humanitarian scientific reflection in Russia coincide with revolutionary and reformist "times of trouble". As long as politics and the economy are united with the state-society in a contradictory but syncretic form, no rational self-knowledge can emerge in estate-based societies.

They speak, respectively, an "economic reformist" or "patriotic" language, which can hardly be used to depict the phenomena of the domestic resource-based life, but serves well to depict the bright future that will emerge after the imported theory materializes. The fact that not a single imported theory of an ideal social order can describe such a unique hybrid of obvious estate stratification and latent class nature as our country was, is and, probably, will always be, does not disturb the reformers and patriots.

A scientific description of Russian realities is impossible because of the different status that scientific knowledge has in an estate-resource-based state and a market economy. In a modern state with a class structure knowledge about this structure is directly or indirectly (through mass media or political institutions) incorporated in the social order, whereas in an estate-based system social knowledge cannot be consolidated and formalized in a way traditional for science. As I have already mentioned, knowledge about the estate-based society-state is scattered among its members. It exists in the form of gossip, rumors, myths, and mythologems expressed in works of fiction and art,[141] but not at all in the form of facts and relating theories. This is primarily knowledge about the origin and estate affiliation of various individuals; their resources and the associates who have access to their distribution; methods by which these resources had been consolidated; who and when had been caught stealing them, and what was the respective punishment. Such knowledge is neither verifiable, nor falsifiable; it is in principle not unscientific—it is pre-scientific. Such knowledge is non-operational, it has intrinsic value and means little outside the context of particular intra- and inter-estate relations. It is produced, replicated, and imposed on members of the existing estates by means of the estate-driven mass media (various propaganda and agitation institutions): through school textbooks, artistic works, TV serials, analytical and news programs, etc. This mythological knowledge largely deter-

---

141 That is why the domestic perception of the world is art-centric (literature-centric). After all, art in general and literature in particular play the same role in it as science does in market societies. I believe it is no coincidence that the most significant worldview findings in our country were obtained, from my point of view, in art criticism. Literature, movies, music, and, especially, art criticism, but not science formed the worldview (if any) of USSR citizens.

mines the estate members' mode of behavior. It is, therefore, a resource for the distribution of which estates keenly compete with each other. Indeed, if knowledge becomes a resource, according to social justice principles it must be handled by respective estates—scientists representing public sector workers and independent professionals. Guided by logic quite adequate for a resource-based social system, members of these estates strive to monopolize the resources of knowledge and to distribute knowledge as such. Since these social scientists can have no own sources of knowledge (there is no empirical research and original mythological constructions are rejected— generally, their authors do not belong to the estate of scientists), they adopt knowledge "from abroad" posing in the public sphere as "progressive" or "patriotic" ideologists, political scientists, sociologists or economists.[142]

Centuries-old attempts to import theories and ideas implement the logic described above, according to which knowledge about the domestic social system can be imported, distributed, and utilized to be later incorporated into the system of national perceptions of the social world, thus likening this world to the "abroad". Such imported knowledge underlies all attempts to reform the estate world order and resource-based economy.

Domestic social sciences are a myth-making substitute of science, which allows intellectual experts on society to display an illusion of knowledge without describing the estate-based reality. Domestic social sciences do not focus on describing reality. Their task is to "remedy shortcomings", "intensify", "modernize", "reform", etc. those aspects of estate life, which the authorities have indicated as imperfect.

---

142 I believe the line of the most significant importers of theories and concepts in modern history starts with Peter the Great, who imported principles of state organization from Holland. He was followed by Catherine II, who in her "Instruction" ("Nakaz") to the Legislative Commission laid the foundation of the domestic estate order based on knowledge about the European social stratification system, which was undergoing transformation into a class structure. Then came Speransky and company, who attempted to revise the estate structure using imported knowledge about what was happening in Europe; Lenin and company, who imported socialist ideas; academicians, corresponding members, doctors and candidates of Marxist-Leninist sciences, who imported the most appealing "progressive economic and political theories" from "the West" to serve as a basis for perestroika and "the construction of capitalism".

The main objective of Russian pro-government economists, political and social scientists is "assisting the authorities" rather than studying reality. Conversely, if they consider themselves to be in opposition, they engage in a mythological struggle with the authorities. In exact accordance with the estate order principles, intellectual experts on society can either facilitate various services and fulfill "the assignments of the party and government" when in service, or support them even as dissidents. No more than that.

In particular, political science with its notions of democracy and law, i.e., formal equality of citizens before the law, is a common tool for describing modern societies. However, distinctions of political science are applicable to our reality only in relatively brief periods of reforms and revolutions. In contrast to democracy, the estate way of life is an organized form of inequality before law experienced by members of different estates. The form of this organization—estate-based principles of coordinating interests—is incompatible with politics and the political order. Perhaps, that is the reason why all attempts to establish democracy in Russia always ended in establishing its non-functional and short-living imitations.

Political scientists also rely on imported perceptions to evaluate the role of the public space, mass media, and the civil society in our socio-state structure. Intellectual journalists, politicians, and scientists, for whom transferring social institutions from the countries they "like" to our reality has become the purpose of their life, never stop talking about the necessity of free media, a civil society, and a transparent government. However, in periods of relative stability, an estate-based society does not and cannot have a public space similar to that in democratic societies, because it is otherwise organized—it has no public and can have no civil society.[143] Openness is incompatible with an estate-based distribution of resources, administrative markets, and estate rent. Openness goes against their nature.

At times other than reforms, various coffee klatches and neighborly get-togethers, estate meetings, clubs-saunas, and other similar institutions serve as a functional equivalent of openness. TV pro-

---

143 For details, see: Kordonsky S. *The state, civil society and corruption.* Otechestvennye Zapiski, No.5 2005.

grams, newspapers, magazines, and other information sources outwardly resembling democratic media do not and cannot contain information about facts, relations, and events important for estate members simply because such information is in principle not available. Instead, they carry rumors, gossip, and anecdotes, which the estate members hear, remember and pass on, thus getting an idea of what is happening and what shortage they should brace themselves for. In times of stability, these rumors and gossip spread by word of mouth, through "samizdat", or, as now, through the Internet. At times of reforms, "glasnost" sets in, and the nuances of inter-estate relations become the subject of public debate and condemnation by "progressive journalists".

Therefore, technical means, which in democratic societies serve to fill the public space with information meaningful for all citizens, in our estate-based society disseminate rumors, gossip, and anecdotes. Not least, they are intended for entertainment adapted by intellectual independent TV and printed media professionals to their perception of the cultural needs of public sector workers, pensioners, merchants, employees, military officers, and various officials. In an estate-based system, experts on society and independent professionals are strictly distinguished according to the service they facilitate or support—state civil, military or law enforcement service.

A special role in supporting the estate-based society is reserved for sociology—a science that in stable times can have no subject in our world order, since it has been developed as a science about class society and does not possess the conceptual framework to describe estate-based systems. At its peak, the USSR had no sociology. Sociological concepts and methods were imported by intellectual experts on society close to government only at the time when even members of the Communist Party Politburo became aware that something was wrong in the country. "Giving the green light to sociology" was a symptom of the system's internal weakness—something that true Marxist-Leninists did not want to acknowledge and, therefore, exerted pressure on the sociologists. Largely because of this pressure, sociology became trendy; it attracted dissidents from all Soviet estates, however, this did not add meaning to the results of their research.

Soviet sociologists studied the population as a statistical aggregate of individuals, entering basic estate characteristics (which respective competent bodies allowed to enter) into questionnaire guides and not reflecting (in my view) on what they were doing. In this way, they researched culture, science, personnel turnover, living standards of the population, migration, reading preferences, theater interests, and the audiences of the communist party mass media. Based on the findings of their research, they sent analytical memoranda to party bodies, which sometimes took respective decisions. The results of sociological research were most spectacularly applied in the 1960s in a decision to optimize the network of rural settlements. By encouraging migration from small villages to rural centers, from rural centers to district centers and so on, this move triggered the social desertification of the country.

What remains of this sociology are organizations conducting statistical research of the public opinion "in general" (which in an estate-based society does not and cannot exist outside of estates) and numerous university departments and institutes. Since these latter have virtually no in-house studies and field research data, their main activity consists in staff members visiting "global sociological centers" abroad, and reading and reproducing orally and in writing the works of foreign classics of sociology (according to their choice of the classics and their understanding of how Russia is organized). Reproducing the methods of their foreign colleagues, sociologists have been vainly trying to find in Russia the subject of their research—the class structure, especially, the middle class.

Public opinion studies consist mainly in respective government and government-related research organizations creating a permanent simulation of elections and associated processes. They ask the respondents to make a choice in a situation simulating elections to various authorities. Based on their responses, the sociologists conclude "who would win" if the elections were to be held the next day. The basic estate structure, which is still open for research (until the moment when the estate order triumphs completely and what our society calls science becomes a part of the ideological mechanism), remains outside the scope of sociologists simply because the works of foreign sociologists that they use as a guide in their polling techniques contain only vague hints at its existence.

The concepts of economics, which is focused on studying free markets and regards shortage-based social systems as anomalies, is another no less significant attribute of imported descriptions.[144] Obviously, it is impracticable to use these concepts to describe and analyze a social system where public life consists in managing, concentrating, storing, distributing, utilizing, and writing off resources. Economic concepts are more or less adequate only during the collapse of the resource-based economy, in the relatively short periods of turmoil. Experience shows that all attempts "to build the market" or "introduce market principles" using theories of intellectual economists ended in a return to the resource-based economy. However, the inapplicability of traditional imported conceptual frameworks to the description of domestic realities only stimulates economists to repeat their attempts, always chanting that the country vitally needs a market and democracy.

It is well know known that economics is based on empirical information, primarily, on economic statistics. Nevertheless, domestic economists have none. Soviet statistics tailored to capture the processes and results of estate-based distribution and utilization of resources has virtually collapsed, and Russian statistics is non-existent, mainly because there is no scientific reflection on the resource-based nature of the Russian economy. Economists try to apply accounting and modeling methods and techniques developed for market economies to processes taking place in the domestic resource-based economy. The result is obvious. There are volumes of figures, which devout liberal economists interpret as the onset of economic disaster[145], whereas bureaucrats facilitating "management of the economy" tend to believe that prosperity is forthcoming—the amount of resources at the state's disposal increases in proportion to the "consolidation of the vertical of power". Servicemen believe that what they take for eco-

---

144 Kornai J. *Shortage*. M., 1992.
145 Illarionov A. *State based on force: preliminary results* // Kommersant. 2007. 12 September

nomic growth is constrained only by an inadequate resource base, therefore, their main concern is to expand it.

The social placelessness specific for domestic scientists is just an outward manifestation of their confused status, because social scientists are either intellectual independent professionals supporting various state services, or old-time public sector workers striving to "carve up" the funds allocated by the state for the development of education, science, culture, and mass media. Ideology, culture, and science in the state-estate unity mainly represent forms of estateness rather than productive activities.

With rare exceptions, members of the estates of scientists and cultural figures are public sector workers, who assert their claims for resources for scientific and other activities. Generally, they lack resources for their core activity—obtaining new knowledge and creating cultural values—and that is the only thing they speak about. Real achievements and results in science and culture emerge, as a rule, in spite of the estate-based state system rather than owing to it. This is evidenced by numerous memoirs of "prominent Soviet scientists and cultural figures" describing how the superiors, resembling by habits and ways despotic feudal lords, interfered with their work.

***

In an estate-based world order, the humanities are mainly engaged in citing recognized and trivial results. It was therefore mandatory that experts on society in the USSR refer to writings of Marxist-Leninist classics, and the key quality parameter of a scientific work was its alignment with the core myths. Similarly, contemporary Russian experts on society must speak English, quote "classics of world science", and refer to recent foreign publications. The culmination of their professional achievements are publications abroad and participation in international scientific events.[146] I believe that productive activities in

---

146 The *Polit.ru* website launched a debate on a conflict at the sociological department of the Moscow State University. Participants of the discussion provided "clear criteria" of the scientific character of modern Russian sociology - knowledge of English, knowledge of the writings of contemporary western sociologists, and scientific publications abroad. No one even mentioned the need to ob-

science and culture are rejected because they produce unapportioned resources in the form of new knowledge. The process of dividing—"carving" them up is so brutal and conflict-prone that it is much easier and safer to utilize the existing "classical" conceptual resources or import knowledge than research the domestic reality. New knowledge obtained from empirical research is usually rejected if it does not fit into the existing patterns of "carving up" resources allocated for social studies—the system of institutes, departments, training courses, and occupations. When creative activity brings new resources that have value for estate building, their distribution generally requires establishing a new estate stratum, institutionalizing an activity new for the system—a research institute, college, department,—and introduce new occupations as a form of estate accounting. However, the overall effect from creating the new resource is in this case minimal, as the outflow of other resources to institutionalize it generally exceeds the potential expansion of the resource base. I believe, that was the reason why the Soviet Union resisted innovations, and why "implementing the achievements of science and technology", as well as scientific, ideological, and artistic creative activity constituted a non-trivial task, most often addressed by importing ideas, technology, and products. In culture and art, the country imported the creations of its emigrants who had preserved the Russian cultural identity. This approach does not require changing the customary pattern of "carving up" resources. When developing the ideological "agenda", the estate politicians today still principally refer to emigrants and dissidents who had served prison terms—Ivan Ilyin, Solonevich, Solzhenitsyn—or to similar le0073s prominent public figures, using them as a source of ideas, concepts, interpretations, and most importantly, social facts.

The situation with empirical knowledge about the country has been paradoxical for many years. On the one hand, resolutions of the Communist Party and the government, presidential decrees and other regulatory acts determined and still determine all aspects of life. On the other hand, few of the authorities' directives are ever fulfilled, and the country lives its own life, often contrary to the official policy. The

---

tain empirical knowledge and conduct sociological research of the domestic reality. See: http://www.polit.ru/story/sozfak_2.html

country is completely known, so that there seems nothing to study other than regulations and their implementation progress. However, it is also completely unknown, so that it is even impossible to formulate research objectives—respective concepts are lacking.

Scientific, technological, and ideological dependence on all kinds of imports has become commonplace and at least four generations of national leaders have been talking about ways to overcome it. Such discourse generally accompanies presentation of plans to build yet another bright future. However, no one has yet attempted to find out the reasons for failures of previous practitioners of estate construction and estate myth-makers, except for charges of treachery, heavy drinking, illness, etc. against leaders already removed from power. Before building something yet again, we should understand why previous generations failed to build a bright future and what impedes our "bad dancers"—the reformers. Besides, it would be useful to clarify the definition of "resources", which only the laziest do not insist on increasing, and the meaning of "state service", which neither the researchers, nor the servicemen mention.

As far as I know, political scientists, sociologists, and economists encumbered by imported stereotypes do not bother to research these phenomena, which are extremely meaningful in our country. Instead, they prefer to personify the reasons of failures or attribute them to inadequate imported theories applied by respective builders of the bright future.

***

Theories of "progressive" social orders with their stratifications had been adopted two hundred, a hundred, and twenty years ago. Operating on the basis of these theories, sociologists today do not think twice about the social structure of our society—they postulate that it is a class (or estate-class) society and search for indicators of class stratification or occupational differentiation. In defiance of the obvious, they assume that social groups in our society form by themselves without the state's participation. These scientists even study occupational differentiation as if it were a natural market phenomenon based on the demand for skilled labor and its supply rather than a product of external management of educational institutions focused primarily on estate socialization. Adopted research methods and techniques do not imply the existence of such obviously "man-made" groups; therefore, research can at best result in knowledge of a certain similarity between domestic and foreign social structures, but definitely not in scientific knowledge about domestic social stratification. Continued attempts to understand (by inadequate means) how our society is arranged are motivated by the emergence of a social structure in Russia (despite the seeming structurelessness of the social order, regardless of numerous attempted reconstructions), which neither the politicians, nor the researchers, whose outlook is determined by imported stereotypes, can grasp. Just like the builders of the "new empire", the builders of democracy and capitalism refuse to accept the existent. They focus on the future and hope their efforts will lead to the emergence of a consumer society with the upper, middle, and lower classes, whose interests will integrate in the political institutions of representative power. Alternatively, a rigid estate structure will appear where the united Russian people will resist its enemies—Zionists, radical Islamists, agents of influence of geopolitical opponents and others.

Currently, various progressionists focused on establishing a class structure occupy virtually the entire "public space", which is shrinking as the estate system develops. Much less known are other builders of the bright future—traditionalists,—who justify the need to return to the estate structure, specific, as they believe, for Imperial Russia. Thus, Aleksandr Eliseev writes, "At a point, the party system emerged as an alternative to the system of estates. The party became a certain laboratory where representatives of different estates created an averaged hybrid human type. One can call this type bourgeois, although it only remotely resembles the "third estate", which existed in a traditional society. Medieval entrepreneurs represented a distinctive cultural type. However, the bourgeoisie sought social hegemony and tried to reshape all the other estates by making them similar to themselves. The result was a cocktail, where bourgeois features were the main component, albeit diluted by other social components. The party was that pot, which brewed the cocktail of modern and contemporary bourgeoisness.

Having emerged in pre-revolutionary Russia, parties became an alternative to the traditional way of life. It is noteworthy that the subversive, progressionist forces started laying the foundation for their regime long before the victory of the revolution. They did not rely on work in the traditional structures of the Russian society, although they did not completely ignore it (thus, the liberals almost completely occupied local (zemstvo) self-government bodies). The main focus, however, was on establishing their social order. Should the liberals and socialists have limited their activity to the zemstvo level, this would have only benefited the tsarist government. The opposition would have let the steam out, thereby strengthening the existing order.

Traditionalists focusing on general civil political structures are doomed to act strictly within the framework of the liberal order opposing nothing to it."[147]

In their analysis and predictions, the traditionalists rely on writings of rather specific imported theorists, such as Othmar Spann,[148] famous, in particular, for substantiating fascism as an ideal corporate state. Perhaps, that is why public discussion of the issues, opportunities, and constraints of the current estate structure is a taboo and does not extend beyond the marginalized groups.

Advocates of democracy and the market relying on liberal imported theories now clearly dominate the public sphere, politics, and rhetoric, whereas the traditionalists that rely on conservative imported theories seem to be marginalized. However, state-building practice is dominated by an unreflected traditionalist paradigm, which underlies the adoption of estate laws and the development of relations between the post-Soviet estates.

The ideology of the estate system is by nature essentially fundamentalist and patriotic, focused on explicating ideas from the past (ideas once imported, but so long ago that no one knows their origin except for narrow specialists) and asserting them in the present. As for the ideology of our market-related domestic democracy, it is essentially progressionist, i.e., focused on the future—regardless of the present and the past.

---

147 Eliseev A. See: http://www.pravaya.ru/look/2135
148 Spann O. See: http://russamos.narod.ru/03-last-2.htm

The current search of Russian scientists, politicians, and ideologists for a national idea is all the more comical that the state has long formulated such an idea and is implementing it in the estate-based reconstruction of our social reality. It seems, however, that the ultimate purpose remains indefinite—either "orthodoxy, autocracy, and nationality" or "social justice".

Socialization and its institutions in an estate-based society[149]

The institution of education plays a special role in an estate-base society. Its functions include providing social mobility, i.e., the opportunity of transition from one estate to another. Education is currently experiencing the most acute conflict between the emerging estate system, on the one hand, and the stagnating market and political system, on the other hand. If education is meant to train specialists for market work, the criticism it is subjected to leads to believe that for different reasons neither the authorities, nor the public, teachers, students, or employers are happy with its current level. In response to this dissatisfaction, the authorities are permanently reforming the system of higher education without any visible progress.

Innovative administrative reforms in no way impede the existing mechanism of higher education, the demand for which is steadily increasing. University and college rectors insist that there is no need to change anything, that the education system in their establishments meets social requirements. They believe it is necessary to increase the amount of allocated resources—enhance compensation to faculty, raise student scholarships, upgrade the material base, and provide housing to young teachers.

According to the general opinion, the system of higher education does not train specialists, with the rare exception of several universities and colleges whose graduates mostly emigrate. More precisely, this system trains specialists for the largely extinct Soviet estate structure. Employers from among market actors have no need for such

---

149   The author used research data obtained by Reuters news agency.

specialists; they require something completely different. According to employers, they have to train the graduates from scratch rather than just retrain them. However, they fail to formulate what exactly they teach the graduates that the latter do not study at universities. In general, employers do not care what knowledge and skills a university graduate possesses. They are mainly interested in the young person's alma mater, his or her soft skills, and the ability to learn and establish business relations. What the employers need is "social training". A university graduate becomes an estate member (subject to adequate social qualities) after lengthy socialization at the workplace.

In spite of its name, the education system actually performs the function of estate socialization. This function is the main, albeit unreflected objective. While studying, the students socialize in a semblance of an "estate environment" simulated at the university or other institution and master the basics of its language (terminology) and behavioral stereotypes. However, not the estate worldview and ideology.

Higher education institutions train young people for the state civil and law enforcement services, for work in ministries, agencies, and supervisory bodies.[150] Some regional universities train personnel for regional state service. The schools of various uniformed agencies prepare for military and law enforcement services, and numerous industry educational institutions train future members of their occupational estates—doctors, agronomists, and builders. The leading uni-

---

150 Conditions are emerging when estate affiliation becomes hereditary. This is happening in the military service, where children of the military have preferences when entering a military educational establishment. This is also true for the law enforcement service, where children of judges, prosecutors, police officers, and drug controllers have more chances to be admitted to respective estate educational establishments and to become members of the law enforcement estate. In general, we can say that the system of training personnel for state service very quickly forms estates with closed membership, which children from non-titular estates find increasingly difficult to penetrate. It may be that the education system already promotes the development of caste-based rather than estate-based social stratification. Basically, that is how it should be, since education institutions create boundaries and increase barriers between social strata due to the professionalism and special knowledge acquired by their graduates. However, the level of knowledge delivered currently by the education system even in the most prestigious universities provides rather for estate ambitions than ensures professionalism.

versities train independent professionals—journalists, actors, and, potentially, clerics.

The universities and colleges are ranked according to the social status their graduates can count on. The status of a metropolitan university graduate means that its holder has received metropolitan upbringing and may qualify for a position of relevance in the metropolitan estate hierarchy. The status of a provincial college graduate captures the graduate's provincialism and fitness—at most—for regional state civil service.

There is, however, an additional channel of vertical estate mobility. This is the system of postgraduate education in such institutions as the Russian Presidential Academy of National Economy and Public Administration (resulted from the merger of the Academy of National Economy under the Government of the Russian Federation and Academy of Public Administration under the President of the Russian Federation), the Financial University (formerly Finance Academy) under the Government of the Russian Federation, and some others. Enrolling in theses institutions gives members of all estates, except for pensioners, prisoners and persons with undetermined estate affiliation, the opportunity to move up the hierarchy of state service estates. These universities have numerous branches in the province, which train personnel for all kinds of service and service facilitation.

Although the education system nominally fulfills the function of estate socialization, it provides no "political literacy" to the graduates. Educated people cannot be considered full-fledged estate members, because they have no distinct estate identity and philosophy. Moreover, the social and philosophical knowledge delivered by the education system is "market-focused and democratic", since it has been imported mainly from the West and is inconsistent with the emerging estate world order. In order to form full-fledged members of contemporary estates, it is necessary to verbalize the relevant worldview and deliver it to the young people, which the education system is still incapable of doing. That may be the reason why contemporary government ideologists set about establishing various movements (My (We), Nashi (Ours), Mestnye (Locals), Idushchiye vmeste (Walking Together), etc.) targeting marginalized young people, who are promised, in particular, educational and occupational benefits and preferences in various state services and organizations. Thus, we may soon face a situation, when a diploma of higher education will be less important for achieving an estate status than the membership card of one of these youth organizations.

Democracy and estate stratification

The estate world order and related non-market distribution of resources are compatible with free markets and class structure under certain conditions specific for each state. They coexist in our state practice as well, however, not in synchrony, as in other states, but only in diachrony, when decades of triumphing estate stratification give way to years of reforms and revolutions. This produces the phenomenon of cyclicity in Russian history—a certain "groundhog century".

Democracy and a party system emerge (when the estate nature is pushed to the sidelines of government) as essential market attributes when the society separates from the state and stratifies into classes—the rich and the poor in the simplest case. As I have already mentioned, democracy is a form of integrating a society split into classes into a political entity and a form of integrating the society and the state into a nation state. A democratic society needs politics as an institution and an activity to reconcile class interests and to represent the nation state in international relations.

The estate-state non-market entity, not divided into classes, needs neither democracy, nor politics, as the estates reconcile their resource interests in the administrative market through administrative bargaining about "carving up" the resources consolidated by the sovereign in the national—all-estate budget. The sovereign—president or monarch—represents the interests of such a state in international relations. By definition, the estate-state entity is not a nation state. It may be an empire or a "state of the whole people" like the Soviet Union, but never a nation state.

A fundamentally undemocratic form of representative power, like the traditional Russian Zemsky Sobor (representative assembly), is typical for a society divided into estates (and for a state not separated from the society). The institution of various intra-estate assemblies, whose members may nominate candidates for the Zemsky Sobor is a prerequisite for sobornost (national unity). Intra-estate community is impossible without the people themselves recognizing that they are divided into estates, with such stratification providing clear estate identity of every individual. Estate members must be distinguishable by apparent attributes and possess estate consciousness.

Ideological education, propaganda, agitation, and the institution of various meetings—Communists Party, Komsomol, trade union,—which involved virtually the entire capable population, ensured estate unity in the USSR. The totality of this system provided for unreflective acceptance of estate identification by Soviet nationals and ensured minimum unity (sobornost) necessary for the existence of a state of the whole people.

In the 1990s, when the estate system disintegrated and a primitive market with its institutions occupied the vacated social space, a new phenomenon emerged—politics and political life as a form of reconciling the interests of social groups left in a structureless social space after the collapse of the estate system, on the one hand, and the new groups of market actors formed in the process of plundering the then ownerless public resources and transforming them into goods and money, on the other hand.

The institution of Soviet estate-based elections, when due to complex calculations and coordinations all Soviet estates were represented in representative authorities, were replaced by free elections, when only those were elected to representative bodies of power, who could pay to be included in a party list or managed to "buy" a majority district. The political parties that appeared at the time of the collapse of the Soviet estate system initially by their form and name represented the interests of Soviet estates (the communist party, the agrarian party and others), but gradually they turned into quasi-political organizations with no definite place either in the developing estate structure or in the stagnating class society. They represent neither the estates, nor the rich or poor classes.

After the adoption of the federal law *On the status of deputies*, members of legislative assemblies of all levels turned into a new post-Soviet estate with legislatively defined privileges and duties. This law introduced a special form of state service—law-making, and the deputies were those people who were engaged in law-making service. This was a failed attempt to integrate democracy and estate stratification by including democratic election institutions in the estate-based structure of resource distribution. As a result, elections in general (and representative power in particular) lost their initial market-democratic sense, and deputies became an estate defending their own interests in resource distribution. This estate is special, because the status of deputy can be "bought" relatively easily compared to membership in other titular estates. Naturally, the estate structure in general cannot remain neutral to such a method of obtaining membership. Largely due to this, the so-called free elections were replaced in recent years by elections by party lists, which impede individuals with inadequate (according to members of other titular estates) origin, citizenship, biography or any other meaningful estate characteristics from gaining access to membership in the deputy estate.

In the process, almost all forms of Soviet estate representation and reconciliation of estate interests disappeared and the place vacated by Soviet propaganda and agitation was taken by consumer-style advertising—an attribute of a class society, which was still not in place. State service in the 1990s still did not make sense, and respective allocated resources no longer covered the social obligations accumulated by the government. For a time, allowances of the remaining servicemen, salaries of public sector workers and employees, retirees' pensions, and all other estate-based forms of distribution became sources of resources plundered by the emerging stratum of entrepreneurs. The political organization of the society, in principle, could not meet the demands of the remnants of Soviet estates simply because the institution of free elections created no conditions for institutionalizing these demands.

The process of differentiation into classes of the rich and the poor went on for fifteen years accompanied by the disintegration of the Soviet estate system. However, in recent years, parallel to the natural emergence of a class structure, the state started institutionalizing service estates and supporting the remnants of the Soviet (non-titular) estates of public sector workers, pensioners, and employees. Consequently, at the beginning of the twenty-first century, trilateral conflicts exist:

- Between the new estates created in the process of implementing the laws on state service and the remnants of Soviet estates
- Between market social groups of the rich and the poor and the remnants of Soviet estates
- Between the new estates and the market groups of the rich and the poor.

These conflicts have not been explicated yet and can be resolved neither by democratic means, nor by specific estate regulating mechanisms. However, if this time Russia is lucky and the estate order will not eliminate the rich to prevent the emergence of the poor, some day these conflicts may give rise to a new social structure balancing estate ambitions and class interests.

In the conflict between the estate and political organization of the society, the "estate nature" is currently suppressing the "class nature". Free elections as an institution disappear due to their non-functionality. Instead, "elections from above" emerge that are somewhat similar to Soviet elections, however, technically and methodologically less elaborate and ideologically completely unsubstantiated.

Gradually, the merchant estate is taking shape. Its function consists in providing services to the budget rather than doing business. Business is ousted by commerce, which has absolutely no need for democracy and its institutions, because merchants work in the administrative market. The "social responsibility of business" becomes a prerequisite for commerce. Because of this responsibility, real business leaves the country or becomes international, which is much better protected from estate "carve-up" and rent than the domestic one.

The political organization of a market society is in no way consistent with estate groups and their inherent forms of coordinating interests. The Federal Assembly is obviously non-functional in what concerns coordinating the activity of the estates, since the estates cannot be represented in it under the effective election laws and because they cannot exist as elements of a democratic system. As long as elections to the Federal Assembly are held based on party lists, attempts to supplement its work by elements of estate representation, known as sovereign democracy (for details see below) are unlikely to succeed. They may succeed only if parties form along estate lines, but then they will cease being political parties even nominally.

Obviously, the country is unlikely to return to the initial Soviet state with fully monopolized resources and their distribution among the estates. On the other hand, it is as unlikely that a truly free market and democratic institutions will be established in the foreseeable future. Therefore, it is inevitable that fragments of a democratic order enabling market activity will coexist with elements of an estate structure including large-scale withdrawal of resources from the market and their distribution according to estate-based social justice criteria. Unconditional domination of the estate nature will lead, ultimately, to yet another overall shortage crisis and disintegration of the state, as happened with the Soviet Union. Domination of the market nature and democracy will result in a disastrous stratification of the society into the rich and the poor and social conflicts also fraught with disintegration of the state.

Obviously, the market and estate systems must coexist in one social space, in synchrony, and be mutually complementary rather than alternative. I believe this requires completing the construction of the estate system and legalizing it ideologically, separating the market components of our statehood from the estate-resource ones structurally, functionally and politically. Only legalization of estate-ness can curb and civilize the resource appetites of numerous members of the service estates and align estate rent rates with estate rules of conduct (morality).

I believe the main problem in the relationship between classes and estates in Russia consists in the following. In order to develop and expand, the market needs the state to minimize withdrawals from it. At the same time, the estate system in general requires maximum withdrawals, an unlimited expansion of the state budget as a resource bank. Evidently, withdrawals are limited to a certain amount after which the market shrinks and shortages of resources distributable among the estates emerge. The estates interpret shortages as a signal to withdraw even more resources from the market. This may eventually lead to a generalization of shortages and social instability, which can destroy the entire system of inter-estate relations. Of course, it is quite possible to consolidate resources and "fight corruption" using mass repressions, but this will hardly justify the inevitable political costs.

Currently, the authorities are testing (largely, unreflectingly) a specific Russian method of integrating the estate and class structures—sovereign democracy. If I correctly understand the logic of its ideologists, it must integrate class and estate interests by limiting the ambitions of both classes and estates. However, the method of implementing sovereign democracy, i.e., the utmost formalization and de-democratization of the electoral process and the quota-based (by party lists) approach to the composition of the Federal Assembly and regional bodies of representative power, considers neither the division of society into the rich and the poor, nor estate ambitions.

The logic of sovereign democracy could be adequate to the emerging world order, if it were possible to clearly separate classes and estates in representative institutions. However, turning the Federal Assembly into an estate-based representative body removes class institutions from politics. Should this logic be realized fully, the agents of the surviving market would be outlawed literally and figuratively. However, should the Federal Assembly lose estate representation currently existing in the form of lobbying the interests of the military, law enforcers, and state civil servants, this will open the door to estate-based arbitrariness regulated neither by law, nor by estate morality.

I have already mentioned that the border between estates and classes passes through the individual rather than between individuals and groups. Sovereign democracy preserves this inner duality of our society members; it is hypocritical in the truest sense of the word. The ideologists of sovereign democracy should recall the well-known Soviet joke about a baptized Jew in a public bath, "Either take the cross off, or put on your pants". The development of sovereign democracy is fraught with a repetition of history and another collapse of the state because of the shortages and inter-estate conflicts caused by them.

Daydreaming. Instead of a conclusion

Social stratification, including the estate one, is adequate and effective only if the external identification of a person's place in the social system more or less coincides with his own perception of who he is. Inconsistency in the inner (self-identification, introspection) and outer (by law or tradition) identification of the people's social status results in anomie. In today's Russian reality the external identification of people's place in the social system is far from transparent. Journalistic categories used to describe the social structure—oligarchs, bandits, bureaucrats, siloviki, ordinary people, etc.—are not operational and serve the purposes of "public policy", largely meaningless in our society, rather than explain the basis of the social world order.

The inner identifications (self-identification) of our compatriots are still blurred and vague (only extremists define themselves as oligarchs or bandits) or such that a person fails to identify himself in the current post-Soviet realities. Instead, he refers to the imperial or Soviet past or to the utmost idealized (to the point of substantive vacuum) progressionist coordinates of the "market economy" and "democratic society". Representatives of contemporary estates are only vaguely aware of their estate status. Rather, estate identification is still veiled by the occupational one. The external (legal) estate identity and self-identity match rather well in the case of military personnel, law enforcers, and Cossacks. However, as far as I know, there has been no direct research of estate self-identification.

In recent years, the state has been enacting laws purposefully and consistently, which, in fact, introduce new post-Soviet estates. Gradually, a foundation emerges, which allows members of the new estates to identify themselves, promotes estate worldviews and serves to transform the estates from nominal (defined only by law) to real, i.e. to agents of the new post-Soviet estate world order. After legislative establishment, the estates start living their own life. Inter-estate relations not stipulated by any initial laws develop. These relations shape the current estate structure, still largely formal, not explicated, and unclear to members of the estate society.

The emerging estate system does not have a description language. Even the ideologists of estate stratification, the conservatives, base their argumentation on imported or archaic (also once imported) methodologies and theories, leaving out of their reasoning and constructions the seemingly public facts about the emergence of a new estate system. The description and understanding of our reality is based on adopted and translated concepts of the (mainly) market world. This has a rather peculiar speculative status in a society that has lost its old estate character and not yet acquired a new one—the market is what we are building, and not what we have now. The estate system is what we had in the past, and not what we have now. Social reality is judged by the degree of compliance with market or conservative ideals, i.e., negatively. This triggers further reformist or conservative efforts on shaping the market and developing market relations or on establishing the estate-based structure. Reformers are impeded by "vestiges of the past"—a term favored by revolutionary raznochintsy (intellectuals of non-noble origin) and by the builders of socialism. Everything "new" that does not fit into the archaic idealized perceptions of estate stratification impedes the conservatives.

The situation is somewhat paradoxical, because the state makes no effort to explain its actions on establishing estates. Apparently, the state is developing the estate structure unreflectively. This means that when drafting and adopting estate laws, those in power and the legislators pursue other goals, such as "restoring order" or "consolidating the vertical of power". Our compatriots yearn for the no longer existent imperial and Soviet social relations, social stability, and social justice in its purely non-market estate version. It seems that the establishment of estates is a by-product of this yearning.

Members of contemporary estates are immersed in a reality that Russia considers a market. In a real market, estate affiliation means little. Relations between the seller and the buyer are not based on mutual service; they are of a "buy-sell" nature. Market relations make some people richer, and the other—poorer. Some start businesses and develop them, the other are less active, but deriving profit is the ultimate goal for both the former and the latter. The market world needs democracy, politics, and other realities functional in a market environment. The market world triggers consumption-based social stratification—the upper, middle, and lower classes. The market world has developed languages of business communication, mass media, interpersonal information exchange, and scientific descriptions.

This market world that the reformers have been attempting to build for many years, definitely exists. It emerged more in spite of the reformers' efforts than owing to them. Its boundaries are much narrower than various progressionists would like to believe. Besides the market, an estate structure, which the state is introducing, also exists. The state alienates resources, withdraws them from the market and distributes among the estates in a non-market way according to its criteria of each estate's social significance. The estate-based state cannot but consider market realities subordinate to the system of mutual estate service, as market distribution of goods and money is not just incompatible with estate-based distribution of resources, but rather opposed to it. At the same time, there is no reflection on the emerging estate system, and the activity on building the estate structure lacks public and accessible justification and interpretation.

The market and estate worlds coexist in the same social space, in the same people. In such a dual world, members of service estates can market their status and privileges—that what the state had granted them when defining their estate affiliation. They can use the advantages provided by their status to gain market preferences. They take from the market what has to be paid for, but they do not pay, because "generals are not expected" to do this. Hussars are well known to take no money from ladies [reference to a Russian joke] and to pay for no services.

Members of the estate society tend to interpret any manifestations of market stratification as corruption, and fight market lawlessness. Members of various service estates consider that the market converts resources into goods and money regardless of the estates' significance, therefore, unfairly. In the course of market transformations, resources are distributed in completely different proportions from those required to achieve estate-based social justice—from each according to his estate status, to each according to his service. According to the estates, the market generates social injustice. It deprives of resources those estates, whose service is insignificant for the market and therefore remains unpaid. The theory and practice of the estate world order consist in fighting injustice—the market, and obtaining scarce goods and services through administrative market institutions. The conflict between market reality and the reality of service, service facilitation, and service support is existential and irresolvable. Neither in our own country nor anywhere else has the class nature completely and finally defeated the estate nature or vice versa. However, unlike Russia, other countries have learned to live with it.

The state is fighting corruption, which is actually the penetration of orderly estate relations by market ones. The market is "buying" the estate system. Its actors are appropriating certain privileges, obtaining estate statuses or using the services of titular estate members, including in security and law enforcement. Service in this case loses its inner meaning; it becomes a shadow market activity, a marketing of services that by definition may not be sold or bought. As a result, there is no estate order and social justice, whatever their meaning, nor is there any market and democracy. There is nothing but a permanent construction of the bright future.

Appendix 1. Classification of threats

Elements of the attributive list of threats (such as, for example, natural, anthropogenic, political, and other threats) are hereinafter referred to as **types of threats**. The types of threats determine the structure of their classification. The list is not exhaustive, and may either expand or shrink.

This section is based on the central hypothesis that the consequences of the threats serve as constitutive features for their classification. Thus, magnetic storms are a natural phenomenon, which has various effects—from an increase in morbidity to global communication and energy supply disruptions. Magnetic storms as such are of interest only to natural scientists, but their consequences pose threats. Similarly, when classifying threats, the amount and forms of utilizing the disposable resources are significant not by themselves, but by the consequences of their shortage—for example, drinking water or energy resource shortages.

Therefore, a classification of threats should include not only the types of threats, but also the consequences of each type, i.e., the relations between the types of threats. Suppose that the number of types of threats is limited, and the consequences of each type are manifested only in relation to the other types of threats also included in the general list. Take, for example, the natural and political types of threats. Natural phenomena are significant (in this context) only because they have threatening political consequences, and political actions are significant because of their environmental (natural) implications.

This hypothesis allows us to build a closed structure (fractal matrix table) formed by relations between the included types of threats.

Take, for example, three types of threats:

1. Natural
2. Technological, and
3. Economic (resource-based).

The names of these types of threats shall form the rows of Table 18, and the respective experts—the columns.

The relations between similarly named rows and columns of the table are interpreted as relevant areas of special knowledge. The relations between differently named rows and columns of the table are interpreted as **types of threats**—the projections of one type of threats on the others, their consequences.

Table 18 Classification of relations between natural, technological, and economic types of threats

Experts on threats / Types of threats	Scientists, experts on natural phenomena	Technologists	Economists, experts on resources
Natural	**Natural sciences**	Natural threats associated with technology development	Natural threats reducing disposable resources
Technological	Technological threats associated with natural phenomena	**Technological sciences**	Technological threats associated with a decrease in disposable resources
Economic (resource-based)	Economic threats associated with natural phenomena	Economic threats associated with technology development	**Economics (science about resources)**

The relation between the "natural threats" row and the "experts on natural phenomena" column is interpreted as "scientific knowledge"; the relation between the technological threats row and "technologists" possessing relevant methods is interpreted as "technological knowledge"; and the relation between the economic threats row and economists possessing relevant methods is interpreted as "economic knowledge".

The table allows presenting threats as a relation between their types, i.e., a result of each type of threat being significant because of its projection on other types of threats. This means that natural threats can have technological and economic consequences. Similarly, economic threats, such as expectations of resource depletion, can have natural and technological implications.

Let us expand Table 18 by introducing one more type of threats—political threats.

Table 19 shows that by introducing one more type of threats we expand substantially the variety of relations between them. Additional threats appear as compared to Table 18 due to the actualization of political implications of natural, technological, and economic types of threats.

There is no limit to introducing new types of threats into the classification.

Table 19   Classification of relations between natural, technological, economic, and political types of threats

Experts on threats Types of threats	Scientists, experts on natural phenomena	Technologists	Economists, experts on resources	Politicians
Natural	**Scientific knowledge**	Natural threats associated with technology development	Natural threats reducing disposable resources	Natural threats with political consequences
Technological	Technological threats associated with natural phenomena	**Technological knowledge**	Technological threats associated with a decrease in disposable resources	Technological threats with political consequences
Economic (resource-based)	Economic threats associated with natural phenomena	Economic threats associated with technology development	**Economic knowledge**	Economic threats with political consequences
Political	Political threats associated with natural phenomena	Political threats associated with technology development	Political threats associated with depletion of resources	**Politics and political science knowledge**

The activity of virtually every service has substantive aspects affecting many types of threats. Thus, natural threats are meant to be neutralized by the Ministry for Emergency Situations, Rospotrebnadzor, the Federal Service for Veterinary and Phytosanitary Supervision, the Federal Service for the Supervision of Healthcare, and the Federal Service for Hydrometeorology and Environmental Monitoring. This means that the services must have appropriate tools to neutralize such threats as "natural threats caused by engineering activities", "natural threats significant for the security of the state", "politicized natural threats (like climate change)", and "natural threats significant for the population (those that provoke everyday fears)".

On the other hand, an expert in a certain field, a "politician", for example, recognizes threats of all types—from "politicized natural threats" to "political threats associated with social groups". Such experts, if they are sufficiently influential, can initiate a flow of information to the leaders of the state justifying the need to neutralize a new threat. This is what happened when "politicians" turned their attention to the content of the information space and decided that this content posed a threat to public safety and morality.

The Federal Service for Supervision of Communications, Information Technology and Mass Media was charged with neutralizing this new threat. However, because of the narrow specialization of this service and its reliance on the historical understanding of information threats, the emergence of a new threat forces the Service to establish inter-departmental bodies (headquarters, commissions, councils) and develop tools to neutralize this type threat. This means a new activity requiring additional resources. The emerging system for neutralizing information threats will have to include commercial partners, regional and municipal agents, which means establishing a new informal corporation for utilizing budgetary resources.

Ranking threats and evaluating the relative amount of resources for their neutralization

Developing threat classifications and using them to structure the information space can eventually provide the basis for comparing scientific and public perceptions of threats with their existing state institutionalization, as embodied in its structure, and for designing a more rational approach to determining the relevance of the threats.

The above classification logic enables ranking the threats. The formal nature of fractal matrix tables allows determining the relative amount of resources needed to neutralize the threats after identifying their relative significance. Experts and officials must take care of the ranking.

Suppose that a group of experts decides that the most significant threats are of a political nature, followed by economic threats, and then technological and natural ones. The level of significance determines the relative amount of resources, which can be utilized in neutralizing the threats. According to the hypothetical think tank, one unit of resources must be allocated to neutralize the lowest-ranking threats (natural), as determined by the expert evaluation, with the higher-ranking threats requiring, respectively, two units (technological), four units (economic), and eight units (political) of resources.

We shall now restructure Table 19 positioning the types of threats in order of relevance from right to left (Table 20).

Suppose that the total amount of resources is equal to 100%. These resources must be divided between the four types of threats so that the ratio between the amounts of resources constitutes 8/4/2/1. This means that 53.3% should be utilized to neutralize political threats, 26.7%—to neutralize economic threats, 13.3%—to neutralize technological threats, and 6.7%—to neutralize natural threats.

Let us indicate the relative amounts of resources required to neutralize the threats in the columns and rows of Table 20.

Please note that we are considering the total amount of resources allocated to neutralize the types of threats. Now we must determine the relative amounts of resources that should be utilized when neutralizing the threats indicated in the cells of the table. The amount of resources utilized for political activity as such, i.e., the diagonal element of the table at the intersection of the "political threats" row with the "politicians" column must constitute 53.3% from 53.3% (28.4% of the total amount of available resources equaling 100%), thus corresponding to the expert threat type ranking.

The relative share of resources that can be utilized when neutralizing the political consequences of economic threats (intersection of the "economic threats" row with the "politicians" column) amounts to 14.2% (26.4% from 53.3%).

Calculation results are presented in Table 21, where the rows show the relative amount of resources that can be utilized to neutralize the threats included in the table.

The relative amounts of resources by rows and columns add up to 100%.

A different ranking of threats or a change in the level of detail will result in another pattern of resource allocation; however, the general principle will remain unchanged. We can describe the above logic as a system of simple mathematical equations.

The cells of the table contain the most general threats. We can itemize the types of threats limiting ourselves only to one category of each type (e.g., select only mass riots from among the political threats, resource shortages—from the economic ones, utility infrastructure failures—from technological threats, and cold winters—from natural threats). In this case, the classification grid will show the political, behavioral, economic, and other consequences of synchronized threats of different categories. After respective ranking, it will be possible to evaluate the relative amount of resources required to neutralize such threats.

Table 20 Ranking relations between the types of threats

Experts on threats \ Types of threats	Politicians	Economists	Technologists	Experts on natural threats
Political	**Political knowledge and politics**	Political threats associated with the economy	Political threats associated with technology	Political threats associated with natural phenomena
Economic	Economic threats associated with politics	**Economic knowledge**	Economic threats associated with technology	Economic threats associated with natural phenomena
Technological	Technological threats associated with politics	Technological threats associated with the economy	**Technological knowledge**	Technological threats associated with natural phenomena
Natural	Natural threats associated with politics	Natural threats associated with the economy	Natural threats associated with technology	**Knowledge about natural phenomena**

Table 21   Ranked relations between types of threats[151]

Types of threats	Experts on threats 53.3	Politicians 53.3	Economists 26.7	Technologists 13.3	Experts on natural threats 6.7	100 %
Political 53.3		Share of resources intended for political activity as such 28.4	Share of resources intended for neutralizing political consequences of economic threats 14.2	Share of resources intended for neutralizing political consequences of technological threats 7.1	Share of resources intended for neutralizing political consequences of natural threats 3.6	53.3
Economic 26.7		Share of resources intended for neutralizing economic consequences of political decisions 14.2	**Share of resources intended for enhancing economic knowledge 7.1**	Share of resources intended for neutralizing economic consequences of technological threats 3.6	Share of resources intended for neutralizing economic consequences of natural threats 1.8	26.7
Technological 13.3		Share of resources intended for neutralizing technological consequences of political decisions 7.1	Share of resources intended for neutralizing technological consequences of economic threats 3.6	**Share of resources intended for developing technology 1.8**	Share of resources intended for neutralizing technological consequences of natural threats 0.9	13.3
Natural 6.7		Share of resources intended for neutralizing natural consequences of political decisions 3.6	Share of resources intended for neutralizing natural consequences of economic threats 1.8	Share of resources intended for neutralizing natural consequences of technological threats 0.9	**Share of resources intended for enhancing knowledge about natural phenomena 0.4**	6.7
Total = 100%		53.3	26.7	13.3	6.7	100

---

151   Calculations made by Dmitry Dekhant and Olga Molyarenko.

Appendix 2. Order of the Administrative Directorate of the President of the Russian Federation

Registered with the Russian Ministry of Justice on 19 August 2010.
Registration No. 18198
Guidelines for applying the Regulation concerning lounges for officials and delegations approved by Decree of the Government of the Russian Federation No. 1116 of 19 September 1996 with regard to lounges for officials and delegations at checkpoints on the state border of the Russian Federation organized at airports (airfields) of Moscow, the Moscow Region, St. Petersburg, and Sochi.
Pursuant to the Decree of the President of the Russian Federation No. 371 of 12 March 1996, *On enhancing the procedure of crossing the state border of the Russian Federation* (Collection of Laws of the Russian Federation, 1996, No. 12, Art. 1059; 2002, No. 31, Art. 3062; 2007, No. 5, Art. 636), Decree of the President of the Russian Federation No. 1370 of 17 September 2008, *On the Administrative Directorate of the President of the Russian Federation* (Collection of Laws of the Russian Federation, 2008, No.38, Art. 4277), Decree of the Government of the Russian Federation No. 1116 of 19 September 1996, *On approving the Regulation concerning lounges for officials and delegations* (Collection of Laws of the Russian Federation, 1999, No.44, Art. 5319; 2002, No.40, Art. 3928; 2007, No.46, Art. 5600), **I hereby order:**
1. To approve the Guidelines for applying the Regulation concerning lounges for officials and delegations approved by Decree of the Government of the Russian Federation No. 1116 of 19 September 1996 with regard to lounges for officials and delegations at checkpoints on the state border of the Russian Federation organized at airports (airfields) of Moscow, the Moscow Region, St. Petersburg, and Sochi (Annex 1 hereto).
2. To approve the list of persons entitled to use the lounges for officials and delegations at checkpoints on the state border of the Russian Federation organized at airports (airfields) of Moscow, the Moscow Region, St. Petersburg, and Sochi (Annex 2 hereto).
3. To repeal Order No. 60 of the Administrative Directorate of the President of the Russian Federation of 21 March 2003, On lounges for officials opened for international travel (international flights) at airports (airfields) of Moscow and the list of persons entitled to use such lounges (Registered with the Russian Ministry of Justice on 21 March 2003, registration No. 4298).

V. Kozhin, Head of the Administrative Directorate
Annex No. 1

Guidelines for applying the Regulation concerning lounges for officials and delegations approved by Decree of the Government of the Russian Federation No. 1116 of 19 September 1996 with regard to lounges for officials and delegations at checkpoints on the state border of the Russian Federation organized at airports (airfields) in Moscow, the Moscow Region, St. Petersburg, and Sochi.
1. The decision to set up lounges for officials and delegations at checkpoints on the state border of the Russian Federation organized at airports (airfields) in Moscow, the

Moscow Region, St. Petersburg, and Sochi (hereinafter, lounges for officials) shall be taken by the Administrative Directorate of the President of the Russian Federation and formalized by an order of the Administrative Directorate of the President of the Russian Federation in coordination with the Ministry of Transport of the Russian Federation, Federal Security Service of the Russian Federation, Federal Customs Services, and the Federal Service for Protecting Consumer Rights and Public Health.

2. The decision to open the lounges for officials shall be taken by the Administrative Directorate of the President of the Russian Federation and formalized by an order of the Administrative Directorate of the President of the Russian Federation in coordination with the Ministry of Transport of the Russian Federation, Ministry of Health and Social Development of the Russian Federation, Ministry of Foreign Affairs of the Russian Federation, Federal Security Service of the Russian Federation, Federal Customs Services, Federal Service for Protecting Consumer Rights and Public Health, and the Federal Guard Service of the Russian Federation.

3. The lounges for officials shall provide services to individuals according to the list of persons entitled to use the lounges for officials and delegations at checkpoints on the state border of the Russian Federation organized at airports (airfields) of Moscow, the Moscow Region, St. Petersburg, and Sochi approved hereby.

4. The Administrative Directorate of the President of the Russian Federation shall supervise the operation of the lounges for officials, including by issuing relevant orders and other regulations.

5. The rules and procedures governing the work of the lounges for officials shall be approved by an order of the Administrative Directorate of the President of the Russian Federation in coordination with the Ministry of Transport of the Russian Federation, Federal Security Service of the Russian Federation, Federal Customs Services, Federal Service for Protecting Consumer Rights and Public Health, and the Federal Guard Service of the Russian Federation.

6. The price for using the lounges for officials operated by the Administrative Directorate of the President of the Russian Federation shall be established on the basis of economically reasonable expenses (costs) associated with arranging service and maintaining the lounges for officials plus a standard profit margin (profitability).

The standard profit margin (profitability) included in the price shall be determined by the Administrative Directorate of the President of the Russian Federation as a percentage of the economically reasonable expenses (costs) associated with arranging service and maintaining the lounges for officials.

7. An organization subordinate to the Administrative Directorate of the President of the Russian Federation shall provide services in the lounges for officials under an agreement signed between the Administrative Directorate of the President of the Russian Federation and its subordinate organization.

8. Lounges for officials shall provide services to individuals indicated in clause 3 hereof, who have tickets for a flight on the day of departure, as well as persons meeting and seeing them off.

9. Generally, services in lounges for officials shall be provided by prior arrangement and upon presentation of the necessary documents and tickets by the individuals indicated in clause 3 hereof.

Persons seeing off and meeting officials shall be admitted to the lounges for officials upon presentation of identification documents or documents confirming their official status, and upon providing information about individuals indicated in clause 3 hereof (flight number, name, and official position).

10. The procedure and deadlines for submitting applications to use the lounges for officials shall be specified in the agreement signed with the organization subordinate to the Administrative Directorate of the President of the Russian Federation that shall be in charge of providing services to individuals indicated in clause 3 hereof .
11. The organization subordinate to the Administrative Directorate of the President of the Russian Federation indicated in clause 7 hereof shall provide services in lounges for officials under applications, guarantee letters, and agreements concluded with entities and individuals.
12. Upon arrival at the lounges for officials, the individuals indicated in clause 3 hereof as well as persons accompanying them shall pay for using the facilities, except for case when such payment had been made earlier or another form of settlement is envisaged.

<u>Annex No. 2</u>
List of persons entitled to use the lounges for officials and delegations at checkpoints on the state border of the Russian Federation organized at airports (airfields) of Moscow, the Moscow Region, St. Petersburg, and Sochi.
1. President of the Russian Federation
2. Chairman of the Government of the Russian Federation and his deputies
3. Chairman of the Federation Council of the Federal Assembly of the Russian Federation and his deputies
4. Chairman of the State Duma of the Federal Assembly of the Russian Federation and his deputies
5. Chairman of the Constitutional Court of the Russian Federation and his deputies
6. Chairman of the Supreme Court of the Russian Federation and his deputies
7. Chairman of the Supreme Arbitration Court of the Russian Federation and his deputies
8. General Director of the Judicial Department of the Supreme Court of the Russian Federation and his deputies
9. Prosecutor General of the Russian Federation and his deputies
10. First deputy Prosecutor General of the Russian Federation - Chairman of the Investigative Committee under the Office of the Prosecutor General of the Russian Federation and his deputies
11. Representative the Russian Federation at the European Court of Human Rights - Deputy Minister of Justice of the Russian Federation
12. Minister of the Russian Federation
13. Chairman of the Accounts Chamber of the Russian Federation and his deputies
14. Chairman of the Central Election Commission of the Russian Federation and his deputies
15. Chairman of the Central Bank of the Russian Federation and his deputies
16. Head of a federal executive authority and his deputies
17. Heads of autonomous structural units of federal executive authorities and their deputies
18. Head of a regional body of a federal executive authority
19. Member of the State Council of the Russian Federation
20. Member of the Security Council of the Russian Federation
21. Member of the Central Election Commission of the Russian Federation
22. Auditor of the Accounts Chamber of the Russian Federation
23. Head of Administration of the President of the Russian Federation
24. First Deputy Head of Administration of the President of the Russian Federation

25. Deputy Head of Administration of the President of the Russian Federation
26. Aide to the President of the Russian Federation
27. Aide to the President of the Russian Federation - Head of a Directorate of the President of the Russian Federation
28. Chief of Protocol of the President of the Russian Federation
29. Press Secretary of the President of the Russian Federation
30. Plenipotentiary Envoy of the President of the Russian Federation to a federal district
31. Plenipotentiary Envoy of the President of the Russian Federation to the Federation Council of the Federal Assembly of the Russian Federation
32. Plenipotentiary Envoy of the President of the Russian Federation to the State Duma of the Federal Assembly of the Russian Federation
33. Plenipotentiary Envoy of the President of the Russian Federation to the Constitutional Court of the Russian Federation
34. Presidential Commissioner for Children's Rights
35. First Deputy Secretary of the Security Council of the Russian Federation
36. Chief of the Chancellery of the President of the Russian Federation
37. Chief of the Speechwriting Office of the President of the Russian Federation
38. Head of Directorate of the President of the Russian Federation
39. Chief of the Secretariat of the Head of Administration of the President of the Russian Federation
40. Deputy Secretary of the Security Council of the Russian Federation
41. Deputy Plenipotentiary Envoy of the President of the Russian Federation to a federal district
42. Deputy Head of Directorate of the President of the Russian Federation
43. Deputy Chief of the Speechwriting Office of the President of the Russian Federation
44. Deputy Chief of the Chancellery of the President of the Russian Federation
45. Deputy Chief of the Secretariat of the Head of Administration of the President of the Russian Federation
46. Deputy Chief of Protocol of the President of the Russian Federation
47. Deputy Press Secretary of the President of the Russian Federation
48. Advisor to the President of the Russian Federation
49. Senior Speechwriter of the President of the Russian Federation
50. Speechwriter of the President of the Russian Federation
51. Aide to the Secretary of the Security Council of the Russian Federation
52. Aide to the Plenipotentiary Envoy of the President of the Russian Federation to a federal district
53. Aide to the Head of Administration of the President of the Russian Federation
54. Assistants of the following subdivisions: Chancellery of the President of the Russian Federation, Speechwriting Office of the President of the Russian Federation, Secretariat of the Head of Administration of the President of the Russian Federation, Office of the Security Council of the Russian Federation, Directorate of the President of the Russian Federation
55. Chief federal inspector
56. Military inspector of the Russian Federation
57. Head of department of the following subdivisions: Office of the Plenipotentiary Envoy of the President of the Russian Federation to a federal district, Chancellery of the President of the Russian Federation, Speechwriting Office of the President of the Russian Federation, Secretariat of the Head of Administration of the President of the

Russian Federation, Office of the Security Council of the Russian Federation, Directorate of the President of the Russian Federation
58. Chief of Staff of the First Deputy Head of Administration of the President of the Russian Federation
59. Chief of Staff of the Deputy Head of Administration of the President of the Russian Federation
60. Chief of Staff of an Aide to the President of the Russian Federation
61. Chief of Staff of the Chief of Protocol of the President of the Russian Federation
62. Chief of Staff of the Press Secretary of the President of the Russian Federation
63. Deputy Head of department of the following subdivisions: Office of the Plenipotentiary Envoy of the President of the Russian Federation to a federal district, Chancellery of the President of the Russian Federation, Speechwriting Office of the President of the Russian Federation, Secretariat of the Head of Administration of the President of the Russian Federation, Office of the Security Council of the Russian Federation, Directorate of the President of the Russian Federation
64. Federal Inspector at the Administration of the President of the Russian Federation
65. Chief Advisor at the Administration of the President of the Russian Federation
66. Advisor at the Administration of the President of the Russian Federation
67. Individuals and delegations, sent abroad or invited by the President of the Russian Federation, Head of Administration of the President of the Russian Federation and his deputies, and Aides to the President of the Russian Federation
68. Chief of Staff of the Federation Council of the Federal Assembly of the Russian Federation
69. Chief of the Secretariat of the Chairman of the Federation Council of the Federal Assembly of the Russian Federation
70. First Deputy Chief of Staff of the Federation Council of the Federal Assembly of the Russian Federation
71. Deputy Chief of Staff of the Federation Council of the Federal Assembly of the Russian Federation
72. Head of Directorate of the Office of the Federation Council of the Federal Assembly of the Russian Federation
73. Head of the Administrative Directorate of the Federation Council of the Federal Assembly of the Russian Federation
74. Chief of the Secretariat of the First Deputy Chairman of the Federation Council of the Federal Assembly of the Russian Federation
75. Deputy Chief of the Secretariat of the Chairman of the Federation Council
76. Chief of the Secretariat of the Deputy Chairman of the Federation Council
77. Deputy Head of Directorate of the Office of the Federation Council
78. Deputy Head of the Administrative Directorate of the Federation Council
79. Chief of the Secretariat of the Chief of Staff of the Federation Council
80. Chief of Staff of a Federation Council committee
81. Chief of Staff of a Federation Council commission
82. Deputy Chief of the Secretariat of the First Deputy Chairman of the Federation Council
83. Aide to the Chairman of the Federation Council of the Federal Assembly of the Russian Federation
84. Press Secretary of the Chairman of the Federation Council
85. Advisor to the Chairman of the Federation Council

86. Assistants of the following subdivisions: Secretariat of the Chairman of the Federation Council, directorate
87. Head of department in a directorate of the Federation Council
88. Aide to a member of the Federation Council in the event of official travel with the member of the Federation Council
89. Chief of Staff of the State Duma
90. First Deputy Chief of Staff of the State Duma
91. Chief of the Secretariat of the Chairman of the State Duma
92. Deputy Chief of Staff of the State Duma
93. Head of a directorate of the State Duma Office
94. Head of the Administrative Directorate of the State Duma
95. Chief of the Secretariat of the First Deputy Chairman of the State Duma
96. Deputy Chief of the Secretariat of the Chairman of the State Duma
97. Deputy Chief of the Secretariat of the Chairman of the State Duma of the Federal Assembly of the Russian Federation - Chief of the Secretariat of the State Duma Council
98. Deputy Head of a directorate of the State Duma Office
99. Deputy Head of the Administrative Directorate of the State Duma
100. Chief of the Secretariat of the Deputy Chairman of the State Duma of the Federal Assembly of the Russian Federation
101. Chief of Staff of a State Duma fraction
102. Chief of Staff of a State Duma committee
103. Chief of Staff of a State Duma commission
104. Chief of the Secretariat of the Chief of Staff of the State Duma of the Federal Assembly of the Russian Federation
105. Deputy Chief of the Secretariat of the First Deputy Chairman of the State Duma of the Federal Assembly of the Russian Federation
106. Aide to the Chairman of the State Duma of the Federal Assembly of the Russian Federation
107. Advisor to the Chairman of the State Duma of the Federal Assembly of the Russian Federation
108. Assistants of the following subdivisions: Secretariat of the Chairman of the State Duma, directorate of the Federal Assembly of the Russian Federation
109. Head of a department of the Secretariat of the Chairman of the State Duma of the Federal Assembly of the Russian Federation
110. Head of a department of a directorate of the State Duma Office
111. Aide to a deputy of the State Duma in the event of official travel together with the deputy of the State Duma of the Federal Assembly of the Russian Federation
112. First Deputy Chairman of the Military-Industrial Commission under the Government of the Russian Federation
113. Deputy Chief of Staff of the Government of the Russian Federation
114. Press Secretary of the Chairman of the Government of the Russian Federation - Deputy Chief of Staff of the Government of the Russian Federation
115. Chief of Protocol of the Chairman of the Government of the Russian Federation - Deputy Chief of Staff of the Government of the Russian Federation
116. Chief of the Secretariat of the Chairman of the Government of the Russian Federation

117. Chief of Staff of the Military-Industrial Commission under the Government of the Russian Federation - Deputy Chief of Staff of the Government of the Russian Federation
118. Chief of the Secretariat of the First Deputy Chairman of the Government of the Russian Federation
119. Plenipotentiary Representative of the Government of the Russian Federation at the Federation Council of the Federal Assembly of the Russian Federation
120. Plenipotentiary Representative of the Government of the Russian Federation at the State Duma of the Federal Assembly of the Russian Federation
121. Plenipotentiary Representative of the Government of the Russian Federation at the Constitutional Court of the Russian Federation, Supreme Court of the Russian Federation, and the Supreme Arbitration Court of the Russian Federation
122. Director of a department of the Office of the Government of the Russian Federation
123. Chairman of the scientific and technical council of the Military-Industrial Commission under the Government of the Russian Federation - Deputy Chairman of the Military-Industrial Commission under the Government of the Russian Federation
124. Member of the Military-Industrial Commission under the Government of the Russian Federation
125. Deputy Chief of the Secretariat of the Chairman of the Government of the Russian Federation
126. Chief of the Secretariat of the Deputy Chairman of the Government of the Russian Federation
127. Chief of the Secretariat of the Deputy Chairman of the Government of the Russian Federation - Chief of Staff of the Government of the Russian Federation
128. Chief of the Secretariat of the Chief of Staff of the Government of the Russian Federation - Minister of the Russian Federation
129. Head of a directorate of the Office of the Government of the Russian Federation
130. Deputy Chief of the Secretariat of the First Deputy Chairman of the Government of the Russian Federation
131. Deputy Director of a department of the Office of the Government of the Russian Federation
132. Deputy Chief of the Secretariat of a Deputy Chairman of the Government of the Russian Federation
133. Deputy Chief of the Secretariat of the Deputy Chairman of the Government of the Russian Federation - Chief of Staff of the Government of the Russian Federation
134. Deputy Chief of the Secretariat of the Chief of Staff of the Government of the Russian Federation - Minister of the Russian Federation
135. Deputy Head of a directorate of the Office of the Government of the Russian Federation
136. Aide to the Chairman of the Government of the Russian Federation
137. Assistant of the Chairman of the Government of the Russian Federation
138. Aide to the First Deputy Chairman of the Government of the Russian Federation
139. Assistant of the First Deputy Chairman of the Government of the Russian Federation
140. Aide to the Deputy Chairman of the Government of the Russian Federation
141. Aide to the Deputy Chairman of the Government of the Russian Federation - Chief of Staff of the Government of the Russian Federation
142. Aide to the Chief of Staff of the Government of the Russian Federation - Minister of the Russian Federation

143. Head of a section in: a department, directorate of the Office of the Government of the Russian Federation
144. Assistants of the following subdivisions: Secretariat of the Chairman of the Government of the Russian Federation, Secretariat of the First Deputy Chairman of the Government of the Russian Federation, Secretariat of the Deputy Chairman of the Government of the Russian Federation, Secretariat of the Deputy Chairman of the Government of the Russian Federation - Chief of Staff of the Government of the Russian Federation, Secretariat of the Chief of Staff of the Government of the Russian Federation - Minister of the Russian Federation, department, directorate of the Office of the Government of the Russian Federation
145. Deputy Head of a section in: a department, directorate of the Office of the Government of the Russian Federation
146. Chief Advisor in a department, directorate of the Office of the Government of the Russian Federation
147. Advisor in a department, directorate of the Office of the Government of the Russian Federation
148. Individuals and delegations, sent abroad or invited by decision of the Government of the Russian Federation
149. Director of a department of the Military-Industrial Commission under the Government of the Russian Federation
150. Deputy Director of a department of the Military-Industrial Commission under the Government of the Russian Federation
151. Head of a department section of the Military-Industrial Commission under the Government of the Russian Federation
152. Assistant of a department of the Military-Industrial Commission under the Government of the Russian Federation
153. First Deputy Federal Minister
154. Deputy Federal Minister
155. Head (Chief) of a federal ministry service
156. Chief of staff of a federal minister
157. Director of a department of a federal ministry office
158. Head (Director) of a department of a federal ministry office
159. Deputy Head (Chief) of a federal ministry service
160. Deputy Chief of staff of a federal minister
161. Chief of a main directorate of a federal ministry office
162. Deputy Director of a department of a federal ministry office
163. Deputy Head (Director) of a department of a federal ministry office
164. First Deputy Chief of a main directorate of a federal ministry office
165. Deputy Chief of a main directorate of a federal ministry office
166. Aide to a Federal Minister
167. Advisor to a Federal Minister
168. Chief of Staff of the Representative the Russian Federation at the European Court of Human Rights - Deputy Minister of Justice of the Russian Federation
169. First Deputy Chief of Staff of the Representative the Russian Federation at the European Court of Human Rights - Deputy Minister of Justice of the Russian Federation
170. Deputy Chief of Staff of the Representative the Russian Federation at the European Court of Human Rights - Deputy Minister of Justice of the Russian Federation
171. Deputy Chief of the General Staff of the Armed Forces of the Russian Federation
172. Chief of an Inspectorate of the Ministry of Defense of the Russian Federation

173. Chief of a Main Directorate of the General Staff of the Armed Forces of the Russian Federation
174. Deputy Chief of an Inspectorate of the Ministry of Defense of the Russian Federation
175. Deputy Chief of a Main Directorate of the General Staff of the Armed Forces of the Russian Federation
176. Deputy Commander-in-Chief of a service branch of the Armed Forces of the Russian Federation
177. Deputy Commander of a service arm of the Armed Forces of the Russian Federation (Railway Troops)
178. Head of the Administrative Directorate of the President of the Russian Federation
179. First Deputy Head of the Administrative Directorate of the President of the Russian Federation
180. Deputy Head of the Administrative Directorate of the President of the Russian Federation
181. Deputy Head of the Administrative Directorate of the President of the Russian Federation - Chief of the Main Medical Division of the Administrative Directorate of the President of the Russian Federation
182. Chief of a Main Division of the Administrative Directorate of the President of the Russian Federation
183. Chief of a Division of the Administrative Directorate of the President of the Russian Federation
184. Deputy Chief of a Main Division of the Administrative Directorate of the President of the Russian Federation
185. Deputy Chief of a Division of the Administrative Directorate of the President of the Russian Federation
186. Aide to the Head of the Administrative Directorate of the President of the Russian Federation
187. Advisor to the Head of the Administrative Directorate of the President of the Russian Federation
188. Individuals and delegations, sent abroad or invited by the Administrative Directorate of the President of the Russian Federation
189. Chief of the Main Directorate for Special Programs of the President of the Russian Federation
190. Deputy Chief of the Main Directorate for Special Programs of the President of the Russian Federation
191. Chief of a division of the Main Directorate for Special Programs of the President of the Russian Federation
192. Deputy Chief of a division of the Main Directorate for Special Programs of the President of the Russian Federation
193. Chief of a section of the Main Directorate for Special Programs of the President of the Russian Federation
194. Head (Director) of a federal service
195. Head (Director) of a federal agency
196. First Deputy Head (Director) of a federal service
197. Deputy Head (Director) of a federal service
198. Deputy Head (Director) of a federal agency
199. Head (Chief) of a federal service function
200. Head of a federal service department

201. Deputy Director of a federal service - Chief of Staff of the State Anti-Drug Committee
202. General Director of the Ministry of Foreign Affairs of the Russian Federation
203. Director of a department of the Ministry of Foreign Affairs of the Russian Federation
204. Ambassador-at-large of the Ministry of Foreign Affairs of the Russian Federation
205. Deputy Director of a department of the Ministry of Foreign Affairs of the Russian Federation
206. Aide to the Minister of Foreign Affairs of the Russian Federation
207. Advisor to the Minister of Foreign Affairs of the Russian Federation
208. Chief of Staff of the Constitutional Court of the Russian Federation
209. Chief of the Secretariat of the Constitutional Court of the Russian Federation
210. Deputy Chief of Staff of the Constitutional Court of the Russian Federation
211. Deputy Chief of the Secretariat of the Constitutional Court of the Russian Federation
212. Chief of the Secretariat of the Chairman of the Constitutional Court of the Russian Federation
213. Chief of the Representative Mission of the Constitutional Court of the Russian Federation
214. Chief of the Secretariat of the Deputy Chairman of the Constitutional Court of the Russian Federation
215. Chief of the Secretariat of the Judge-Secretary of the Constitutional Court of the Russian Federation
216. Head of a directorate of the Office of the Constitutional Court of the Russian Federation
217. Head of the Administrative Directorate of the Constitutional Court of the Russian Federation
218. Deputy Chief of the Secretariat of the Chairman of the Constitutional Court of the Russian Federation
219. Deputy Chief of the Representative Mission of the Constitutional Court of the Russian Federation
220. Deputy Head of a directorate of the Office of the Constitutional Court of the Russian Federation
221. Deputy Head of the Administrative Directorate of the Constitutional Court of the Russian Federation
222. Head of a section of the Office of the Constitutional Court of the Russian Federation
223. Aide to the Chairman of the Constitutional Court of the Russian Federation
224. Advisor to the Chairman of the Constitutional Court of the Russian Federation
225. Legal Adviser at the Constitutional Court of the Russian Federation
226. Chief of the Secretariat of the Chairman of the Supreme Court of the Russian Federation
227. Chief of the Secretariat of the First Deputy Chairman of the Supreme Court of the Russian Federation
228. Deputy Chief of the Secretariat of the Chairman of the Supreme Court of the Russian Federation
229. Head of a directorate of the Office of the Supreme Court of the Russian Federation
230. Head of the Administrative Directorate of the Supreme Court of the Russian Federation

231. Deputy Head of a directorate of the Office of the Supreme Court of the Russian Federation
232. Deputy Head of the Administrative Directorate of the Supreme Court of the Russian Federation
233. Head of a section of the Office of the Supreme Court of the Russian Federation
234. Aide to the Chairman of the Supreme Court of the Russian Federation
235. Advisor to the Chairman of the Supreme Court of the Russian Federation
236. Chief of a Main Directorate of the Judicial Department at the Supreme Court of the Russian Federation
237. Chief of a Directorate of the Judicial Department at the Supreme Court of the Russian Federation
238. Head of the Administrative Directorate of the Judicial Department at the Supreme Court of the Russian Federation
239. Chief of Staff - Administrator of the Supreme Arbitration Court of the Russian Federation
240. Deputy Chief of Staff of the Supreme Arbitration Court of the Russian Federation
241. Chief of the Secretariat of the Chairman of the Supreme Arbitration Court of the Russian Federation
242. Deputy Chief of the Secretariat of the Chairman of the Supreme Arbitration Court of the Russian Federation - Aide to the Chairman of the Supreme Arbitration Court of the Russian Federation
243. Head of a directorate of the Office of the Supreme Arbitration Court of the Russian Federation
244. Head of the Administrative Directorate of the Supreme Arbitration Court of the Russian Federation
245. Deputy Head of a directorate of the Office of the Supreme Arbitration Court of the Russian Federation
246. Deputy Head of the Administrative Directorate of the Supreme Arbitration Court of the Russian Federation
247. Head of a section of the Office of the Supreme Arbitration Court of the Russian Federation
248. Aide to the Chairman of the Supreme Arbitration Court of the Russian Federation
249. Advisor to the Chairman of the Supreme Arbitration Court of the Russian Federation
250. Head of a directorate of the Office of the Prosecutor General of the Russian Federation
251. Deputy Head of a directorate of the Office of the Prosecutor General of the Russian Federation
252. Chief of Staff of the Office of the Prosecutor General of the Russian Federation
253. Deputy Chief of Staff of the Office of the Prosecutor General of the Russian Federation
254. Head of the Administrative Directorate of the Office of the Prosecutor General of the Russian Federation
255. Deputy Head of the Administrative Directorate of the Office of the Prosecutor General of the Russian Federation
256. Head of a main directorate of the Investigative Committee under the Office of the Prosecutor General of the Russian Federation
257. Deputy Head of a main directorate of the Investigative Committee under the Office of the Prosecutor General of the Russian Federation

258. Head of a directorate of the Investigative Committee under the Office of the Prosecutor General of the Russian Federation
259. Chief of Staff of the Accounts Chamber of the Russian Federation
260. Deputy Chief of Staff of the Accounts Chamber of the Russian Federation
261. Chief of the Secretariat of the Chairman of the Accounts Chamber of the Russian Federation
262. Chief of the Secretariat of the Deputy Chairman of the Accounts Chamber of the Russian Federation
263. Director of a department of the Office of the Accounts Chamber of the Russian Federation
264. Deputy Director of a department of the Office of the Accounts Chamber of the Russian Federation
265. Deputy Chief of the Secretariat of the Chairman of the Accounts Chamber of the Russian Federation
266. Head of an inspectorate of the Office of the Accounts Chamber of the Russian Federation
267. Chief of Staff of the Central Election Commission of the Russian Federation
268. Deputy Chief of Staff of the Central Election Commission of the Russian Federation
269. Head of a directorate of the Office of the Accounts Chamber of the Russian Federation
270. Deputy Head of a directorate of the Office of the Accounts Chamber of the Russian Federation
271. Head of the Administrative Directorate of the Commissioner for Human Rights of the Russian Federation
272. Chief of the Secretariat of the Commissioner for Human Rights of the Russian Federation
273. Deputy Head of the Administrative Directorate of the Commissioner for Human Rights of the Russian Federation
274. Head of a directorate in the Office of the Commissioner for Human Rights of the Russian Federation
275. Deputy Chief of the Secretariat of the Commissioner for Human Rights of the Russian Federation
276. Deputy Head of a directorate in the Office of the Commissioner for Human Rights of the Russian Federation
277. Director of the Federal Service for Technical and Export Control
278. First Deputy Director of the Federal Service for Technical and Export Control
279. Deputy Director of the Federal Service for Technical and Export Control
280. Head of a main directorate of the Federal Service for Technical and Export Control
281. Head of a directorate of the Federal Service for Technical and Export Control
282. First Deputy Head of a main directorate of the Federal Service for Technical and Export Control
283. Deputy Head of a main directorate of the Federal Service for Technical and Export Control
284. Deputy Head of a directorate of the Federal Service for Technical and Export Control
285. Head of division in a main directorate of the Federal Service for Technical and Export Control
286. Representative of the Government of the Russian Federation

287. Head of a government body of the Russian Federation
288. Deputy Representative of the Government of the Russian Federation
289. Deputy Head of a government body of the Russian Federation
290. Holder of the highest office in a constituent entity of the Russian Federation (head of the supreme executive body of state authority of a constituent entity of the Russian Federation) and his deputies
291. Head of an executive body of state authority of a constituent entity of the Russian Federation
292. Minister of an executive body of state authority of a constituent entity of the Russian Federation
293. Deputy of the legislative (representative) body of state authority of a constituent entity of the Russian Federation
294. Chairman of the Supreme Court of a constituent entity of the Russian Federation and his deputies
295. Chairman of the Arbitration Court of a constituent entity of the Russian Federation and his deputies
296. Prosecutor of a constituent entity of the Russian Federation and his deputies
297. Head of a directorate (main directorate) of internal affairs of a constituent entity of the Russian Federation and his deputies
298. Head of a Federal Security Service directorate in a constituent entity of the Russian Federation and his deputies
299. Head of the investigative directorate of the Investigative Committee under the Office of the Prosecutor General of the Russian Federation for a constituent entity of the Russian Federation and his deputies
300. Head of an administrative center (capital) of a constituent entity of the Russian Federation and his deputies
301. Aide to the holder of the highest office in a constituent entity of the Russian Federation, head of an executive body of state authority of a constituent entity of the Russian Federation, chairman of the legislative (representative) body of state authority of a constituent entity of the Russian Federation
302. Director of a department at the Central Bank of the Russian Federation
303. Chairman of the Management Board of Pension Fund of the Russian Federation and his deputies
304. Chairman of the Social Insurance Fund of the Russian Federation and his deputies
305. President of the Russian Academy of Sciences
306. Vice-President of the Russian Academy of Sciences
307. Chief Academic Secretary of the Presidium of the Russian Academy of Sciences
308. Academician-Secretary of a branch of the Russian Academy of Sciences
309. Chairman of a regional branch of the Russian Academy of Sciences
310. Full member of the Russian Academy of Sciences
311. Other officials appointed and dismissed by the President of the Russian Federation or the Chairman of the Government of the Russian Federation
312. Patriarch of Moscow and All Russia
313. Permanent member of the Holy Synod of the Russian Orthodox Church
314. Chief Rabbi of Russia
315. Chairman of the Council of Muftis of Russia
316. Marshal of the Soviet Union
317. Marshal of the Russian Federation
318. Chief Marshal of a service arm of the Armed Forces of the Russian Federation

319. Marshal of a service arm of the Armed Forces of the Russian Federation
320. Army General
321. Navy Admiral
322. Commander-in-Chief of a service branch of the Armed Forces of the Russian Federation and his first deputies
323. Commander of a service arm of the Armed Forces of the Russian Federation and his first deputies
324. Commander of the troops of a military district (fleet) and his first deputies
325. Commander of regional troops and his first deputies
326. Pilot-cosmonaut
327. Hero of Russia
328. Hero of the Soviet Union
329. Hero of Socialist Labor
330. Individuals awarded the Order of Glory (first, second, or third class)
331. Individuals awarded the Order "For Merit to the Fatherland" (first or second class)
332. Ambassador Extraordinary and Plenipotentiary of the Russian Federation in a foreign state
333. Envoy Extraordinary and Minister Plenipotentiary
334. Head of a diplomatic mission accredited in the Russian Federation and members of his family
335. Russian delegations and foreign delegations led by officials of the Russian Federation, constituent entities of the Russian Federation, and foreign states
336. Leader of a foreign state
337. Head of government of a foreign state
338. Government minister of a foreign state
339. Head of an administrative-territorial entity of a foreign state and his deputies
340. Minister of an executive authority of an administrative-territorial entity of a foreign state
341. City mayor of a foreign state and his deputies leading foreign delegations
342. Foreign diplomatic and consular couriers
343. Officers of the Federal Guard Service of the Russian Federation performing official duties when accompanying individuals under state protection and (or) traveling abroad for official purposes on the instructions of the Federal Guard Service of the Russian Federation
344. Chairman of the Executive Committee of the Union of the Red Cross Societies and his deputies
345. Persons meeting and seeing off officials, family members of the officials, as well as accompanying persons according to the application of the official
346. Leaders of political parties represented in the State Duma of the Federal Assembly of the Russian Federation and their deputies
347. Commissioner for Human Rights of the Russian Federation
348. State Secretary of the Union State and his deputies
349. Secretary General of the Collective Security Treaty Organization and his deputies
350. Chairman of the Executive Committee - Executive Secretary of the Commonwealth of Independent States and his deputies
351. President of the Chamber of Commerce and Industry of the Russian Federation and his vice-presidents
352. Member of the Public Chamber of the Russian Federation approved by the President of the Russian Federation and persons accompanying him on his official trip

353. Persons entitled to state protection upon decision of the President of the Russian Federation
354. Individuals and delegations from foreign states arriving at the invitation of the Federal Guard Service of the Russian Federation

Literature

«Административно-территориальное деление России: история и современность». Под редакцией А. Пыжикова. М. Олма-пресс. 2003

The administrative-territorial division of Russia: History and modernity. Edited by A. Pyzhikov. M.: Olma-Press. 2003

А. Рождение ГУЛАГа: дискуссии в верхних эшелонах власти // Исторический архив. 1997. № 4.

A. *The birth of GULAG: Discussion in the upper echelons of power* // Istoricheskiy arkhiv. 1997. N°. 4.

Авраамова Е.М., Михайлюк М.В., Ниворожкина Л.И., Овсянников А.А., Овчарова Л.Н., Радаев В.В., Рощина Я.М., Сурков С.В., Фирсова Н.Ю. Средние классы в России: экономические и социальные стратегии / Ред.: Малева Т.М. - Москва: Гендальф, 2003.

Avraamova E.M., Mikhailyuk M.V., Nivorozhkina L.I., Ovsyannikov A.A., Ovcharova L.N., Radaev V.V., Roshchina Ya.M., Surkov S.V., Firsova N.Yu. *The middle classes in Russia: Economic and social strategies* / Ed.: Maleva T. M. - Moscow: Gendalf, 2003.

Азарх Э.Д. Кордонский С.Г. Социологическое содержание некоторых проблем здоровья и здравоохранения в исследовании уровня жизни населения. В "Опыт социологического исследования уровня жизни: методические аспекты". Новосибирск 1986

Azarkh E.D. Kordonsky S.G. Sociological aspects of some health and healthcare issues in studying the living standards of the population. In *Experience of sociological research of the living standard: Methodological aspects.* Novosibirsk 1986

Аристотель. Никомахова этика. / пер. Брагинская Н. М.: ЗАО «Издательство «Эксмо-Пресс», 1997

Aristotle. *Nicomachean ethics* / translated by Braginskaya N. M.: IBA Izdatel'stvo Eksmo-Press, 1997

Аристотель. Политика. III, V, 8 // Аристотель. Политика. Афинская полития. М.: Мысль, 1997

Aristotle. *Politics.* III, V, 8 // Aristotle. *Politics. Constitution of Athens.* M.: Mysl', 1997

Арутюнян Ю. В. Социальная структура сельского населения СССР. М., 1971.

Arutyunyan Yu. V. *The social structure of rural population in the USSR.* M., 1971

Балабанов С. С. Социальные типы и социальная стратификация // Социологический журнал. 1995. № 2. С. 116.

Balabanov S. S. *Social types and social stratification* // Sotsiologicheskiy zhurnal. 1995. № 2. p. 116.

Бергер П., Лукман Т. Социальное конструирование реальности. Трактат по социологии знания. М., 1995.

Berger P., Luckmann T. *The Social Construction of Reality. A Treatise on Sociology of Knowledge.* M., 1995.

Бердинский В. Спецпоселенцы. М., 2005.

Berdinsky V. *Deportees.* M., 2005.

Бердяев Н. А. Истоки и смысл русского коммунизма. М., 1990.

Berdyaev N. A. *The origin of Russian communism.* M., 1990.

Берхин И.Б. Экономическая политика советского государства в первые годы советской власти. Москва 1979

Berkhin I.B. *Economic policy of the Soviet state in the first years of Soviet power.* Moscow 1979

Бессонова О. Раздаточная экономика России. М., 2007.

Bessonova O. *The Russian distributive economy.* M., 2007.

Бессонова О. Э. Институты раздаточной экономики России: ретроспективный анализ. Новосибирск, 1997.

Bessonova O. E. *Institutions of the Russian distributive economy. A retrospective analysis.* Novosibirsk, 1997.

Бессонова О. Э., Кирдина С. Г., О'Салливан Р. Рыночный эксперимент в раздаточной экономике России. Новосибирск, 1996.

Bessonova O. E., Kirdina S. G., O'Sullivan P. *Market experiment in Russia's distributive economy.* Novosibirsk, 1996.

Блюм А., Меспуле М. Бюрократическая анархия. Статистика и власть при Сталине. М., 2006.

Blum A., Mespoulet M. *Bureaucratic anarchy: Statistics and power under Stalin.* М., 2006.

Богомолова Т. Ю., Тапилина В. С., Михеева А. Р. Социальная структура: неравенство в материальном благосостоянии. Новосибирск, 1992.

Bogomolova T. Yu., Tapilina V. S., Mikheeva A. R. *Social structure: Inequality in material well-being.* Novosibirsk, 1992.

Борисова Л. И. Трудовые отношения в советской России (1918–1924 гг.) М., 2006.

Borisova L. I. *Labor relations in Soviet Russia (1918–1924)* М., 2006.

Бородкин Л. И., Соколов А. К., Хлевнюк О. В. и др. ГУЛАГ: Экономика принудительного труда / Под ред. Л.И. Бородкина, П. Грегори, О.В. Хлевнюка. М., 2005.

Borodkin L. I., Sokolov A. K., Khlevnyuk O. V. et al. *GULAG: The economy of forced labor* / Edited by L.I. Borodkin, P. Gregory, O.V. Khlevnyuk. М., 2005.

Борхес Х. Л. Аналитический язык Джона Уилкинса. Проза разных лет. М., 1989.

Borges J. L. *The Analytical Language of John Wilkins. Collected prose.* М., 1989.

Боулдинг К. Общая теория систем - скелет науки // Исследования по общей теории систем. - М.: Прогресс, 1969 - с.106–124.
Boulding K. *General systems theory—The skeleton of science* // Issledovaniya po obschey teorii sistem. - M.: Progress, 1969 - pp.106–124.

Бруцкус Б.Д. Социалистическое хозяйство. Теоретические мысли по поводу русского опыта. М., 1999.
Brutskus B.D. *The socialist economy. Theoretical reflections on the Russian experience*. M., 1999.

Бурдье П. Практический смысл. СПб., 2001.
Bourdieu P. *Practical reason*. SPb., 2001.

Бурдье П. Социология политики. М., 1993.
Bourdieu P. *Sociology of politics*. M., 1993.

Бурдье П. Университетская докса и творчество: против схоластических делений // Socio-Logos'96. Альманах Российско-французского центра социологических исследований Института социологии Российской Академии наук. М., 1996.
Bourdieu P. *University Doxa and creativity: Against scholastic divisions* // Socio-Logos'96. Al'manakh Rossiysko-frantsuzskogo tsentra sotsiologicheskikh issledovaniy Instituta sotsiologii Rossiyskoy Akademii nauk. M., 1996.

В.И. Ленин и ВЧК. Москва 1975
V.I. *Lenin and the VChK*. Moscow 1975

Ваганов Ф. Правый уклон в ВКП(б) и его разгром. Москва 1970
Vaganov F. *The right deviation in the CPSU(b) and its defeat*. Moscow 1970

Вагин В.В. Городская социология: Учеб. пособие для муницип. управляющих. М., 2000.
Vagin V.V. *Urban sociology: Manual for municipal managers*. M., 2000.

Вагин В.В. Русский провинциальный город: ключевые элементы жизнеустройства // Мир России. 1997. № 4. С. 53–88.

Vagin V.V. *The Russian provincial town: Key elements of town-life organization* // Mir Rossii. 1997. № 4. pp. 53–88.

Вебер М. Основные понятия стратификации // СОЦИС. 1994. No. 5. С. 169–183

Weber M. *Key concepts on social stratification* // SOTsIS. 1994. No. 5. pp. 169–183

Веблен Т. Теория праздного класса. М., 1984.

Veblen T. *The theory of the leisure class*. M., 1984.

Вернадский В.И. Избранные труды по истории науки. - М.: Наука, 1981 - с.289.

Vernadsky V.I. *Collected works on the history of science*. - M.: Nauka, 1981 - p.289.

Веселовский В. Классы, слои и власть. М., 1981.

Veselovsky V. *Classes, strata, and government*. M., 1981.

Волков В.В. Силовое предпринимательство. М., 2002.

Volkov V.V. *Violent entrepreneurship*. M., 2002.

Волков В.В. Советская цивилизация как повседневная практика: возможности и пределы трансформации // Куда идет Россия? Общее и особенное в современном развитии. М., 1997.

Volkov V.V. *Soviet civilization as daily practice: transformation opportunities and limits* // Kuda idyot Rossiya? Obschee i osobennoe v sovremennom razvitii. M., 1997.

Восленский М. Номенклатура. Москва 1991

Voslensky M. *The Nomenklatura*. Moscow 1991

Восленский М. Феодальный социализм. Место номенклатуры в истории // Новый мир. 1991. № 9.

Voslensky M. *Feudal socialism. The role of nomenklatura in history* // Novy mir. 1991. № 9.

Восленский М.С. Номенклатура. Господствующий класс Советского Союза. М., 1991.
Voslensky M.S. *Nomenklatura. The Soviet ruling class.* M., 1991.

Вылцан М.А. Депортация народов в годы Великой отечественной войны // Этнографическое обозрение. 1995. №3
Vyltsan M.A. *Deportation of ethnic groups during the Great Patriotic War* // Etnograficheskoe obozrenie. 1995. №3

Вышинский А. Я. Судебные речи. Москва 1953
Vyshinsky A. Ya. *Court speeches.* Moscow 1953

Галковский Д. Русская политика и русская философия. Иное. Том 3. Москва 1995
Galkovsky D. *Russian politics and Russian philosophy.* Other. Vol. 3. Moscow 1995

Геллнер Э. Условия свободы: гражданское общество и его соперники. М., 1995.
Gellner E. *Conditions of liberty: Civil society and its rivals.* M., 1995.

Герцен А.И. Письма об изучении природы. - М.: Худ. лит., 1965 - с.305
Herzen A.I. *Letters on the study of nature.* - M.: Khud. lit., 1965 - p.305

Гидденс Э. Стратификация и классовая структура // Социологические исследования. 1992. № 9.
Giddens A. *Stratification and class structure* // Sotsiologicheskie issledovaniya. 1992. № 9.

Гинзбург Л. Литература в поисках реальности. Ленинград 1987
Ginzburg L. *Literature in search of reality.* Leningrad 1987

Глазычев В.Л. Глубинная Россия: 2000–2002. М., 2002.
Glazychev V.L. *Russia's Remote Areas*: 2000–2002. M., 2002.

Гоббс Т. Левиафан, или Материя, форма и власть государства церковного и гражданского. Гл. XV // Гоббс Т. Левиафан. М.: Мысль, 2001

Hobbes T. *Leviathan, or the Matter, Forme, and Power of a Common Wealth, Ecclesiasticall and Civil.* Chapter XV // Hobbes T. Leviathan. M.: Mysl', 2001

Голенкова З.Т., Гридчин Ю.В., Игитханян Е.Д. (Ред.). Трансформация социальной структуры и стратификация российского общества. М., 1998.

Golenkova Z.T., Gridchin Yu.V., Igitkhanyan E.D. (ed.). *Transformation of the social structure and stratification of the Russian society.* M., 1998.

Гольденберг И.А. Хозяйственно-социальная иерархия в России до и после перестройки // СОЦИС. 1995. № 4.

Goldenberg I.A. *The economic social hierarchy in Russia before and after perestroika* // SOTsIS. 1995. № 4.

Гордон Л.А., Клопов Э.В. Человек после работы. М., 1972.

Gordon L.A., Klopov E.V. *Man after work.* M., 1972.

Горшкова М.К., Тихонова Н.Е., Чепуренко А.Ю. (Ред.). Средний класс в современном российском обществе. М., 1999.

Gorshkova M.K., Tikhonova N.Ye., Chepurenko A.Yu (ed.). *The middle class in modern Russian society.* M., 1999.

Громова Р.Г. Социальные группы как участники трансформационного процесса // Куда идет Россия? Власть, общество, личность. М., 2000.

Gromova R.G. *Social groups as participants of the transformation process* // Kuda idyot Rossiya? Vlast', obschestvo, lichnost'. M., 2000.

Гумилев Л. Этносфера: история людей и история природы. Ленинград 1991

Gumilyov L. *Ethnosphere: Human history and natural history.* Leningrad 1991

Дворкин Р. Либерализм // Современный либерализм: Ролз, Берлин, Дворкин, Кимлика, Сэндел, Тейлор, Уолдрон / пер. с англ. Л.Б. Макеевой. М.: Дом интеллектуальной книги, Прогресс. Традиция, 1998
Dworkin R. *Liberalism* // Contemporary liberalism: Rawls, Berlin, Dworkin, Kymlicka, Sandel, Taylor, Waldron / translated by L.B. Makeeva. M.: Dom intellektual'noy knigi, Progress. Traditsiya, 1998

Демографическая модернизация России 1900-2000 / Под ред. А. Вишневского М., 2006.
Demographic modernization in Russia 1900-2000 / edited by A. Vishnevsky M., 2006.

Джеффри Ч. Биологическая номенклатура. М., 1980.
Jeffrey Ch. *Biological Nomenclature*. M., 1980.

Джилас М. Лицо тоталитаризма. М., 1992.
Djilas M. *The face of totalitarianism*. M., 1992.

Дзержинский Ф. Э. Избранные произведения. Том 1. Москва 1957
Dzerzhinsky F. E. *Selected works*. Vol. 1. Moscow 1957

Диалектический и исторический материализм. Москва 1934
Dialectical and Historical Materialism. Moscow 1934

Дилигенский Г.Г. Люди среднего класса - Москва: Институт Фонда Общественное мнение, 2003
Diligensky G.G. *The middle-class people*—Moscow: Institut Fonda Obschestvennoe mnenie, 2003

Добкин А.И. Лишенцы (1918–1936) // Звенья. М.; СПб.1992. (Исторический альманах. 2nd issue).
Dobkin A.I. *Lishentsy (1918–1936)* // Zven'ya. M.; SPb.1992. (Istoricheskiy al'manakh. Вып. 2).

Добренко Е. Политэкономия соцреализма. М., 2007.
Dobrenko E. *The political economy of socialist realism*. M., 2007.

Дэвис К., Мур У. Некоторые принципы стратификации // Социальная стратификация / Вып. 1. Отв. ред. С.А. Белановский. М., 1992.

Davis K., Moore W. *Some principles of stratification* // Sotsial'naya stratifikatsiya / 1st issue. Publishing editor S.A. Belanovsky. M., 1992.

Дюркгейм Э. О разделении общественного труда - Москва: Канон, 1996.

Durkheim E. *The Division of Labour in Society* - Moscow: Kanon, 1996.

Дюркгейм Э. О разделении общественного труда. Метод социологии. Москва 1991

Durkheim E. *The Division of Labour in Society. Sociological method*. Moscow 1991

Дюркгейм Э. Самоубийство. М., 1994.

Durkheim E. *Suicide*. M., 1994.

Ерошкин Н.П. История государственных учреждений дореволюционной России. М., 1983.

Yeroshkin N.P. *The history of state institutions in pre-revolutionary Russia*. M., 1983.

Ефимов В.М. Эволюционный анализ русской аграрной институциональной системы // Мир России. № 1 2009

Yefimov V.M. *Evolutionary analysis of the Russian agrarian institutional system* // Mir Rossii. № 1 2009

Жиромская В.Б. После революционных бурь: Население России в первой половине 20-х годов. М.: Наука, 1996

Zhiromskaya V.B. *After the revolutionary storms: Russia's population in the first half of the 1920s*. M.: Nauka, 1996

Жувенель де Бертран Этика перераспределения. Москва 1995

De Jouvenel B. *The ethics of redistribution*. Moscow 1995

Замогильный С.И. Динамика социальной дифференциации. Саратов, 1991.
Zamogil'ny S.I. *The dynamics of social differentiation.* Saratov, 1991.

Замогильный С.И. Эволюция теорий классов и современность. Саратов, 1989.
Zamogil'ny S.I. *Evolution of class theories and the present.* Saratov, 1989.

Заславская Т. Российское общество на социальном изломе: взгляд изнутри. М., 1997.
Zaslavskaya T. *The Russian society at the social fracture: insight.* M., 1997.

Заславская Т., Рывкина Р. Социология экономической жизни. Очерки теории. Новосибирск 1991
Zaslavskaya T., Ryvkina R. *The sociology of economic life. Essays on theory.* Novosibirsk 1991

Заславская Т.И. О социальных функциях миграции сельского населения в городе // Урбанизация и рабочий класс в условиях научно–технической революции. М., 1970.
Zaslavskaya T.I. *On the social functions of the migration of the rural population in the city* // Urbanizatsiya i rabochiy klass v usloviyakh nauchno-technicheskoy revolyutsii. M., 1970.

Заславская Т.И. Трансформация российского общества как предмет мониторинга // Экономические и социальные перемены: Мониторинг общественного мнения. 1993. № 2.
Zaslavskaya T.I. *Transformation of the Russian society as a subject of monitoring* // Ekonomicheskie i sotsial'nye peremeny: Monitoring obschestvennogo mneniya. 1993. № 2.

Заславская Т.И., Громова Р.Г. К вопросу о «среднем классе» российского общества // Мир России. 1998. N 4.
Zaslavskaya T.I., Gromova R.G. *On the issue of the Russian "middle class"* // Mir Rossii. 1998. N 4.

Зверев. А.Г. Записки министра. М., 1973.

Zverev A.G. *A minister's notes*. М., 1973.

Земсков В.Н. Заключенные в 1930-е годы: социально-демографические проблемы // Отечественная история. 1997. № 5.

Zemskov V.N. *Prisoners of the 1930s: socio-demographic problems* // Otechestvennaya istoriya. 1997. № 5.

Земсков В.Н. Спецпереселенцы // СОЦИС. 1990. № 11.

Zemskov V.N. *Deportees* // SOTsIS. 1990. № 11.

Земсков В.Н. Судьба «кулацкой ссылки» (1930–1954) // Отечественная история. 1994. № 1.

Zemskov V.N. *Fate of "Kulak exile" (1930–1954)* // Otechestvennaya istoriya. 1994. № 1.

Зиммель Г. Социальная дифференциация. М., 1909.

Simmel G. *On social differentiation*. М., 1909.

Зиновьев А. Зияющие высоты. Москва 1990 том 1–2

Zinoviev A. *Gaping heights*. Moscow 1990 Vol. 1–2

Иванова Н. А., Желтова В. П. Сословно-классовая структура России в конце XIX - начале XX века. М., 2004.

Ivanova N. A., Zheltova V. P. *The estate and class structure of Russia in the late nineteenth–early twentieth centuries*. М., 2004.

Ивницкий Н. А. Коллективизация и раскулачивание (начало 30-х гг.). М., 1994.

Ivnitsky N.A. *Collectivization and dekulakization (the early 1930s)*. М., 1994.

Изменение социально-классовой структуры общества в условиях его трансформации / Якуба Е. А., Куценко О. Д., Хижняк Л. М., Безносов М. А., Евдокимова И. А. Харьков, 1997.

Changes in the social and class structure of the society during its transformation / Yakuba E. A., Kutsenko O. D., Khizhnyak L. M., Beznosov M. A., Yevdokimova I. A. Kharkov, 1997.

Изменение социальной структуры советского общества: в 2 кн. М., 1976.
Changes in the social structure of the Soviet society: in 2 vol. M., 1976.

Изменения социальной структуры советского общества. 1921- середина 30 годов. Москва 1979
Changes in the social structure of the Soviet society. 1921-mid-1930s. Moscow 1979

Ильин В., Хосуева Н. Социальная мобильность региональной административной элиты в переходный период // Рубеж: Альманах социальных исследований. 1997. Вып.10/11.
Ilyin V., Khosueva N. Social mobility of the regional administrative elite in the transition period // Rubezh: Al'manakh sotsial'nykh issledovaniy. 1997. Issue 10/11.

Ильин В.И. «Белые воротнички» в современной России: новые средние слои или конторский пролетариат? // Рубеж: Альманах социальных исследований. 1996. Вып. 8/9.
Ilyin V.I. "White collar workers" in modern Russia: The new middle strata or office proletariat? // Rubezh: Al'manakh sotsial'nykh issledovaniy. 1996. Issue 8/9.

Ильин В.И. Власть и уголь. Сыктывкар, 1998.
Ilyin V.I. Government and coal. Syktyvkar, 1998.

Ильин В.И. Государство и социальная стратификация советского и постсоветского обществ. 1917–1996 гг. Опыт конструктивистско-структуралистского анализа. Сыктывкар, 1996.
Ilyin V.I. The state and social stratification of Soviet and post-Soviet societies. 1917–1996. Experience of a constructivist-structuralist analysis. Syktyvkar, 1996.

Ильин В.И. Методологические проблемы анализа классовой структуры // Куда идет Россия? Власть, общество, личность. М., 2000.

Ilyin V.I. *Methodological issues of class structure analysis* // Kuda idyot Rossiya? Vlast', obschestvo, lichnost'. M., 2000.

Ильин В.И. Поведение потребителей. СПб., 2000.

Ilyin V.I. *Consumer behavior.* SPb., 2000.

Ильин В.И. Социальная группа как фактор потребительского поведения // Маркетинг и маркетинговые исследования в России. 1999. № 4 (22).

Ilyin V.I. *The social group as a factor of consumer behavior* // Marketing i marketingovye issledovaniya v Rossii. 1999. № 4 (22).

Ильин В.И. Социальная стратификация. Сыктывкар: Издательство СГУ, 1991

Ilyin V.I. *Social stratification.* Syktyvkar: Izdatel'stvo SGU, 1991

Ильин В.И. Социальное конструирование национального меньшинства // Этнические стереотипы в меняющемся мире / Под ред. Батьянова Е. П. и Калабанова А. Н. М., 1998.

Ilyin V.I. *The social modeling of a national minority* // Etnicheskie stereotypy v menyayuschemsya mire / Edited by Bat'yanova E. P. and Kalabanova A. N. M., 1998.

Ильин В.И. Социальное неравенство. М., 2000.

Ilyin V.I. *Social inequality.* M., 2000.

Ильин В.И. Хрестоматия: теория социального неравенства в западной социологии - Сыктывкар: Сыктывкарский государственный университет, 2002.

Ilyin V.I. *Anthology: The theory of social inequality in Western sociology* - Syktyvkar: Syktyvkarskiy gosudarstvenny universitet, 2002.

Ильин В.И. Классовая структура: проблема методологии анализа // Рубеж (альманах социальных исследований). 2000. N 15. С. 86–109.

Ilyin V.I. *Class structure: Analysis methodology* // Rubezh (al'manakh sotsial'nykh issledovaniy). 2000. N 15. pp. 86–109.

Иноземцев В.Л. Социальное неравенство как проблема становления постэкономического общества // Полис. 1999, № 5.

Inozemtsev V.L. *Social inequality as a problem of the postindustrial society* // Polis. 1999, № 5.

Ионин Л., Шкаратан О. Паркинсон и бюрократы: Послесловие // Паркинсон С.Н. Законы Паркинсона: М., 1989.

Ionin L., Shkaratan O. *Parkinson and bureaucrats: Afterword* // Parkinson S.N. The laws of Parkinson: M., 1989.

Исаев И.А. История государства и права России. М., 1993.

Isaev I.A. *History of state and law in Russia.* M., 1993.

Источник. Документы русской истории. Разделы "Подоплека событий. Версии" и "Старая площадь. Вестник архива Президента России". № 1–12, 1994–1996 годы.

Source. Documents of Russian history. Sections "The background of events. Versions" and "Staraya Ploshchad. Bulletin of the archive of the President of Russia". № 1–12, 1994–1996.

Каганский В.Л. Культурный ландшафт и советское обитаемое пространство. - М.: Новое литературное обозрение, 2001.

Kagansky V.L. *The cultural landscape and Soviet inhabited space.* - M.: Novoe literaturnoe obozrenie, 2001.

Каганский В.Л. Советское пространство: конструкция, деструкция и трансформация // Общественные науки, 1995, N 1–2.

Kagansky V.L. *Soviet space: construction, destruction, and transformation* // Obschestvennye nauki, 1995, N 1–2.

Канарш Г.Ю. Социальная справедливость: философские концепции и российская ситуация: монография // Г.Ю. Канарш, М.: Изд-во Моск. гуманит. ун-та, 2011. - 316с.

Kanarsh G.Yu. *Social justice: Philosophical concepts and the situation in Russia: Monograph* // G.Yu. Kanarsh, M.: Izd-vo Mosk. gumanit. un-ta, 2011. - 316 p.

Кант И. О поговорке «Может быть, это и верно в теории, но не годится для практики» // Кант Иммануил. Соч. в 4 томах на немецком и русском языках. Том 1: Трактаты и статьи (1784–1796). Подготовлен к изданию Н. Мотрошиловой (Москва) и Б. Тушлингом (Марбург). М.: Издательская фирма АО «Ками», 1993

Kant I. *"On the common saying: This may be true in theory but it does not apply in practice"* // Kant Immanuel. Collected works in four volumes in German and Russian. Vol.1: Treatises and Articles (1784–1796). Podgotovlen k izdaniyu N. Motroshilovoy (Moskva) i B. Tushlingom (Marburg). M.: Izdatel'skaya firma AO Kami, 1993

Кивинен М. Перспективы развития среднего класса в России // Социологический журнал. 1994. № 2.

Kivinen M. *Prospects for the emergence of the middle class in Russia* // Sotsiologicheskiy zhurnal. 1994. № 2.

Киш А. Социальная структура социалистического общества: мифы и реальность. Москва 1981

Kish A. *Social structure of the socialist society: Myths and reality.* Moscow 1981

Клайн М. Математика. Утрата определенности. - М.: Мир, 1984 - с.446.

Kline M. *Mathematics: Loss of certainty*. - М.: Mir, 1984 - p.446.

Кларк С. Классовая структура России в переходный период // Рубеж: Альманах социальных исследований. 1997. Вып. 10/11.

Clarke S. *The Class Structure of Russia in Transition* // Rubezh: Al'manakh sotsial'nykh issledovaniy. 1997. Issue 10/11.

Ключевский В.О. История сословий в России. Полный курс лекций. М., 2007.
Klyuchevsky V.O. *The history of estates in Russia. Full course of lectures.* M., 2007.

Кобищанов Ю.М. Теория большой феодальной формации // Вопросы истории. 1992. № 4-5.
Kobischanov Yu.M. *Theory of a big feudal formation* // Voprosy istorii. 1992. № 4-5.

Комаров М.С. Социальная стратификация и социальная структура // Социологические исследования. 1992, № 7.
Komarov M.S. *Social stratification and the social structure* // Sotsiologicheskie issledovaniya. 1992, № 7.

Конрад Д., Селеньи И. Интеллигенция и власть в посткоммунистических обществах // Венгерский меридиан. 1991. № 1.
Konrad G., Szelenyi I. *Intellectuals and power in post-communist societies* // Vengerskiy meridian. 1991. № 1.

Кордонский С. Рынки власти. Административные рынки СССР и России. М. 2006 ОГИ
Kordonsky S. *Markets for power. Administrative markets of the USSR and Russia.* M. 2006 OGI

Кордонский С. В реальности и на самом деле // Логос: Философ.-лит. журнал / РГГУ. Философский факультет. Центр феноменологической философии. М.: РГГУ, 2000, № 5/6 (26).
Kordonsky S. *In reality and in fact* // Logos: Filosof.-lit. zhurnal / RGGU. Filosofskiy fakul'tet. Tsentr fenomenologicheskoy filosofii. M.: RGGU, 2000, № 5/6 (26).

Кордонский С. В реальности и на самом деле // Ресурсное государство. М. Регнум 2007

Kordonsky S. *In reality and in fact* // Resource-based state. M. Regnum 2007

Кордонский С. Г. Министерство правды // Век XX и мир, №2 1989

Kordonsky S. G. *The Ministry of Truth* // Vek XX i mir, №2 1989

Кордонский С. Г. Партия и Советы. Возможные действия на локальных рынках // Vestnik Postfaktuma. № 4, 10 августа 1990

Kordonsky S. G. *The Party and Soviets. Potential actions on local markets* // Vestnik Postfaktuma. № 4, 10 august 1990

Кордонский С. Г. Сценарий игрек // Век XX и мир, №3 1990

Kordonsky S. G. *The Y Scenario* // Vek XX i mir, №3 1990

Кордонский С. Г. Три мифа и четыре кита перестройки // Век XX и мир, № 4 1990

Kordonsky S. G. *The three myths and four whales of perestroika* // Vek XX i mir, № 4 1990

Кордонский С. Государство, гражданское общество и коррупция // Отечественные записки, №5 2005

Kordonsky S. *The state, civil society, and corruption* // Otechestvennye zapiski, №5 2005

Кордонский С. Ресурсное государство. М. Регнум 2007.

Kordonsky S. *The resource-based state*. M. Regnum 2007.

Кордонский С. Социальная структура постсоветской России. М. ФОМ. 2008

Kordonsky S. *The social structure of post-Soviet Russia*. M. FOM. 2008

Кордонский С. Циклы деятельности и идеальные объекты. М., 2000.

Kordonsky S. *Activity cycles and ideal objects*. M., 2000.

Кордонский С.Г (Виктор Алтаев) Государственная безопасность // Век XX и мир, № 8 1989

Kordonsky S.G. (Viktor Altaev) *State security* // Vek XX i mir, № 8 1989

Кордонский С.Г. Вариант исчисления административных весов в исполнительской и представительской иерархиях власти // Кентавр, № 2–3 1995

Kordonsky S.G. *Way of measuring the administrative weight in the executive and representative power hierarchies* // Kentavr, № 2–3 1995

Кордонский С.Г. Знание о людях и понимание людей // Проблемы гуманитарного познания. - Новосибирск: Наука, 1986.

Kordonsky S.G. *Knowledge about people and understanding people* // Problemy gumanitarnogo poznaniya. - Novosibirsk: Nauka, 1986.

Кордонский С.Г. Интеллигенция в роли национальной интеллектуальной элиты // Пределы власти, № 1 Москва 1994

Kordonsky S.G. *Intelligentsia in the role of the national intellectual elite* // Predely vlasti, № 1 Moscow 1994

Кордонский С.Г. Исследовательские программы в биологии. Проблема соответствия парадигмальных представлений практике исследований // Методология исследовательских программ. - Новосибирск: Наука, 1987 - с.120–145.

Kordonsky S.G. *Research programs in biology. Reconciling paradigms with research practice* // Metodologiya issledovatel'skikh programm. - Novosibirsk: Nauka, 1987 - pp. 120–145.

Кордонский С.Г. Кристалл и кисель. М., 2002.

Kordonsky S.G. *Crystal and jelly.* M., 2002.

Кордонский С.Г. Построение научной онтологии // Проблемы методологии науки. - Новосибирск: Наука, 1985 - с.111–124.

Kordonsky S.G. *Building a scientific ontology* // Problemy metodologii nauki. - Novosibirsk: Nauka, 1985 - pp.111–124.

Кордонский С.Г. Принципы зоны // Век XX и мир, №8 1989

Kordonsky S.G. *Prison-camp principles* // Vek XX i mir, №8 1989

Кордонский С.Г. Рынки власти. Административные рынки СССР и России. М., 2006.

Kordonsky S.G. *Markets for power. Administrative markets of the USSR and Russia.* М., 2006.

Кордонский С.Г. Социальная структура и механизм торможения / Постижение, Москва 1989

Kordonsky S.G. *The social structure and braking mechanism* / Postizhenie, Moscow 1989

Кордонский С.Г. Способы формирования теоретических объектов разного типа. - Новосибирск: НЭТИ, 1983 - с.106–121. - Деп. в ИНИОН АН СССР 18.05.1984, N 16767.

Kordonsky S.G. *Methods of forming various theoretical objects.* - Novosibirsk: NETI, 1983 - pp.106–121. - Dep. v INION AN SSSR 18.05.1984, N 16767.

Кордонский С.Г. Таксоны и аналитические объекты как системы // Системный метод и современная наука. - Новосибирск: изд. НГУ, 1983 - с.141–150.

Kordonsky S.G. *Taxa and analytical objects as systems* // Sistemny metod i sovremennaya nauka. - Novosibirsk: izd. NGU, 1983 - pp.141–150.

Кордонский С.Г. Теневая экономика в теневом обществе // Пределы власти, №4 Москва 1994

Kordonsky S.G. *Shadow economy in a shadow society* // Predely vlasti, №4 Moscow1994

Кордонский С. Поместная федерация. М.: 2010.

Kordonsky S. *Manorial federation.* М.: 2010.

Корнаи Я. Дефицит. Москва 1990
Kornai J. *Shortage*. Moscow 1990

Кочетов А. Истоки «новой» социальной структуры // Свободная мысль. 1993. № 9.
Kochetov A. *The origins of the "new" social structure* // Svobodnaya mysl'. 1993. № 9.

Красильников С. СЕРП И МОЛОХ. Крестьянская ссылка в Западной Сибири в 1930-е годы. М., 2003.
Krasil'nikov S. *THE SICKLE AND THE MOLOKH. Peasant exile in West Siberia in the 1930s*. М., 2003.

Красильников С.А. Политическая ссылка в 1920-е гг.: некоторые проблемы и задачи изучения // Социально-политические проблемы истории Сибири XVII–XX вв. Новосибирск, 1994.
Krasil'nikov S.A. *Political exile in the 1920s: research challenges and objectives* // Sotsial'no-politicheskie problemy istorii Sibiri XVII–XX vv. Novosibirsk, 1994.

Красильников С.А. Спецпереселенцы в Нарыме в 1931–1932 гг. // История Сибири: человек, общество, государство. Новосибирск, 1995.
Krasil'nikov S.A. *Deportees in Narym in 1931–1932* // Istoriya Sibiri: chelovek, obschestvo, gosudarstvo. Novosibirsk, 1995.

Красильников С.А. Ссылка в 1920-е годы. // Минувшее. М.; СПб., 1997. (Ист. альманах. Вып. 21).
Krasil'nikov S.A. *Exile in the 1920s* // Minuvshee. M.; SPb., 1997. (Ist. al'manakh. Issue 21).

Красильников С.А. Тылоополченцы // ЭКО. 1994. № 3.
Krasil'nikov S.A. *Tyloopolchentsy* // EKO. 1994. № 3.

Кривов А., Крупнов Ю. Дом в России. Национальная идея. ОЛМА-ПРЕСС, 2004 г.
Krivov A., Krupnov Yu. *Home in Russia. The national idea*. OLMA-PRESS, 2004.

Кронрод Я.А. Законы политической экономии социализма. М., 1966.

Kronrod Ya.A. *Laws of the political economy of socialism*. M., 1966.

Кржижановский С. Страны, которых нет. Москва 1994

Krzhizhanovsky S. *Non-existing countries*. Moscow1994

Крыштановская О. Трансформация старой номенклатуры в новую российскую элиту // Общественные науки и современность. 1995. № 1.

Kryshtanovskaya O. *Transformation of the old nomenklatura into the new Russian elite* // Obschestvennye nauki i sovremennost'. 1995. № 1.

Крыштановская О.В. Анатомия российской элиты. М., 2004

Kryshtanovskaya O.V. *Anatomy of the Russian elite*. M., 2004

Кузнецов И.Н. Компетенция высших органов власти и управления СССР. Москва

Kuznetsov I.N. *Competence of the Supreme bodies of power and government of the USSR*. Moscow

Кузьмичев В. Организация общественного мнения. М., 1929.

Kuz'michev V. *Organizing public opinion*. M., 1929.

Куценко О.Д. Общество неравных. Харьков, 2000.

Kutsenko O.D. *Society of unequals*. Kharkov, 2000.

Лакшин В. Читатель. Писатель. Критик // Новый мир, № 12 1969

Lakshin V. *Reader. Writer. Critic* // Novy mir, № 12 1969

Лебедев А. Чаадаев. Москва 1966

Lebedev A. *Chaadayev*. Moscow 1966

Леви-Стросс К. Структурная антропология. Москва 1985

Levi-Strauss C. *Structural anthropology*. Moscow 1985

Лейн Д. Преобразование государственного социализма в России: от «хаотической» экономики к кооперативному капитализму, координируемому государством? // Мир России. 2000. № 1.
Lane D. *The transformation of state socialism in Russia: from "chaotic" economy to state-led cooperative capitalism?* // Mir Rossii. 2000. № 1.

Ленинизм и диалектика общественного развития. Москва 1970
Leninism and dialectics of social development. Moscow 1970

Локк Дж. Два трактата о правлении. Кн. II Гл. 2 // Локк Дж. Два трактата о правлении: пер. с англ.; ред. и сост., автор вступ. статьи и примеч. А. Л. Субботин. М.: «Канон+» РООИ «Реабилитация», 2009
Locke J. *Two treatises of government. Book II Chapter 2* // Locke J. *Two treatises of government*: translation from English. Editor and compiler, author of the foreword and notes A.L. Subbotin. M.: «Kanon+» ROOI «Reabilitatsiya», 2009

Лотман Ю. М. Беседы о русской культуре. Быт и традиции русского дворянства (XVIII-начало XIX века). М., 2006.
Lotman Yu. M. *Conversations about Russian culture. Life and traditions of the Russian nobility (Eighteenth-early nineteenth century).* M., 2006.

Макинтайр А. После добродетели: Исследования теории морали / пер. с англ. В.В. Целищева. М.: Академический Проект; Екатеринбург: Деловая книга, 2000
MacIntyre A. *After virtue: A study in moral theory* / translated by V.V. Tselischev. M.: Akademicheskiy Proekt; Yekaterinburg: Delovaya kniga, 2000

Мамардашвили М. Закон инаконемыслия // Здесь и теперь, 1992 №1
Mamardashvili M. *The non-dissidence law* // Zdes' i teper', 1992 №1

Мамут Л.С. Социальное государство с точки зрения права // Государство и право: Ежемесячный журнал. - 2001. - № 7. - С. 5–14.

Mamut L.S. The welfare state from the legislative perspective // Gosudarstvo i pravo: Yezhemesyachny zhurnal. - 2001. - № 7. - pp. 5–14.

Манин Ю.И. Доказуемое и недоказуемое. - М.: Сов. радио, 1979 - с.168.

Manin Yu. I. The provable and unprovable. - M.: Sov. radio, 1979 - p.168.

Маргиналы в социуме. Маргиналы как социум. Сибирь – 1920–1930 годы. Новосибирск, 2007.

Marginalized in the community. Marginalized as a community. Siberia—1920s–1930s. Novosibirsk, 2007.

Махрова А.Г., Нефедова Т.Г., Трейвиш А.И. Московская область сегодня и завтра: тенденции и перспективы пространственного развития. Москва: Новый хронограф, 2008

Makhrova A.G., Nefedova T.G., Treyvish A.I. The Moscow Region today and tomorrow: trends and prospects of spatial development. Moscow: Novy khronograf, 2008

Медушевский А.Н. Демократия и авторитаризм: российский конституционализм в сравнительной перспективе. М., 1998.

Medushevsky A.N. Democracy and authoritarianism: Russian constitutionalism in a comparative perspective. M., 1998.

Межуев В. Социалистическая идея—шанс на будущее // Красные холмы. Альманах. М., 1999.

Mezhuev V. Socialist idea—chance for the future // Krasnye kholmy. Al'manakh. M., 1999.

Межуев В. Традиция самовластия в современной России // Свободная мысль. 2000. № 4.

Mezhuev V. *Tradition of autocracy in contemporary Russia* // Svobodnaya mysl'. 2000. № 4.

Мейен С.В., Шрейдер Ю.А. Методологические аспекты теории классификации // Вопр. философии. - 1976 - N 12 - с.67–79.

Meyen S.V., Shreyder Yu. A. *Methodological aspects of the theory of classification* // Vopr. filosofii. - 1976 - N 12 - pp.67–79.

Мизес Л. фон. Социализм. Экономический и социологический анализ М., 1994.

Von Mises L. *Socialism: an economic and sociological analysis.* M., 1994.

Миллс Ч.Р. Властвующая элита. М., 1959.

Mills Ch.W. *The power elite.* M., 1959.

Миронов Б. Н. Социальная история России периода империи (XVIII–начало XX вв.): Генезис личности, демократической семьи, гражданского общества и правового государства. СПб., 1999.

Mironov B. N. *The social history of Russia at the times of the empire (18th-early 20th centuries): Genesis of the individual, democratic family, civil society and the rule of law.* SPb., 1999.

Моральный кодекс строителя коммунизма. М., 1979.

The moral code of the builder of communism. M., 1979.

Найшуль В. Высшая и последняя стадия социализма. "Погружение в трясину". Москва 1991

Naishul V. *The supreme and last stage of socialism. "Sinking into the bog".* Moscow 1991

Найшуль В. О приватизации государственных обязательств. О современных концепциях рынка // Вестник московской школы политических исследований, № 3 1995

Naishul V. *On the privatization of state obligations. On modern market concepts* // Vestnik moskovskoy shkoly politicheskikh issledovaniy, № 3 1995

Нефедова Т. Г. Сельская Россия на перепутье (географические очерки). М., 2003.

Nefedova T.G. *Rural Russia at the crossroads (geographical essays).* М., 2003.

Нефедова Т., Пэллот. Дж. Неизвестное сельское хозяйство. Зачем нужна корова. М., 2006.

Nefedova T., Pallot J. *Unknown agriculture. Why one needs a cow.* М., 2006.

Нефедова Т.Г, Полян П.М., Трейвиш А.И. Город и деревня в Европейской России: сто лет перемен. Москва: ОГИ, 2001.

Nefedova T.G., Polyan P.M., Treyvish A.I. *The city and village in European Russia: One hundred years of change.* Moscow: OGI, 2001.

Нуреев Р.М. Экономический строй докапиталистических формаций. Душанбе, 1989.

Nureev R.M. *The economic system of pre-capitalist formations.* Dushanbe, 1989

Одиннадцатый съезд Российской коммунистической партии (большевиков). Стенографический отчет. Москва 1922

The Eleventh Congress of the Russian Communist Party (Bolsheviks). Verbatim records. Moscow 1922

Опыт словаря нового мышления. Москва 1989

Vocabulary of new thinking. Moscow 1989

Осокина Е. За фасадом «сталинского изобилия». Распределение и рынок в снабжении населения в годы индустриализации 1927-1941. М., 1999.

Osokina E. *Behind the facade of "Stalin's abundance". The role of distribution and the market in consumer supplies during industrialization.* 1927–1941. M., 1999.

Осокина Е.А. Иерархия потребления. О жизни людей в условиях сталинского снабжения. 1928-1935 годы. М., 1993.

Osokina E.A. *The hierarchy of consumption. Life under Stalin's supply system. 1928-1935.* M., 1993.

Павленко Ю.В. Раннеклассовые общества: генезис и пути развития. Киев, 1989.

Pavlenko Yu.V. *Early class societies: genesis and ways of development.* Kiev, 1989.

Павлов Д. В. Стойкость. М., 1983.

Pavlov D.V. *Resistance.* M., 1983.

Паперный В. Культура Два. Анн Арбор: Ардис Паблишинг 1985

Paperny V. *Culture Two.* Ann Arbor: Ardis Publishing 1985

Парсонс Т. Понятие общества: компоненты и их взаимоотношения // Тезис. 1993. Т. 1. № 2. С. 94–122.

Parsons T. *Concept of society: components and their relation* // Tezis. 1993. Vol. 1. № 2. pp. 94–122.

Партийная этика. Дискуссии 20 годов. Москва 1989

Party ethics. Discussion of the 1920s. Moscow 1989

Пахомов И.Б., Орлов С.А. Ряженые капиталисты на нэповском празднике жизни. М., 2007.

Pakhomov I.B., Orlov S.A. *Capitalists in disguise at the NEP feast of life.* M., 2007.

Первый всесоюзный съезд советских писателей. Стенографический отчет. Москва ГиХЛ 1934
First All-Union Congress of Soviet Writers. Verbatim records. Moscow GiKhL 1934

Петров Н.В. Политические элиты в центре и на местах // Российский монитор: архив современной политики. М., 1995. вып. 5.
Petrov N.V. *Central and local political elites* // Rossiyskiy monitor: arkhiv sovremennoy politiki. M., 1995. issue 5.

Пивоваров Ю. Полная гибель всерьез. М., 2004.
Pivovarov Yu. *Complete collapse in earnest*. M., 2004.

Пивоваров Ю. Русская политика в ее историческом и культурном отношениях. М., 2004.
Pivovarov Yu. *Russian politics in its historical and cultural aspects*. M., 2004.

Пивоваров Ю., Фурсов А. Русская власть, русская система, русская история // Красные холмы: Альманах. М., 1999.
Pivovarov Yu., Fursov A. *Russian government, Russian system, Russian history* // Krasnye kholmy: Al'manakh. M., 1999.

Пименов А.В. Дряхлый Восток и светлое будущее // Мир России. 1999. № 1–2.
Pimenov A.V. *The decrepit East and the bright future* // Mir Rossii. 1999. № 1–2.

Платон. Государство. 557–562 // Платон. Государство. СПб.: Наука, 2005
Plato. *The Republic*. 557–562 // Plato. The Republic. SPb.: Nauka, 2005

Политическая экономия. Учебник. Москва 1954
Political economy. Textbook. Moscow 1954

Полиция и милиция России: страницы истории. М., 1995.
Police and militia in Russia: Pages of history. M., 1995.

Полтерович В.М., Катышев П.К. Политика реформ, начальные условия и трансформационный спад // Экономика и математические методы. 2006. Т. 42. вып.4.

Polterovich V.M., Katyshev P.K. *Reform policies, initial conditions, and transformational recession* // Ekonomika i matematicheskie metody. 2006. Vol. 42. Issue 4.

Попов В.П. Государственный террор в советской России в 1920-1940 // Отечественные архивы. 1992. № 2.

Popov V.P. *State terror in Soviet Russia in 1920-1940* // Otechestvennye arkhivy. 1992. № 2.

Попов В.П. Паспортная система в СССР (1932–1976) // СОЦИС, № 8–9 1995

Popov V.P. *The passport system in the USSR (1932–1976)* // SOTsIS, № 8–9 1995

Поппер К. Логика и рост научного знания. - М.: Прогресс, 1983 - с.605.

Popper K. *The logic of scientific discovery*. - M.: Progress, 1983 - p.605.

Практикум по советскому трудовому праву. Москва. 1986

Workshop on Soviet labor law. Moscow. 1986

Проблема классов в современной социологии (интервью с Эриком Райтом) // Рубеж: Альманах социальных исследований. 1995. № 6/7.

The issue of classes in contemporary sociology (interview with Erik Wright) // Rubezh: Al'manakh sotsial'nykh issledovaniy. 1995. № 6/7.

Проблемы системного изучения деревни / Ред. Заславская Т.И., Рывкина Р.В. Новосибирск, 1975.

Systemic research of the village: Challenges / Edited by Zaslavskaya T.I., Ryvkina R.V. Novosibirsk, 1975.

Программа коммунистической партии Советского Союза. Москва 1967.

Program of the Communist Party of the Soviet Union. Moscow 1967.

Радаев В. В. Социология рынков: к формированию нового направления. М., 2003.

Radaev V. V. *Sociology of markets: towards formation of a new approach.* М., 2003.

Радаев В. В. Формирование новых российских рынков: трансакционные издержки, формы контроля и деловая этика. М., 1998.

Radaev V. V. *Forming new Russian markets: Transaction costs, forms of control, and business ethics.* М., 1998.

Радаев В.В., Шкаратан О.И. Социальная стратификация. М.: Аспект Пресс, 1996.

Radaev V.V., Shkaratan O.I. *Social stratification.* М.: Aspect Press, 1996.

Радаев В.В. Власть и собственность // СОЦИС. 1991. № 1.

Radaev V.V. *Power and property* // SOTsIS. 1991. № 1.

Разуваев В. Время удельных князей // Свободная мысль, №4 1996

Razuvaev V. *The time of appanage princes* // Svobodnaya mysl', №4 1996

Рашин А. Г. Население России за 100 лет (1811–1913 гг.). Статистические очерки. М., 1956.

Rashin A. G. *The population of Russia over 100 years (1811–1913). Statistical essays.* М., 1956.

Региональные элиты Северо-Запада России: политические и экономические ориентации / Под. ред. А.В.Дука. СПб., 2001.

Regional elites of Russia's North-West: Political and economic orientation / Edited by A.V. Duk. SPb., 2001.

Роговин В.З. Л.Д. Троцкий о социальных отношениях в СССР // СОЦИС. 1990. № 5.

Rogovin V.Z. *Leo Trotsky on social relations in the USSR* // SOTsIS. 1990. № 5.

Роговин В.З. Социальная политика в развитом социалистическом обществе. Москва 1980

Rogovin V.Z. *Social policy in a developed socialist society*. Moscow 1980

Ролз Д. Теория справедливости / пер. и науч. ред.: Целищев В.В. Новосибирск: Изд-во Новосиб. Ун-та, 1995

Rawls J. A *Theory of Justice* / translated and edited by Tselischev V.V. Novosibirsk: Izd-vo Novosib. Un-ta, 1995

Россия сегодня. Политический портрет в документах 1991–1992. Москва 1993

Russia today. Political portrait in documents, 1991–1992. Moscow 1993

Глазычев В., Щедровицкий П. Россия: принципы пространственного развития. Доклад Центра стратегических исследований Приволжского федерального округа, 2004

Glazychev V., Schedrovitsky P. *Russia: Principles of spatial development. Report of the Center for Strategic Research of the Volga Federal District*, 2004

Ротбард М. О реконструкции экономической теории полезности и благосостояния. М., 2004.

Rothbard M. *Toward a reconstruction of utility and welfare economics*. М., 2004.

Русский узел евразийства: Восток в русской мысли: Сб. трудов евразийцев. М., 1997.

The Russian Eurasianism knot: the Orient in Russian thought: Collected works of Eurasianists. М., 1997.

Руссо Ж.-Ж. Об общественном договоре, или Принципы политического права. Гл. I // Руссо Ж.-Ж. Об общественном договоре. Трактаты: пер. с фр. М.: «КАНОН пресс», «Кучково поле», 1998

Rousseau J.-J. *Of the social contract, or Principles of political right. Chapter I* // Rousseau J.-J. Of the social contract. Treatises: translation from French. M.: KANON press, Kuchkovo pole, 1998

Рывкина Р.В. Экономическая социология переходной России. М., 1998.

Ryvkina R.V. *Economic sociology of Russia in transition*. M., 1998.

Рыклин М. Пространство ликования. М., 2002.

Ryklin M. *Space of jubilation*. M., 2002.

Сводный список книг, подлежащих исключению из библиотек и книготорговой сети. Части 1–2. Москва 1961

Consolidated list of books to be withdrawn from libraries and bookstores. Parts 1–2. Moscow 1961

Семигин Г. Ю. Социальная справедливость и право. Современная экономика и право. М.. 2008.

Semigin G. Yu. *Social justice and law. Contemporary economy and law*. M.. 2008.

Сен А. Развитие как свобода: пер. с англ.; под ред. и с послесл. Р.М. Нуреева. М.: Новое издательство, 2004

Sen A. *Development as freedom*: Translation from English; Editor and author of the afterword R.M. Nureev. M.: Novoe izdatel'stvo, 2004

Сен Мартен М. де. Реконверсия и трансформация элит // Socio-Logos '96. Альманах Российско-французского центра социологических исследований Института социологии Российской Академии наук. М., 1996.

De Saint Martin M. *Reconversion and transformation of elites* // Socio-Logos '96. Al'manakh Rossiysko-frantsuzskogo tsentra sotsiologicheskikh issledovaniy Instituta sotsiologii Rossiyskoy Akademii nauk. M., 1996.

Смелсер Н. Социология. Москва 1994

Smelser N. *Sociology*. Moscow 1994

Советская демократия / Под ред. Ю. Стеклова. М., 1929.

Soviet democracy / Edited by Yu. Steklov. M., 1929.

Советский простой человек. Опыт социального портрета на рубеже 90-х / Под. ред. Ю. Левады. М., 1993.

An ordinary Soviet citizen. Social portrait at the turn of the 1990s / Edited by Yu. Levada. M., 1993.

Советское административное право. Управление в области административно-политической деятельности. Москва 1979

Soviet administrative law. Management of administrative-political activity. Moscow 1979

Советское административное право. Управление социально-культурным строительством. Москва 1980

Soviet administrative law. Management of socio-cultural processes. Moscow 1980

Сокольников Г.Я. Финансовая политика революции. Т. 1–2. М., 2006.

Sokolnikov G.Ya. *The revolution's financial policy*. Vol. 1–2. M., 2006.

Сорокин П. Система социологии. тома 1–2. Москва 1991

Sorokin P. *A system of sociology*. Vol. 1–2. Москва 1991

Сорокин П. Человек, цивилизация, общество. М., 1992.

Sorokin P. *Personality, civilization*, society. M., 1992.

Сорокин П. А. Социальная мобильность / Пер. с англ. М. В. Соколовой. - Москва: Academia: LVS, 2005.

Sorokin P. A. *Social mobility* / translated by M. V. Sokolova. - Moscow: Academia: LVS, 2005.

Средний класс в российском обществе. М., 1999.

The middle class in Russian society. M., 1999.

Сталин И.В. О проекте Конституции Союза ССР: Доклад на Чрезвычайном VIII Всесоюзном съезде Советов 25 ноября 1936 года // Сочинения. Т. 14. М., 1997.

Stalin J.V. *On the Draft Constitution of the USSR. Report Delivered at the Extraordinary Eighth Congress of Soviets of the USSR on 25 November 1936* // Collected works. Vol. 14. M., 1997.

Стариков Е.Н. Маргиналы // Знамя. 1989. № 10

Starikov E.N. *The marginalized* // Znamya. 1989. № 10

Стариков Е.Н. Общество—казарма от фараонов до наших дней. Новосибирск, 1996

Starikov E.N. *Society—Kaserne from the Pharaohs to our days.* Novosibirsk, 1996

Статистические очерки. М., 1956.

Statistical essays. M., 1956.

Страхов А.П. Глубокие корни: Выборное начало и российская государственность // Свободная мысль. 1999. № 5.

Strakhov A.P. *Deep roots: Elective principle and Russian statehood* // Svobodnaya mysl'. 1999. № 5.

Струмилин С.Г. На плановом фронте. Москва 1958

Strumilin S.G. *At the planning front.* Moscow 1958

Струмилин С.Г. Проблемы экономики труда. М., 1984.
  Strumilin S.G. *Issues of labor economics.* М., 1984.

Струмилин С.Г. Промышленный переворот в России. М., 1944.
  Strumilin S.G. *Industrial revolution in Russia.* М., 1944.

Сусоколов А.А. Русский этнос в XX веке: этапы кризиса экстенсивной культуры // Мир России. 1994. № 2.
  Susokolov A.A. *The Russian ethnos in the XX century: Phases of the extensive culture crisis* // Mir Rossii. 1994. № 2.

Сыроежин И. Планомерность. Планирование. План. Москва 1986
  Syroyezhin I. *Balanced development. Planning. Plan.* Moscow 1986

Тархов С. Изменение административно-территориального деления России в XIII-XX веках // Логос № 1 (46) 2005, С. 65
  Tarkhov S. *Changes in the administrative-territorial division of Russia in the XIII-XX centuries* // Logos № 1 (46) 2005, p. 65

Телефонный справочник ЦК КПСС. Москва 1990
  Telephone Directory of the CPSU Central Committee. Moscow 1990

Тилкиджиев Н. Слоевая структура социалистического общества // Социологические проблемы. 1987. № 3.
  Tilkidzhiyev N. *Stratified structure of the socialist society* // Sotsiologicheskie problemy. 1987. № 3.

Тихонова Н.Е. Социальная стратификация в современной России. Опыт эмпирического анализа - М.: Институт социологии РАН, 2007. - 320 с.
  Tikhonova N.E. *Social stratification in modern Russia. Empirical analysis* - М.: Institut sotsiologii RAN, 2007. - 320 p.

Тихонова Н.Е. Факторы стратификации в условиях перехода к рыночной экономике. М., 1999.
  Tikhonova N.E. *Stratification factors in the context of transition to a market economy.* М., 1999.

Трейвиш А. И. Географическая полимасштабность развития России (город, район, страна и мир). Докторская диссертация. Регистрационный номер ВНТИЦ: 0520060182

Treyvish A. I. *The geographic multidimensionality of Russia's development (city, district, country, and the world)*. Doctoral thesis. Registration number VNTITs: 0520060182

Троцкий Л. Преданная революция. М., 1991.

Trotsky L. *The Revolution Betrayed*. M., 1991.

XV съезд Всесоюзной коммунистической партии (б). Стенографический отчет. Москва 1928

XV Congress of the All-Union Communist Party (Bolsheviks). Verbatim records. Moscow 1928

Умов В.И. Российский средний класс: социальная реальность и политический фактор // Полис. 1993. № 4.

Umov V.I. *The Russian middle class: social reality and political factor* // Polis. 1993. № 4.

Уорнер Л. Социальный класс и социальная структура. Янки Сити // Рубеж. 1999. Т. 10, вып. 11.

Warner L. *Social class and social structure. Yankee City* // Rubezh. 1999. Vol. 10, issue 11.

Фельдман. Д.М. Терминология власти. Советские политические термины в историко-культурном контексте. М., 2006.

Feldman D.M. *The terminology of government. Soviet political terms in the historical and cultural context*. M., 2006.

Филиппов А.Ф. О понятии социального пространства // Куда идет Россия? Социальная трансформация постсоветского пространства / Под общ. ред. Т.И. Заславской. М., 1996.

Filippov A.F. *On the concept of social space* // Kuda idyot Rossiya? Sotsial'naya transformatsiya postsovetskogo prostranstva / Edited by T.I. Zaslavskaya. M., 1996.

Филиппов А.Ф. Смысл империи: К социологии политического пространства // Иное. Т. 3. Россия как идея. М., 1995.

Filippov A.F. *The meaning of empire: On the sociology of political space* // Inoe. Vol. 3. Rossiya kak ideya. M., 1995.

Филиппов А.Ф. Элементарная социология пространства // Социологический журнал. 1995. № 1.

Filippov A.F. *Elementary sociology of space* // Sotsiologicheskiy zhurnal. 1995. № 1.

Фитцпатрик Ш. Классы и классовая принадлежность в Советской России в 1920-е гг. // Вопросы истории. 1990. № 8.

Fitzpatrick S. *Classes and class identity in Soviet Russia in the 1920s* // Voprosy istorii. 1990. № 8.

Франкфорт Г., Франкфорт Г.А., Уилсон Дж., Якобсен Т. В преддверии философии. - М.: Наука, 1984 - с.236.

Frankfort H., Frankfort H.A., Wilson J., Jacobsen T. *Before philosophy*. - M.: Nauka, 1984 - p.236.

Френкель А., Бар-Хиллел И. Основания теории множеств. - М.: Мир, 1966 - с.5

Fraenkel A., Bar-Hillel Y. *Foundations of set theory*. - M.: Mir, 1966 - p.5

Хахулина Л. Социальное неравенство в российском обществе: мнения и оценки // Мониторинг общественного мнения. 1999. № 4 (42).

Khakhulina L. *Social inequality in Russian society: Opinions and judgments* // Monitoring obschestvennogo mneniya. 1999. № 4 (42).

XVI конференция всесоюзной коммунистической партии (б). Стенографический отчет. Москва 1929

XVI Conference of the All-Union Communist Party (Bolsheviks). Verbatim records. Moscow 1929

Чаянов А.В. Избранные труды. М., 1991.

Chayanov A.V. *Selected works*. M., 1991.

Черепнин Л.В. Земские Соборы русского государства в XVI–XVII вв. М., 1978.

Cherepnin L.V. *Zemsky Sobors of the Russian state in the XVI–XVII centuries*. M., 1978.

Черников В. За завесой секретности или строительство 859. Озерск 1995

Chernikov V. *Behind a veil of secrecy or the construction of 859*. Ozyorsk 1995

Чечулин А. В., Решетников М. М. Общественное признание: опыт поощрения лучших и признания заслуг в дореволюционной и современной России. СПб., 2000.

Chechulin A. V., Reshetnikov M. M. *Public recognition: experience of promoting the best performers and acknowledging merits in pre-revolutionary and contemporary Russia*. SPb., 2000.

Швеков Г.В. Первый советский уголовный кодекс. Москва 1970

Shvekov G.V. *The first Soviet criminal code*. Moscow 1970

Шибутани Т. Социальная психология. Москва 1969

Shibutani T. *Social psychology*. Moscow 1969

Шкаратан О.И., Ильин В.И. Социальная стратификация России и Восточной Европы. Сравнительный анализ. М.: Издательский дом ГУ ВШЭ, 2006.

Shkaratan O.I., Ilyin V.I. *Social stratification in Russia and Eastern Europe. Comparative analysis*. M.: Izdatel'skiy dom GU VShE, 2006.

Шкаратан О.И. Проблемы социальной структуры рабочего класса СССР. М., 1970.

Shkaratan O.I. *The social structure of the USSR working class*. M., 1970.

Шкаратан О.И. От этакратизма к гражданскому обществу // Рабочий класс и современный мир. 1990. № 3.

Shkaratan O.I. *From etacratism to a civil society* // Rabochiy klass i sovremenny mir. 1990. № 3.

Шкаратан О.И., Коломиец В.П. Крах во спасение (Социально-генетические преступления советского режима) // Мир России. 1993. № 1.
Shkaratan O.I., Kolomiets V.P. *Collapse for the sake of salvation (Socio-genetic crimes of the Soviet regime)* // Mir Rossii. 1993. № 1.

Шкаратан О.И., Радаев В.В. Правда этакратизма против мифа о социализме // Квинтэссенция: Философский альманах. 1991. М., 1992.
Shkaratan O.I., Radaev V.V. *The truth of etacratism against the myth of socialism* // Kvintessentsiya: Filosovskiy al'manakh. 1991. М., 1992.

Шкаратан О.И., Рукавишников В.О. Социальные слои в классовой структуре социалистического общества // Социологические исследования. 1977. № 2.
Shkaratan O.I., Rukavishnikov V.O. *Social strata in the class structure of the socialist society* // Sotsiologicheskie issledovaniya. 1977. № 2.

Шкаратан О.И., Сергеев Н.В. Реальные группы: концептуальный подход, эмпирическое исследование // Общественные науки и современность. 2000. № 5.
Shkaratan O.I., Sergeev N.V. *Real groups: Conceptual approach, empirical research* // Obschestvennye nauki i sovremennost'. 2000. № 5.

Штомпка П. Социология социальных изменений. М., 1996.
Sztompka P. *The sociology of social change.* М., 1996.

Шульгина О.В. Административно-территориальное деление России в XX веке (историко-географический аспект): Дис. д-ра ист. наук. Москва, 2005 419 с. РГБ ОД, 71:06-7/19
Shul'gina O.V. *Administrative-territorial division of Russia in the XX century (historical and geographical aspect):* Doctoral thesis (history). Moscow, 2005 419 p. RGB OD, 71:06-7/19

Шютц А. Равенство и смысловая структура социального мира // Социологический журнал. 2002. N 4. С. 5–45.

Schutz A. *Equality and the meaning structure of the social world* // Sotsiologicheskiy zhurnal. 2002. N 4. pp. 5–45.

Элдерсфельд С.Д. Политические элиты в современных обществах: эмпирические исследования и демократическая теория. М., 1992.

Eldersfeld S.D. *Political elites in modern societies: Empirical research and democratic theory.* M., 1992.

Яременко Ю. Экономические беседы. Диалоги с С. Белановским. М., 1999 г.

Yaremenko Yu. *Economic conversations. Dialogues with S. Belanovsky.* M., 1999 г.

Social Stratification and Mobility in the USSR / Eds M. Yanowitch and W.A. Fisher. With commentary by S.M. Lipset // International Journal

Freeze G. *The soslovian (estate) paradigm in Russian social history* // American historical review. 1986.

Horvat B. *The Political economy of socialism. A Marxist social theory.* N., 1982.

Konrad J., Szelenyi I. *The intellectuals on the road to class power: A sociological study of the role of the intelligentsia in socialism.* N., 1979.

Nussbaum M. *Aristotelian social democracy* // Liberalism and the Good / R. B. Douglass et al. (eds.). N.Y., 1990

Nowak St. *Changes of social structure in social consciousness* // The Polish Sociological Bulletin. 1964. N 2.

Nozick R. *Anarchy, State, and Utopia.* New York. Basic Books, 1974

Ossowski St. *Structura klasowa spolecznej swiadomsci.* Lodz, 1957.

Radaev V., Shkaratan O. *Power and property—Evidence from the Soviet experience* // International Sociology. 1992. N 3.

Rawls J. *A Theory of Justice.* Oxford University Press, 1972. P. 351

Shkaratan O. *The old and the new masters of Russia. From power relations to proprietary relations* // Sociological Research. 1992. N 5.

Teckenberg W. *Die soziale Struktur der sowjetischen Arbeiterklasse im internationalen Vergleich. Auf dem Wege zur industrialisierten Standegesellschaft?* Munchen, Wien, 1977.

Teckenberg W. *The social structure of the Soviet working class. Toward an estatist society?* // International Journal of Sociology. 1981-1982. Vol XI, N 4.

Teckenberg W. *The stability of occupational structures, social mobility and interest formation: The USSR as an estatist society in comparison with class societies* // Ibid. 1989. Vol. 19, N 232.

The social structure of the USSR. Recent Soviet studies / Ed. by M. Yanowitch. N., 1986.

Thompson, William; Joseph Hickey (2005). *Society in focus.* Boston, MA: Pearson.

Wesolowski W., Slomczynski K. *Social stratification in Polish cities* // Social Stratification

SOVIET AND POST-SOVIET POLITICS AND SOCIETY

Edited by Dr. Andreas Umland

ISSN 1614-3515

1   *Андреас Умланд (ред.)*
Воплощение Европейской
конвенции по правам человека в
России
Философские, юридические и
эмпирические исследования
ISBN 3-89821-387-0

2   *Christian Wipperfürth*
Russland – ein vertrauenswürdiger
Partner?
Grundlagen, Hintergründe und Praxis
gegenwärtiger russischer Außenpolitik
Mit einem Vorwort von Heinz Timmermann
ISBN 3-89821-401-X

3   *Manja Hussner*
Die Übernahme internationalen Rechts
in die russische und deutsche
Rechtsordnung
Eine vergleichende Analyse zur
Völkerrechtsfreundlichkeit der Verfassungen
der Russländischen Föderation und der
Bundesrepublik Deutschland
Mit einem Vorwort von Rainer Arnold
ISBN 3-89821-438-9

4   *Matthew Tejada*
Bulgaria's Democratic Consolidation
and the Kozloduy Nuclear Power Plant
(KNPP)
The Unattainability of Closure
With a foreword by Richard J. Crampton
ISBN 3-89821-439-7

5   *Марк Григорьевич Меерович*
Квадратные метры, определяющие
сознание
Государственная жилищная политика в
СССР. 1921 – 1941 гг
ISBN 3-89821-474-5

6   *Andrei P. Tsygankov, Pavel
A.Tsygankov (Eds.)*
New Directions in Russian
International Studies
ISBN 3-89821-422-2

7   *Марк Григорьевич Меерович*
Как власть народ к труду приучала
Жилище в СССР – средство управления
людьми. 1917 – 1941 гг.
С предисловием Елены Осокиной
ISBN 3-89821-495-8

8   *David J. Galbreath*
Nation-Building and Minority Politics
in Post-Socialist States
Interests, Influence and Identities in Estonia
and Latvia
With a foreword by David J. Smith
ISBN 3-89821-467-2

9   *Алексей Юрьевич Безугольный*
Народы Кавказа в Вооруженных
силах СССР в годы Великой
Отечественной войны 1941-1945 гг.
С предисловием Николая Бугая
ISBN 3-89821-475-3

10   *Вячеслав Лихачев и Владимир
Прибыловский (ред.)*
Русское Национальное Единство,
1990-2000. В 2-х томах
ISBN 3-89821-523-7

11   *Николай Бугай (ред.)*
Народы стран Балтии в условиях
сталинизма (1940-е – 1950-е годы)
Документированная история
ISBN 3-89821-525-3

12   *Ingmar Bredies (Hrsg.)*
Zur Anatomie der Orange Revolution
in der Ukraine
Wechsel des Elitenregimes oder Triumph des
Parlamentarismus?
ISBN 3-89821-524-5

13   *Anastasia V. Mitrofanova*
The Politicization of Russian
Orthodoxy
Actors and Ideas
With a foreword by William C. Gay
ISBN 3-89821-481-8

14 *Nathan D. Larson*
Alexander Solzhenitsyn and the
Russo-Jewish Question
ISBN 3-89821-483-4

15 *Guido Houben*
Kulturpolitik und Ethnizität
Staatliche Kunstförderung im Russland der
neunziger Jahre
Mit einem Vorwort von Gert Weisskirchen
ISBN 3-89821-542-3

16 *Leonid Luks*
Der russische „Sonderweg"?
Aufsätze zur neuesten Geschichte Russlands
im europäischen Kontext
ISBN 3-89821-496-6

17 *Евгений Мороз*
История «Мёртвой воды» – от
страшной сказки к большой
политике
Политическое неоязычество в
постсоветской России
ISBN 3-89821-551-2

18 *Александр Верховский и Галина
Кожевникова (ред.)*
Этническая и религиозная
интолерантность в российских СМИ
Результаты мониторинга 2001-2004 гг.
ISBN 3-89821-569-5

19 *Christian Ganzer*
Sowjetisches Erbe und ukrainische
Nation
Das Museum der Geschichte des Zaporoger
Kosakentums auf der Insel Chortycja
Mit einem Vorwort von Frank Golczewski
ISBN 3-89821-504-0

20 *Эльза-Баир Гучинова*
Помнить нельзя забыть
Антропология депортационной травмы
калмыков
С предисловием Кэролайн Хамфри
ISBN 3-89821-506-7

21 *Юлия Лидерман*
Мотивы «проверки» и «испытания»
в постсоветской культуре
Советское прошлое в российском
кинематографе 1990-х годов
С предисловием Евгения Марголита
ISBN 3-89821-511-3

22 *Tanya Lokshina, Ray Thomas, Mary
Mayer (Eds.)*
The Imposition of a Fake Political
Settlement in the Northern Caucasus
The 2003 Chechen Presidential Election
ISBN 3-89821-436-2

23 *Timothy McCajor Hall, Rosie Read
(Eds.)*
Changes in the Heart of Europe
Recent Ethnographies of Czechs, Slovaks,
Roma, and Sorbs
With an afterword by Zdeněk Salzmann
ISBN 3-89821-606-3

24 *Christian Autengruber*
Die politischen Parteien in Bulgarien
und Rumänien
Eine vergleichende Analyse seit Beginn der
90er Jahre
Mit einem Vorwort von Dorothée de Nève
ISBN 3-89821-476-1

25 *Annette Freyberg-Inan with Radu
Cristescu*
The Ghosts in Our Classrooms, or:
John Dewey Meets Ceauşescu
The Promise and the Failures of Civic
Education in Romania
ISBN 3-89821-416-8

26 *John B. Dunlop*
The 2002 Dubrovka and 2004 Beslan
Hostage Crises
A Critique of Russian Counter-Terrorism
With a foreword by Donald N. Jensen
ISBN 3-89821-608-X

27 *Peter Koller*
Das touristische Potenzial von
Kam''janec'–Podil's'kyj
Eine fremdenverkehrsgeographische
Untersuchung der Zukunftsperspektiven und
Maßnahmenplanung zur
Destinationsentwicklung des „ukrainischen
Rothenburg"
Mit einem Vorwort von Kristiane Klemm
ISBN 3-89821-640-3

28 *Françoise Daucé, Elisabeth Sieca-
Kozlowski (Eds.)*
Dedovshchina in the Post-Soviet
Military
Hazing of Russian Army Conscripts in a
Comparative Perspective
With a foreword by Dale Herspring
ISBN 3-89821-616-0

29 *Florian Strasser*
    Zivilgesellschaftliche Einflüsse auf die
    Orange Revolution
    Die gewaltlose Massenbewegung und die
    ukrainische Wahlkrise 2004
    Mit einem Vorwort von Egbert Jahn
    ISBN 3-89821-648-9

30 *Rebecca S. Katz*
    The Georgian Regime Crisis of 2003-
    2004
    A Case Study in Post-Soviet Media
    Representation of Politics, Crime and
    Corruption
    ISBN 3-89821-413-3

31 *Vladimir Kantor*
    Willkür oder Freiheit
    Beiträge zur russischen Geschichtsphilosophie
    Ediert von Dagmar Herrmann sowie mit
    einem Vorwort versehen von Leonid Luks
    ISBN 3-89821-589-X

32 *Laura A. Victoir*
    The Russian Land Estate Today
    A Case Study of Cultural Politics in Post-
    Soviet Russia
    With a foreword by Priscilla Roosevelt
    ISBN 3-89821-426-5

33 *Ivan Katchanovski*
    Cleft Countries
    Regional Political Divisions and Cultures in
    Post-Soviet Ukraine and Moldova
    With a foreword by Francis Fukuyama
    ISBN 3-89821-558-X

34 *Florian Mühlfried*
    Postsowjetische Feiern
    Das Georgische Bankett im Wandel
    Mit einem Vorwort von Kevin Tuite
    ISBN 3-89821-601-2

35 *Roger Griffin, Werner Loh, Andreas
    Umland (Eds.)*
    Fascism Past and Present, West and
    East
    An International Debate on Concepts and
    Cases in the Comparative Study of the
    Extreme Right
    With an afterword by Walter Laqueur
    ISBN 3-89821-674-8

36 *Sebastian Schlegel*
    Der „Weiße Archipel"
    Sowjetische Atomstädte 1945-1991
    Mit einem Geleitwort von Thomas Bohn
    ISBN 3-89821-679-9

37 *Vyacheslav Likhachev*
    Political Anti-Semitism in Post-Soviet
    Russia
    Actors and Ideas in 1991-2003
    Edited and translated from Russian by Eugene
    Veklerov
    ISBN 3-89821-529-6

38 *Josette Baer (Ed.)*
    Preparing Liberty in Central Europe
    Political Texts from the Spring of Nations
    1848 to the Spring of Prague 1968
    With a foreword by Zdeněk V. David
    ISBN 3-89821-546-6

39 *Михаил Лукьянов*
    Российский консерватизм и
    реформа, 1907-1914
    С предисловием Марка Д. Стейнберга
    ISBN 3-89821-503-2

40 *Nicola Melloni*
    Market Without Economy
    The 1998 Russian Financial Crisis
    With a foreword by Eiji Furukawa
    ISBN 3-89821-407-9

41 *Dmitrij Chmelnizki*
    Die Architektur Stalins
    Bd. 1: Studien zu Ideologie und Stil
    Bd. 2: Bilddokumentation
    Mit einem Vorwort von Bruno Flierl
    ISBN 3-89821-515-6

42 *Katja Yafimava*
    Post-Soviet Russian-Belarussian
    Relationships
    The Role of Gas Transit Pipelines
    With a foreword by Jonathan P. Stern
    ISBN 3-89821-655-1

43 *Boris Chavkin*
    Verflechtungen der deutschen und
    russischen Zeitgeschichte
    Aufsätze und Archivfunde zu den
    Beziehungen Deutschlands und der
    Sowjetunion von 1917 bis 1991
    Ediert von Markus Edlinger sowie mit einem
    Vorwort versehen von Leonid Luks
    ISBN 3-89821-756-6

44 *Anastasija Grynenko in Zusammenarbeit mit Claudia Dathe*
Die Terminologie des Gerichtswesens der Ukraine und Deutschlands im Vergleich
Eine übersetzungswissenschaftliche Analyse juristischer Fachbegriffe im Deutschen, Ukrainischen und Russischen
Mit einem Vorwort von Ulrich Hartmann
ISBN 3-89821-691-8

45 *Anton Burkov*
The Impact of the European Convention on Human Rights on Russian Law
Legislation and Application in 1996-2006
With a foreword by Françoise Hampson
ISBN 978-3-89821-639-5

46 *Stina Torjesen, Indra Overland (Eds.)*
International Election Observers in Post-Soviet Azerbaijan
Geopolitical Pawns or Agents of Change?
ISBN 978-3-89821-743-9

47 *Taras Kuzio*
Ukraine – Crimea – Russia
Triangle of Conflict
ISBN 978-3-89821-761-3

48 *Claudia Šabić*
"Ich erinnere mich nicht, aber L'viv!"
Zur Funktion kultureller Faktoren für die Institutionalisierung und Entwicklung einer ukrainischen Region
Mit einem Vorwort von Melanie Tatur
ISBN 978-3-89821-752-1

49 *Marlies Bilz*
Tatarstan in der Transformation
Nationaler Diskurs und Politische Praxis 1988-1994
Mit einem Vorwort von Frank Golczewski
ISBN 978-3-89821-722-4

50 *Марлен Ларюэль (ред.)*
Современные интерпретации русского национализма
ISBN 978-3-89821-795-8

51 *Sonja Schüler*
Die ethnische Dimension der Armut
Roma im postsozialistischen Rumänien
Mit einem Vorwort von Anton Sterbling
ISBN 978-3-89821-776-7

52 *Галина Кожевникова*
Радикальный национализм в России и противодействие ему
Сборник докладов Центра «Сова» за 2004-2007 гг.
С предисловием Александра Верховского
ISBN 978-3-89821-721-7

53 *Галина Кожевникова и Владимир Прибыловский*
Российская власть в биографиях I
Высшие должностные лица РФ в 2004 г.
ISBN 978-3-89821-796-5

54 *Галина Кожевникова и Владимир Прибыловский*
Российская власть в биографиях II
Члены Правительства РФ в 2004 г.
ISBN 978-3-89821-797-2

55 *Галина Кожевникова и Владимир Прибыловский*
Российская власть в биографиях III
Руководители федеральных служб и агентств РФ в 2004 г.
ISBN 978-3-89821-798-9

56 *Ileana Petroniu*
Privatisierung in Transformationsökonomien
Determinanten der Restrukturierungs-Bereitschaft am Beispiel Polens, Rumäniens und der Ukraine
Mit einem Vorwort von Rainer W. Schäfer
ISBN 978-3-89821-790-3

57 *Christian Wipperfürth*
Russland und seine GUS-Nachbarn
Hintergründe, aktuelle Entwicklungen und Konflikte in einer ressourcenreichen Region
ISBN 978-3-89821-801-6

58 *Togzhan Kassenova*
From Antagonism to Partnership
The Uneasy Path of the U.S.-Russian Cooperative Threat Reduction
With a foreword by Christoph Bluth
ISBN 978-3-89821-707-1

59 *Alexander Höllwerth*
Das sakrale eurasische Imperium des Aleksandr Dugin
Eine Diskursanalyse zum postsowjetischen russischen Rechtsextremismus
Mit einem Vorwort von Dirk Uffelmann
ISBN 978-3-89821-813-9

60 Олег Рябов
«Россия-Матушка»
Национализм, гендер и война в России XX века
С предисловием Елены Гощило
ISBN 978-3-89821-487-2

61 Ivan Maistrenko
Borot'bism
A Chapter in the History of the Ukrainian Revolution
With a new introduction by Chris Ford
Translated by George S. N. Luckyj with the assistance of Ivan L. Rudnytsky
ISBN 978-3-89821-697-5

62 Maryna Romanets
Anamorphosic Texts and Reconfigured Visions
Improvised Traditions in Contemporary Ukrainian and Irish Literature
ISBN 978-3-89821-576-3

63 Paul D'Anieri and Taras Kuzio (Eds.)
Aspects of the Orange Revolution I
Democratization and Elections in Post-Communist Ukraine
ISBN 978-3-89821-698-2

64 Bohdan Harasymiw in collaboration with Oleh S. Ilnytzkyj (Eds.)
Aspects of the Orange Revolution II
Information and Manipulation Strategies in the 2004 Ukrainian Presidential Elections
ISBN 978-3-89821-699-9

65 Ingmar Bredies, Andreas Umland and Valentin Yakushik (Eds.)
Aspects of the Orange Revolution III
The Context and Dynamics of the 2004 Ukrainian Presidential Elections
ISBN 978-3-89821-803-0

66 Ingmar Bredies, Andreas Umland and Valentin Yakushik (Eds.)
Aspects of the Orange Revolution IV
Foreign Assistance and Civic Action in the 2004 Ukrainian Presidential Elections
ISBN 978-3-89821-808-5

67 Ingmar Bredies, Andreas Umland and Valentin Yakushik (Eds.)
Aspects of the Orange Revolution V
Institutional Observation Reports on the 2004 Ukrainian Presidential Elections
ISBN 978-3-89821-809-2

68 Taras Kuzio (Ed.)
Aspects of the Orange Revolution VI
Post-Communist Democratic Revolutions in Comparative Perspective
ISBN 978-3-89821-820-7

69 Tim Bohse
Autoritarismus statt Selbstverwaltung
Die Transformation der kommunalen Politik in der Stadt Kaliningrad 1990-2005
Mit einem Geleitwort von Stefan Troebst
ISBN 978-3-89821-782-8

70 David Rupp
Die Rußländische Föderation und die russischsprachige Minderheit in Lettland
Eine Fallstudie zur Anwaltspolitik Moskaus gegenüber den russophonen Minderheiten im „Nahen Ausland" von 1991 bis 2002
Mit einem Vorwort von Helmut Wagner
ISBN 978-3-89821-778-1

71 Taras Kuzio
Theoretical and Comparative Perspectives on Nationalism
New Directions in Cross-Cultural and Post-Communist Studies
With a foreword by Paul Robert Magocsi
ISBN 978-3-89821-815-3

72 Christine Teichmann
Die Hochschultransformation im heutigen Osteuropa
Kontinuität und Wandel bei der Entwicklung des postkommunistischen Universitätswesens
Mit einem Vorwort von Oskar Anweiler
ISBN 978-3-89821-842-9

73 Julia Kusznir
Der politische Einfluss von Wirtschaftseliten in russischen Regionen
Eine Analyse am Beispiel der Erdöl- und Erdgasindustrie, 1992-2005
Mit einem Vorwort von Wolfgang Eichwede
ISBN 978-3-89821-821-4

74 Alena Vysotskaya
Russland, Belarus und die EU-Osterweiterung
Zur Minderheitenfrage und zum Problem der Freizügigkeit des Personenverkehrs
Mit einem Vorwort von Katlijn Malfliet
ISBN 978-3-89821-822-1

75 Heiko Pleines (Hrsg.)
    Corporate Governance in post-
    sozialistischen Volkswirtschaften
    ISBN 978-3-89821-766-8

76 Stefan Ihrig
    Wer sind die Moldawier?
    Rumänismus versus Moldowanismus in
    Historiographie und Schulbüchern der
    Republik Moldova, 1991-2006
    Mit einem Vorwort von Holm Sundhaussen
    ISBN 978-3-89821-466-7

77 Galina Kozhevnikova in collaboration
    with Alexander Verkhovsky and
    Eugene Veklerov
    Ultra-Nationalism and Hate Crimes in
    Contemporary Russia
    The 2004-2006 Annual Reports of Moscow's
    SOVA Center
    With a foreword by Stephen D. Shenfield
    ISBN 978-3-89821-868-9

78 Florian Küchler
    The Role of the European Union in
    Moldova's Transnistria Conflict
    With a foreword by Christopher Hill
    ISBN 978-3-89821-850-4

79 Bernd Rechel
    The Long Way Back to Europe
    Minority Protection in Bulgaria
    With a foreword by Richard Crampton
    ISBN 978-3-89821-863-4

80 Peter W. Rodgers
    Nation, Region and History in Post-
    Communist Transitions
    Identity Politics in Ukraine, 1991-2006
    With a foreword by Vera Tolz
    ISBN 978-3-89821-903-7

81 Stephanie Solywoda
    The Life and Work of
    Semen L. Frank
    A Study of Russian Religious Philosophy
    With a foreword by Philip Walters
    ISBN 978-3-89821-457-5

82 Vera Sokolova
    Cultural Politics of Ethnicity
    Discourses on Roma in Communist
    Czechoslovakia
    ISBN 978-3-89821-864-1

83 Natalya Shevchik Ketenci
    Kazakhstani Enterprises in Transition
    The Role of Historical Regional Development
    in Kazakhstan's Post-Soviet Economic
    Transformation
    ISBN 978-3-89821-831-3

84 Martin Malek, Anna Schor-
    Tschudnowskaja (Hrsg.)
    Europa im Tschetschenienkrieg
    Zwischen politischer Ohnmacht und
    Gleichgültigkeit
    Mit einem Vorwort von Lipchan Basajewa
    ISBN 978-3-89821-676-0

85 Stefan Meister
    Das postsowjetische Universitätswesen
    zwischen nationalem und
    internationalem Wandel
    Die Entwicklung der regionalen Hochschule
    in Russland als Gradmesser der
    Systemtransformation
    Mit einem Vorwort von Joan DeBardeleben
    ISBN 978-3-89821-891-7

86 Konstantin Sheiko in collaboration
    with Stephen Brown
    Nationalist Imaginings of the
    Russian Past
    Anatolii Fomenko and the Rise of Alternative
    History in Post-Communist Russia
    With a foreword by Donald Ostrowski
    ISBN 978-3-89821-915-0

87 Sabine Jenni
    Wie stark ist das „Einige Russland"?
    Zur Parteibindung der Eliten und zum
    Wahlerfolg der Machtpartei
    im Dezember 2007
    Mit einem Vorwort von Klaus Armingeon
    ISBN 978-3-89821-961-7

88 Thomas Borén
    Meeting-Places of Transformation
    Urban Identity, Spatial Representations and
    Local Politics in Post-Soviet St Petersburg
    ISBN 978-3-89821-739-2

89 Aygul Ashirova
    Stalinismus und Stalin-Kult in
    Zentralasien
    Turkmenistan 1924-1953
    Mit einem Vorwort von Leonid Luks
    ISBN 978-3-89821-987-7

90 Leonid Luks
    Freiheit oder imperiale Größe?
    Essays zu einem russischen Dilemma
    ISBN 978-3-8382-0011-8

91 Christopher Gilley
    The 'Change of Signposts' in the
    Ukrainian Emigration
    A Contribution to the History of
    Sovietophilism in the 1920s
    With a foreword by Frank Golczewski
    ISBN 978-3-89821-965-5

92 Philipp Casula, Jeronim Perovic
    (Eds.)
    Identities and Politics
    During the Putin Presidency
    The Discursive Foundations of Russia's
    Stability
    With a foreword by Heiko Haumann
    ISBN 978-3-8382-0015-6

93 Marcel Viëtor
    Europa und die Frage
    nach seinen Grenzen im Osten
    Zur Konstruktion ‚europäischer Identität' in
    Geschichte und Gegenwart
    Mit einem Vorwort von Albrecht Lehmann
    ISBN 978-3-8382-0045-3

94 Ben Hellman, Andrei Rogachevskii
    Filming the Unfilmable
    Casper Wrede's 'One Day in the Life
    of Ivan Denisovich'
    Second, Revised and Expanded Edition
    ISBN 978-3-8382-0044-6

95 Eva Fuchslocher
    Vaterland, Sprache, Glaube
    Orthodoxie und Nationenbildung
    am Beispiel Georgiens
    Mit einem Vorwort von Christina von Braun
    ISBN 978-3-89821-884-9

96 Vladimir Kantor
    Das Westlertum und der Weg
    Russlands
    Zur Entwicklung der russischen Literatur und
    Philosophie
    Ediert von Dagmar Herrmann
    Mit einem Beitrag von Nikolaus Lobkowicz
    ISBN 978-3-8382-0102-3

97 Kamran Musayev
    Die postsowjetische Transformation
    im Baltikum und Südkaukasus
    Eine vergleichende Untersuchung der
    politischen Entwicklung Lettlands und
    Aserbaidschans 1985-2009
    Mit einem Vorwort von Leonid Luks
    Ediert von Sandro Henschel
    ISBN 978-3-8382-0103-0

98 Tatiana Zhurzhenko
    Borderlands into Bordered Lands
    Geopolitics of Identity in Post-Soviet Ukraine
    With a foreword by Dieter Segert
    ISBN 978-3-8382-0042-2

99 Кирилл Галушко, Лидия Смола
    (ред.)
    Пределы падения – варианты
    украинского будущего
    Аналитико-прогностические исследования
    ISBN 978-3-8382-0148-1

100 Michael Minkenberg (ed.)
    Historical Legacies and the Radical
    Right in Post-Cold War Central and
    Eastern Europe
    With an afterword by Sabrina P. Ramet
    ISBN 978-3-8382-0124-5

101 David-Emil Wickström
    Rocking St. Petersburg
    Transcultural Flows and Identity Politics in
    the St. Petersburg Popular Music Scene
    With a foreword by Yngvar B. Steinholt
    Second, Revised and Expanded Edition
    ISBN 978-3-8382-0100-9

102 Eva Zabka
    Eine neue „Zeit der Wirren"?
    Der spät- und postsowjetische Systemwandel
    1985-2000 im Spiegel russischer
    gesellschaftspolitischer Diskurse
    Mit einem Vorwort von Margareta Mommsen
    ISBN 978-3-8382-0161-0

103 Ulrike Ziemer
    Ethnic Belonging, Gender and
    Cultural Practices
    Youth Identitites in Contemporary Russia
    With a foreword by Anoop Nayak
    ISBN 978-3-8382-0152-8

104 Ksenia Chepikova
,Einiges Russland' - eine zweite
KPdSU?
Aspekte der Identitätskonstruktion einer
postsowjetischen „Partei der Macht"
Mit einem Vorwort von Torsten Oppelland
ISBN 978-3-8382-0311-9

105 Леонид Люкс
Западничество или евразийство?
Демократия или идеократия?
Сборник статей об исторических дилеммах
России
С предисловием Владимира Кантора
ISBN 978-3-8382-0211-2

106 Anna Dost
Das russische Verfassungsrecht auf dem
Weg zum Föderalismus und zurück
Zum Konflikt von Rechtsnormen und
-wirklichkeit in der Russländischen
Föderation von 1991 bis 2009
Mit einem Vorwort von Alexander Blankenagel
ISBN 978-3-8382-0292-1

107 Philipp Herzog
Sozialistische Völkerfreundschaft,
nationaler Widerstand oder harmloser
Zeitvertreib?
Zur politischen Funktion der Volkskunst
im sowjetischen Estland
Mit einem Vorwort von Andreas Kappeler
ISBN 978-3-8382-0216-7

108 Marlène Laruelle (ed.)
Russian Nationalism, Foreign Policy,
and Identity Debates in Putin's Russia
New Ideological Patterns after the Orange
Revolution
ISBN 978-3-8382-0325-6

109 Michail Logvinov
Russlands Kampf gegen den
internationalen Terrorismus
Eine kritische Bestandsaufnahme des
Bekämpfungsansatzes
Mit einem Geleitwort von
Hans-Henning Schröder
und einem Vorwort von Eckhard Jesse
ISBN 978-3-8382-0329-4

110 John B. Dunlop
The Moscow Bombings
of September 1999
Examinations of Russian Terrorist Attacks
at the Onset of Vladimir Putin's Rule
Second, Revised and Expanded Edition
ISBN 978-3-8382-0388-1

111 Андрей А. Ковалёв
Свидетельство из-за кулис
российской политики I
Можно ли делать добро из зла?
(Воспоминания и размышления о
последних советских и первых
послесоветских годах)
With a foreword by Peter Reddaway
ISBN 978-3-8382-0302-7

112 Андрей А. Ковалёв
Свидетельство из-за кулис
российской политики II
Угроза для себя и окружающих
(Наблюдения и предостережения
относительно происходящего после 2000 г.)
ISBN 978-3-8382-0303-4

113 Bernd Kappenberg
Zeichen setzen für Europa
Der Gebrauch europäischer lateinischer
Sonderzeichen in der deutschen Öffentlichkeit
Mit einem Vorwort von Peter Schlobinski
ISBN 978-3-89821-749-1

114 Ivo Mijnssen
The Quest for an Ideal Youth in
Putin's Russia I
Back to Our Future! History, Modernity, and
Patriotism according to *Nashi*, 2005-2013
With a foreword by Jeronim Perović
Second, Revised and Expanded Edition
ISBN 978-3-8382-0368-3

115 Jussi Lassila
The Quest for an Ideal Youth in
Putin's Russia II
The Search for Distinctive Conformism in the
Political Communication of *Nashi*, 2005-2009
With a foreword by Kirill Postoutenko
Second, Revised and Expanded Edition
ISBN 978-3-8382-0415-4

116 Valerio Trabandt
Neue Nachbarn, gute Nachbarschaft?
Die EU als internationaler Akteur am Beispiel
ihrer Demokratieförderung in Belarus und der
Ukraine 2004-2009
Mit einem Vorwort von Jutta Joachim
ISBN 978-3-8382-0437-6

117 *Fabian Pfeiffer*
Estlands Außen- und Sicherheitspolitik I
Der estnische Atlantizismus nach der
wiedererlangten Unabhängigkeit 1991-2004
Mit einem Vorwort von Helmut Hubel
ISBN 978-3-8382-0127-6

118 *Jana Podßuweit*
Estlands Außen- und Sicherheitspolitik II
Handlungsoptionen eines Kleinstaates im
Rahmen seiner EU-Mitgliedschaft (2004-2008)
Mit einem Vorwort von Helmut Hubel
ISBN 978-3-8382-0440-6

119 *Karin Pointner*
Estlands Außen- und Sicherheitspolitik III
Eine gedächtnispolitische Analyse estnischer
Entwicklungskooperation 2006-2010
Mit einem Vorwort von Karin Liebhart
ISBN 978-3-8382-0435-2

120 *Ruslana Vovk*
Die Offenheit der ukrainischen
Verfassung für das Völkerrecht und
die europäische Integration
Mit einem Vorwort von Alexander
Blankenagel
ISBN 978-3-8382-0481-9

121 *Mykhaylo Banakh*
Die Relevanz der Zivilgesellschaft
bei den postkommunistischen
Transformationsprozessen in mittel-
und osteuropäischen Ländern
Das Beispiel der spät- und postsowjetischen
Ukraine 1986-2009
Mit einem Vorwort von Gerhard Simon
ISBN 978-3-8382-0499-4

122 *Michael Moser*
Language Policy and the Discourse on
Languages in Ukraine under President
Viktor Yanukovych (25 February
2010–28 October 2012)
ISBN 978-3-8382-0497-0 (Paperback edition)
ISBN 978-3-8382-0507-6 (Hardcover edition)

123 *Nicole Krome*
Russischer Netzwerkkapitalismus
Restrukturierungsprozesse in der
Russischen Föderation am Beispiel des
Luftfahrtunternehmens "Aviastar"
Mit einem Vorwort von Petra Stykow
ISBN 978-3-8382-0534-2

124 *David R. Marples*
'Our Glorious Past'
Lukashenka's Belarus and
the Great Patriotic War
ISBN 978-3-8382-0574-8 (Paperback edition)
ISBN 978-3-8382-0675-2 (Hardcover edition)

125 *Ulf Walther*
Russlands "neuer Adel"
Die Macht des Geheimdienstes von
Gorbatschow bis Putin
Mit einem Vorwort von Hans-Georg Wieck
ISBN 978-3-8382-0584-7

126 *Simon Geissbühler (Hrsg.)*
Kiew – Revolution 3.0
Der Euromaidan 2013/14 und die
Zukunftsperspektiven der Ukraine
ISBN 978-3-8382-0581-6 (Paperback edition)
ISBN 978-3-8382-0681-3 (Hardcover edition)

127 *Andrey Makarychev*
Russia and the EU
in a Multipolar World
Discourses, Identities, Norms
With a foreword by Klaus Segbers
ISBN 978-3-8382-0629-5

128 *Roland Scharff*
Kasachstan als postsowjetischer
Wohlfahrtsstaat
Die Transformation des sozialen
Schutzsystems
Mit einem Vorwort von Joachim Ahrens
ISBN 978-3-8382-0622-6

129 *Katja Grupp*
Bild Lücke Deutschland
Kaliningrader Studierende sprechen über
Deutschland
Mit einem Vorwort von Martin Schulz
ISBN 978-3-8382-0552-6

130 *Konstantin Sheiko, Stephen Brown*
History as Therapy
Alternative History and Nationalist
Imaginings in Russia, 1991-2014
ISBN 978-3-8382-0665-3

131 Elisa Kriza
     Alexander Solzhenitsyn: Cold War
     Icon, Gulag Author, Russian
     Nationalist?
     A Study of the Western Reception of his
     Literary Writings, Historical Interpretations,
     and Political Ideas
     With a foreword by Andrei Rogatchevski
     ISBN 978-3-8382-0589-2 (Paperback edition)
     ISBN 978-3-8382-0690-5 (Hardcover edition)

132 Serghei Golunov
     The Elephant in the Room
     Corruption and Cheating in Russian
     Universities
     ISBN 978-3-8382-0570-0

133 Manja Hussner, Rainer Arnold (Hgg.)
     Verfassungsgerichtsbarkeit in
     Zentralasien I
     Sammlung von Verfassungstexten
     ISBN 978-3-8382-0595-3

134 Nikolay Mitrokhin
     Die "Russische Partei"
     Die Bewegung der russischen Nationalisten in
     der UdSSR 1953-1985
     Aus dem Russischen übertragen von einem
     Übersetzerteam unter der Leitung von Larisa Schippel
     ISBN 978-3-8382-0024-8

135 Manja Hussner, Rainer Arnold (Hgg.)
     Verfassungsgerichtsbarkeit in
     Zentralasien II
     Sammlung von Verfassungstexten
     ISBN 978-3-8382-0597-7

136 Manfred Zeller
     Das sowjetische Fieber
     Fußballfans im poststalinistischen
     Vielvölkerreich
     Mit einem Vorwort von Nikolaus Katzer
     ISBN 978-3-8382-0757-5

137 Kristin Schreiter
     Stellung und Entwicklungspotential
     zivilgesellschaftlicher Gruppen in
     Russland
     Menschenrechtsorganisationen im Vergleich
     ISBN 978-3-8382-0673-8

138 David R. Marples, Frederick V. Mills
     (eds.)
     Ukraine's Euromaidan
     Analyses of a Civil Revolution
     ISBN 978-3-8382-0660-8

139 Bernd Kappenberg
     Setting Signs for Europe
     Why Diacritics Matter for
     European Integration
     With a foreword by Peter Schlobinski
     ISBN 978-3-8382-0663-9

140 René Lenz
     Internationalisierung, Kooperation
     und Transfer
     Externe bildungspolitische Akteure in der
     Russischen Föderation
     Mit einem Vorwort von Frank Ettrich
     ISBN 978-3-8382-0751-3

141 Juri Plusnin, Yana Zausaeva, Natalia
     Zhidkevich, Artemy Pozanenko
     Wandering Workers
     Mores, Behavior, Way of Life, and Political
     Status of Domestic Russian Labor Migrants
     Translated by Julia Kazantseva
     ISBN 978-3-8382-0653-0

142 Matthew Kott, David J. Smith (eds.)
     Latvia – A Work in Progress?
     100 Years of State- and Nation-building
     ISBN 978-3-8382-0648-6

143 Инна Чувычкина (ред.)
     Экспортные нефте- и газопроводы
     на постсоветском пространстве
     Анализ трубопроводной политики в свете
     теории международных отношений
     ISBN 978-3-8382-0822-0

144 Johann Zajaczkowski
     Russland – eine pragmatische
     Großmacht?
     Eine rollentheoretische Untersuchung
     russischer Außenpolitik am Beispiel der
     Zusammenarbeit mit den USA nach 9/11 und
     des Georgienkrieges von 2008
     Mit einem Vorwort von Siegfried Schieder
     ISBN 978-3-8382-0837-4

145 Boris Popivanov
     Changing Images of the Left in
     Bulgaria
     The Challenge of Post-Communism in the
     Early 21st Century
     ISBN 978-3-8382-0667-7

146 Lenka Krátká
A History of the Czechoslovak Ocean
Shipping Company 1948-1989
How a Small, Landlocked Country Ran
Maritime Business During the Cold War
ISBN 978-3-8382-0666-0

147 Alexander Sergunin
Explaining Russian Foreign Policy
Behavior
Theory and Practice
ISBN 978-3-8382-0752-0

148 Darya Malyutina
Migrant Friendships in
a Super-Diverse City
Russian-Speakers and their Social
Relationships in London in the 21st Century
With a foreword by Claire Dwyer
ISBN 978-3-8382-0652-3

149 Alexander Sergunin, Valery Konyshev
Russia in the Arctic
Hard or Soft Power?
ISBN 978-3-8382-0753-7

150 John J. Maresca
Helsinki Revisited
A Key U.S. Negotiator's Memoirs
on the Development of the CSCE into the
OSCE
With a foreword by Hafiz Pashayev
ISBN 978-3-8382-0852-7

151 Jardar Østbø
The New Third Rome
Readings of a Russian Nationalist Myth
With a foreword by Pål Kolstø
ISBN 978-3-8382-0870-1

152 Simon Kordonsky
Socio-Economic Foundations of the
Russian Post-Soviet Regime
The Resource-Based Economy and Estate-
Based Social Structure of Contemporary
Russia
With a foreword by Svetlana Barsukova
ISBN 978-3-8382-0775-9

153 Duncan Leitch
Assisting Reform in Post-Communist
Ukraine 2000–2012
The Illusions of Donors and the Disillusion of
Beneficiaries
With a foreword by Kataryna Wolczuk
ISBN 978-3-8382-0844-2

154 Abel Polese
Limits of a Post-Soviet State
How Informality Replaces, Renegotiates, and
Reshapes Governance in Contemporary
Ukraine
With a foreword by Colin Williams
ISBN 978-3-8382-0845-9

155 Mikhail Suslov (ed.)
Digital Orthodoxy in the Post-Soviet
World
The Russian Orthodox Church and Web 2.0
ISBN 978-3-8382-0871-8